REFLECTIONS ON TURKEY

The Turkish-American-Israeli Relations and the Middle East

REFLECTIONS ON TURKEY

The Turkish-American-Israeli Relations
and the Middle East

Mehmet Kalyoncu

BLUE DOME

Published by Blue Dome Press
535 Fifth Avenue, Ste.601
New York, NY 10017-8019

www.bluedomepress.com

Library of Congress Cataloging-in-Publication Data Available

ISBN: 978-1-935295-19-8

Printed by
Çağlayan A.Ş., Izmir - Turkey

Contents

IRAQ, IRAN AND
THE ARMENIAN RESOLUTION

Turkey's Burgeoning Civil Society and
Transforming Foreign Policy[1]

O ct. 10, 2007 is the date when the so-called genocide resolution is brought to a vote by the US House of Representatives Committee on Foreign Affairs.

The Armenian diaspora is keen to see the long-awaited resolution passing not only in the committee but also in the full House and the Senate, in that order. In the meantime the Senate Democrats and Republicans have agreed that it would be the best option to split Iraq into three autonomous Kurdish, Sunni and Shiite regions and withdraw from Iraq, while Ankara is still too busy to realize what this means for Turkish interests in northern Iraq, as it is overwhelmed with the question of whether Turkey is becoming Malaysia or not. Last but not least, the possibility of a military showdown between yet-to-nuclearize Tehran and the Washington-Jerusalem coalition is more real than ever.

The Armenian resolution, the future of Iraq and the looming crisis with Iran are the three foreign policy issues likely to strain relations between Ankara and Washington in the short term. The ways Ankara will have to deal with these issues are quite different from the ways it would normally have done a decade or more ago, for two reasons.

First NGOs such as business associations, think tanks and civil society organizations that are able to and do influence both the government's domestic and foreign policies have proliferated in recent years. Secondly, the Turkish military's institutional democratization, which

---

[1]   First appeared in *Today's Zaman* daily on October 10, 2007

started with the former chiefs of General Staff Gen. Hüseyin Kıvrıkoğlu and Gen. Hilmi Özkök, has almost matured with current Chief of General Staff Gen. Yaşar Büyükanıt. These two concurrent and ongoing progresses in favor of civil society have changed not only the way Turkish foreign policy is formulated but also the foreign policy decision making process itself.

Ankara: from elite rule to citizen rule

One of the most insightful sources in terms of understanding Turkey is the accounts of foreign correspondents who have covered Turkey for decades while living in Turkey; their accounts are critical but yet remain immune to official scrutiny. In his book, *Crescent and Star*, former Istanbul Bureau Chief for *The New York Times* Stephen Kinzer captures the essence of the classical power-relation between the elite and the masses that prevailed for decades. He depicts the resistance of the former to change as follows:

> The ruling elite, however, refuses to embrace this new nation or even admit that it exists. Military commanders, prosecutors, security officers, narrow-minded bureaucrats, lapdog newspaper editors, rigidly conservative politicians and other members of this sclerotic cadre remain psychologically trapped in the 1920s. They see threats from across every one of Turkey's eight borders and, most dangerously, from within the country itself. In their minds Turkey is still a nation under siege. To protect it from mortal danger, they feel obliged to run it themselves. They not only ignore but actively resist intensifying pressure from educated, worldly Turks who want their country to break free of its shackles and complete its march toward the democracy that was Atatürk's dream.

Similarly, in their *Turkey Unveiled*, referring to the elite's dominance of political and economic sphere, Nicole Pope, who covered Turkey for *Le Monde*, and Hugh Pope, former *Wall Street Journal* bureau chief in Istanbul, note that "until the Democrats' victory, the country had been dominated not just by the army but by an elitist and tyrannical bureaucracy whose rule went back to the latter days of the Ottoman empire" and "the attitude of disdain of the educated classes and the state towards the 'little people' is still evident, several decades after the DP's [Democrat Party] success served the bureaucracy its first notice."

In addition to the above-mentioned reasons, the lack of educated individuals skilled in multiple Western languages within the general public who would qualify to join the highly selective diplomatic corps left the Turkish foreign policy making and implementation to a small group of elite members. For the foreign capitals, dealing with Turkey meant simply dealing with that group which had remained generally unchanged, even if the individuals within it changed.

However, the late 1990s witnessed a rapid human development within the general public, with increasing numbers of university graduates gaining advanced degrees in the West, and the proliferation of NGOs that directly or indirectly influence both the government's domestic and foreign policy. For this reason, Ankara's foreign policy-making has been different from the past in recent years and will be different from now on with regard to the issues of Iraq, Iran and the Armenian resolution at hand.

The question of Iraq: united versus divided Iraq?

On Sept. 26, the United States Senate passed a non-binding resolution suggesting that the United States should support a political settlement among Iraqis based on a federal system of government, which would create Sunni Arab, Shiite Arab and Kurdish regions with a viable but limited central government in Baghdad. Earlier, at one of his town hall meetings for his 2008 Presidential campaign, Senator Joseph Biden (D-DE), the chief sponsor of the resolution, had suggested that a wall like the one separating the Palestinian territories from the Israeli settlements which would separate the Kurds, the Sunnis and the Shiites would be useful to minimize possible ethno-religious violence once the federal system is installed.

The plan is viewed infeasible, for it would require, as Arizona's Republican Senator John McCaine argues, splitting the intermarried families of the Kurds, the Sunnis and the Shiites. On his way back to Baghdad after his appearance at the UN General Assembly in New York, Iraqi Prime Minister Nouri al-Maliki condemned the idea of splitting

Iraq into federal regions, "Iraqis are eager for Iraq's unity...Dividing Iraq is a problem and a decision like that would be a catastrophe." Along similar lines, Ali al-Jaroush, the Arab League's head of the Arab Relations Department, insisted that the idea was "hostile to Arab interests" and the best response would be to help the Iraqi people drive occupying forces out of the country.

Ankara joins Maliki in believing that there would be catastrophic consequences of dividing Iraq in one way or another not only for the Kurds, the Sunnis and the Shiites, but also more so for the Turkmens within Iraq and for Turkey itself, bringing it to a collision course with the Kurdistan regional administration in northern Iraq over the issue of Kurdistan Workers' Party (PKK) terror as well as the status of Kirkuk. The idea of creating a federal system in Iraq which leaves the north to the Kurds with lucrative oil resources is likely to take deeper root in the minds of US policy makers. However, once the Bush administration is gone, Ankara is likely to primarily demand more cooperation from Washington to root the terrorist PKK out of northern Iraq and secondarily pressure on both Washington and Baghdad to preserve Iraq's unity as to secure Turkmens who would otherwise be left out as a minority vulnerable to the Kurdish majority.

If it was the 1990s or before, Ankara would either willingly or unwillingly be complacent with the partition of Iraq and consequently build up its military presence on the Iraqi border, putting all of southeastern Turkey under "emergency rule." As some would argue, this would be a more than welcome development for the infamous elite because it would curb the authority of the civilian administration on the grounds of the so-called security threat emanating from both inside and outside. This is not the case anymore. That is, a vast majority of society and civil society organizations are quite vocal about and reactionary toward the government's policies.

The online polls conducted by recently emerged survey companies for such major newspapers as *Zaman*, *Hürriyet*, *Milliyet* and *Yeni Şafak*, among others, create a direct channel of communication between the government and the public who elected it. Therefore the government is no longer as independent as before in foreign policy making nor immune to public scrutiny, and as such any foreign policy preference that would dramatically contradict public opinion would simply mean a farewell to office in the next elections. Second, the Turkish military is no longer as interested, as some would argue, as before to override the civilian administration's foreign policy preferences—as proven multiple times before and during the US invasion of Iraq.

The question of Iran: will Turks be cooperative?

The frequent argument within Washington's neoconservative circles about Iran's posing an imminent threat to both regional and global order and therefore its being dealt with militarily before it acquires nuclear capabilities is unlikely to convince Turks to pledge support to any possible US or US–Israeli operation against Iran for several reasons.

First of all, unlike the US invasion of Iraq, where Saddam's dictatorship and army were already eliminated in the early days of the invasion, a possible military conflict with Iran would spark a state-to-state war, as Zbigniew Brzezinski, the former National Security Advisor to President Jimmy Carter, suggests, and as such rapidly destabilize the entire region. Second, even with the hard-line President Mahmoud Ahmadinejad, Iran is a containable threat. In his *Hidden Iran*, Ray Takeyh suggests that in quest for returning back to the roots of the Islamic Revolution, the new generation Iranian clergy is hostile to establishing dialogue with the United States and is indifferent to doing so with Europe. Yet the grim economic realities, such as increasing unemployment and the raised cost of living across Iran make it imperative for Tehran to work with the few allies it has left. According to the recent energy agreement between Ankara and Tehran, the two will bring Turkmenistan's natural gas through Iran and Turkey, and Iran's gas through Turkey, to the European markets. Additionally, Ankara is to assist Tehran to develop its gas field in the Persian Gulf province of Assaluyeh.

Thirdly, the Turkish-speaking Azeri Iranians that constitute 24 percent of Iran's 65 million-population would also be a considerable concern to the Turkish public in the event of what may soon turn into a full-fledged war. Even if their plight may not suffice to make Ankara stand in the way of Washington, the rapid surge of anti-Americanism among the public would not avail the government to cooperate with

Washington on any other matter either. Fourthly, according to the German Marshall Fund's survey "Transatlantic Trends 2006," while 56 percent of the Turkish respondents view Iran's developing nuclear weapons as being normal, only 10 percent supports military action against it. Finally, if not the general public, the intellectuals are well aware of the impact of the political intervention in 1953 and how it sowed the seeds of the Islamic Revolution in Iran.

The Armenian resolution: a new civilian approach

Thanks to burgeoning civil society and public debate on even the most dogma-ridden subjects, Turks are ever-closer to understanding that fierce attacks on Turkey and seeking means to inflict pain on her and her people is likely to be the only way in which the Armenian diaspora, especially its second and third generations, is familiar with as a way to serve their perceived Armenian cause. Some argue that it is for this very reason that, as Kinzer notes, in the 1970s and 1980s, terrorists calling themselves Justice Commandos against Armenian Genocide (JCAG) assassinated not only 75 Turkish diplomats in the United States and Europe but also their relatives, wives, children and the mere bystanders, and bombed targets like the Turkish Airline (THY) counter at Orly Airport in Paris. Again, it may be for this very reason that Armenia has long supported the terrorist PKK—to bleed Turkey to death. For Turks the answer to "Why do they hate us?" may not necessarily be that Armenians are inherently hostile to Turks, which is certainly quite unlikely given the ongoing dialogue between non-fanatical Turks and Armenians, but that "those who hate us" have no ability to sympathize with Turks because their mental image of Turkey and Turks is associated with nothing but the massacres they heard of one way or another. Therefore the Armenian diaspora's relentless campaign for the resolutions such as H. Res. 106 in the US Congress may be tolerated.

However, the failure of Turkish civil society, including Turks and Armenians, to show the Armenian diaspora how to better serve the Armenian cause cannot be tolerated. Therefore, Turks and Armenians of Turkey have recently started to allocate at least part of their time and resources to help the Armenian diaspora realize how to better serve the Armenian interests, instead of solely countering its attacks. It goes without saying that the foremost of those interests are respectively to better the socioeconomic and political conditions of Armenians in Turkey and help Armenia settle its disputes with its neighbors and prosper economically. During his recent trip to Washington, D.C., the Turkish-Armenian Patriarch Mesrob II, whose speech at Georgetown University was allegedly cancelled due to the security threats voiced by fanatical Armenian groups, stated that the primary need of the Turkish-Armenians is to open a theological school where they can educate their priests. In addition the Patriarchate needs to be able to procure income through means other than member donations, which is not allowed under the current legal framework. Therefore it is widely held that it would be more reasonable for the Armenian diaspora to donate the financial resources they use for lobbying, at least partially, to the Patriarchate.

Similarly it would be more rational for Armenian Foreign Minister Vartan Oskanian to seek ways to solve his country's problems with the neighboring Azerbaijan, 20 percent of the land of which is currently under Armenian occupation, instead of protesting the letter of the eight US Secretaries of State by advising House Speaker Nancy Pelosi that the resolution would not affect Turkish-Armenian relations, simply because there are no such relations. He is indeed right that Turkish-Armenian relations are plagued primarily by the latter's partial occupation of Azerbaijan, as Suat Kınıklıoğlu, deputy of the ruling Justice and Development (AK Party), puts it. Nevertheless, Yerevan's goodwill efforts on the so-called genocide debate would certainly encourage Ankara to be more proactive in solving Armenia's regional problems.

Otherwise, even if passing the genocide resolution in the US Congress would satisfy the collective ego of the diaspora and for a short period of time relieve Congress members of the Armenian lobby's ceaseless pressure, it will have disastrous impact not only on American–Turkish relations but also on Armenian-Turkish relations. The impact on the former is highly likely to be enduring, because the Turkish public opinion is that the US Congress has nothing to do with the so-called genocide issue and is further politicizing the issue by bringing it to the vote.

ARMENIAN RESOLUTION TAKES
US–TURKISH RELATIONS HOSTAGE - 1

Will Turks Lose the Battle They Have Never Fought?[2]

Rumors vary regarding the possibility of the so-called genocide bill, HR-106, coming to the House floor to be voted on by the US Congress. According to some accounts, in September the Armenian diaspora will do whatever it takes to pass the bill, which seems possible given that the number of HR-106 co-sponsors suffices to do that and the House Speaker Nancy Pelosi was one of the early sponsors of the bill. According to others, Congress will not bring up the genocide issue for at least the rest of 2007, as Washington needs Ankara's full cooperation to implement its partial troop withdrawal from Iraq.

Nevertheless, the genocide bill's not coming up in the foreseeable future does not necessarily solve the most pressing problem affecting US–Turkish relations. Not only to immunize US–Turkish relations against the artificial genocide debate, which erratically breaks out, but also to relieve themselves of a great burden of being accused of genocide, Turks should pursue a just and final solution to the genocide debate. There is no better time than now to launch and wind the battle of ideas, given the American public's increased awareness of the Armenian diaspora's efforts to conceal crucial facts about the Turkish-Armenian atrocities during World War I and of its efforts to inhibit free speech on the subject.

---

[2] First appeared in *Today's Zaman* daily on September 26, 2007.

An anatomy of the so-called genocide allegation

Not necessarily the entire Armenian diaspora in the United States, but the militant groups within it, label any language or conversation that calls to investigate the allegations regarding the so-called genocide a form of an outright denial of what they call "genocide." They seek to justify their unrelenting attitude on this most politicized issue by suggesting that it would be similar and, as such, meaningless to investigating the credibility of the Holocaust, which cost the lives of some 6 million Jews in Nazi Germany.

Beside its undermining of the Holocaust, and its motivation to exploit the Jews' deep sorrow, on a moral and intellectual ground, these militant groups' attitude itself is already self-defeating enough. One is naturally inclined to wonder why it would not be normal to investigate "a truth," while doing so would only affirm it if it is really "the truth." In addition to the diaspora's inhibition of freedom of conscience and speech, the very fact that it is only the Armenian archives, which are vital to research in order to understand what really happened in 1915 and the following years, that remain closed, while the Turkish ones and all others—including Russian, British, French and American—are wide open to any researchers of any ethno-national origin, raises questions about the credibility of the Armenian allegations of genocide.

Moreover, that these archives are kept in Boston, MA, under the custody of an Armenian foundation headquartered in Toronto, Canada, and that they are inaccessible not only to Turkish but also to American researchers who are not ethnic Armenians further challenges the credibility of the Armenian allegations. According to Dr. Yusuf Halacoğlu, head of the Turkish Historical Society (TTK) in Ankara, one frequently cited excuse for these archives remaining inaccessible to researchers is that they have not been organized yet. Dr. Halacoğlu noted that he offered to donate $20 million to the Foundation out of TTK's own budget, as opposed to the Turkish government's budget, in order to expedite the process of organizing these archives and opening them to research, and yet his offer has been refused by foundation officials.

The US Congress under pressure

The statistical data indicating that the surge in support for the HR-106 resolution in the month it was introduced (January 2007) and the plummeting support thereafter suggests that the Congress members' support for the resolution is driven primarily by Democrat peer pressure, if not by their commitment to fulfilling their pre-election promises to their Armenian American fundraisers and the fear of losing electoral support in the next elections. The mid-term congressional elections took place in November 2006 after which the Democrats seized the majority and California's Democrat Congresswoman Nancy Pelosi, a staunch supporter of the Armenian genocide allegations, assumed the position of speaker of the House of Representatives in January 2007.

On Jan. 30, California's Democrat Representative Adam Schiff whose constituency, and hence campaign sponsors, consist of Armenian Americans of Glendale, CA, introduced the HR-106 bill which "calls upon the president to ensure that the foreign policy of the United States reflects appropriate understanding and sensitivity concerning issues related to human rights, ethnic cleansing, and genocide documented in the United States record relating to the Armenian genocide and the consequences of the failure to realize a just resolution" and "calls upon the president in the president's annual message commemorating the Armenian genocide issued on or about April 24, to accurately characterize the systematic and deliberate annihilation of 1,500,000 Armenians as genocide and to recall the proud history of United States intervention in opposition to the Armenian genocide." The bill has been co-sponsored by five other representatives whose respective constituencies consist of a sizeable community of Armenian American voters. These co-sponsors include respectively George Radanovich (R-CA), Frank Pallone (D-NJ), Joseph Knollenberg (R-MI), Brad Sherman (D-CA) and Thaddeus McCotter (R-MI). On Jan. 31, some 158 members of Congress, including those who withdrew their support later on, signed onto the HR-106. The number of representatives pledging support for the bill has plummeted in the months that followed, averaging 10 per month adding up to the total of 226 as of today.

One misinterpretation of these numbers would be that more than half of the House of Representatives (226 out of 435) believe that what happened in 1915 was "genocide," as the bill suggest, while the other would be that those who did not sign up onto the bill do not think what happened in 1915 was not "genocide." In addition, interpreting these numbers as that the US Congress does not value its Turkish ally would probably be the most misleading one. Similarly, blaming the possible recognition of the so-called genocide in the US Congress on the Jewish American community, by the example of the Anti-Defamation League's (ADL) recent recognition of it, would not only be equally misleading, but also amount to shooting oneself in the foot and ironically rewarding the Armenian diaspora by giving up an enduring ally in the United States. No need to mention that it has been the Jewish-American Congress members and community leaders who have long advocated Turkish theses on this pressing genocide debate.

ARMENIAN RESOLUTION TAKES
US–TURKEY RELATIONS HOSTAGE - 2
Will Turks Lose the Battle They Have Never Fought?[3]

B oth psychological and contextual reasons lay behind the somewhat incomprehensible ready support for the Armenian allegations in both public and political circles in the United States.

First of all, the primary reason for the relevant representatives' introducing the HR-106 bill was not their own convictions about the Turks
or the Ottoman Empire, but the insistence of their Armenian-American constituency for them to do so. After all, the representatives are supposed to be the voice of the very constituency who has elected them,
be they right or wrong. A legislative aide to one of the chief sponsors
of HR-106 noted, "We do not have a commitment to pass this bill, but
to bring it up and keep it alive." Similarly, conversations with both members of Congress and their political advisors reveal that the majority
of co-sponsors of the HR-106 bill are not even aware of its content,
but have pledged their support due either to the request of their fellow colleagues who introduced the bill, or most likely to get rid of the
ceaseless pressure of the Armenian lobbyists, which in some case appear
in the form of the threat of lost votes in the next elections.

Secondly, as explicit in the relentless attitude of the Armenian
diaspora, those members who do not acknowledge the so-called Armenian genocide, let alone call for an objective investigation of it, are readily accused of being on the payroll of the Turkish government, as if, as
some would argue, those who acknowledge it are not on that of mem-

---

[3]   First appeared in *Today's Zaman* daily on September 27, 2007.

bers of the wealthy Armenian diaspora. Thirdly, under the influence of the constructed "Terrible Turk" image, just like any ordinary American, the Congress members are inclined to believe that the Turkish Ottoman state may well have carried out genocide against the Christian Armenians. One should not undermine the impact of the "Terrible Turk" image; especially so given that movies such as "Lawrence of Arabia" and "Midnight Express," are still screened in some movie theaters across the United States. Finally, the silence of the Turkish-Americans in the whole genocide debate and their sluggishness to even call their representatives to express their objection to the HR-106 only encourages Congress members to support the resolution and move on.

The very fact that the battle of ideas in the so-called genocide debate has been fought by the official Turkey, meaning primarily Turkish diplomats and the Foreign Ministry, vis-à-vis the allegedly "underdog" people of the Armenian diaspora has undermined the credibility of the Turkish theses on what happened in 1915 and Turks' commitment to finalize this prolonged debate. Illustrative of the general Armenian diaspora, in his article titled "Armenian Patriarch of Turkey in US on Turkish Propaganda Tour Once Again," and published in the California Courier, Harut Sassounian alleges that His Beatitude Mesrob II Mutafyan's visit to the United States and speaking engagements at various prestigious institutions such as the Capitol and Georgetown University is organized by the Turkish government to prevent the possible voting on the infamous HR-106 genocide bill in the House of Representatives. He continued to proudly explain how the Armenian-American Church had previously pressured the Southern Methodist University administration, a co-sponsor of a conference titled, "Turkish-Armenian Question: What to do now?" to withdraw its sponsorship, and succeeded in its endeavor. Yet, with almost complete denial or disregard of how the Armenian diaspora inhibits "free speech," Sassounian accuses the Turkish government of inhibition of "free speech." Apparently, according to him as well as a marginal, but noisy, political faction within the Armenian-American community, "free speech" is allowed only if what is to be said is what they want to hear.

However, not only the American public and members of Congress, but also the majority of the Armenian-American community is fed-up with and sick of the militantly hostile attitude of certain Armenian organizations, such as the Armenian National Committee of America (ANCA), and with their efforts to inhibit a possible reconciliation between Armenians and Turks. The Turkish-American organizers of the conference held in Dallas note that most of the Armenian scholars invited to speak at the conference had to decline the invitation, complaining about the likely attack on them to be launched by organizations such as ANCA and other militant Armenian-American groups. Similarly the members of Congress who have not signed on to support the infamous HR-106 bill complain about the Armenian lobby's manipulation of the US Congress and about some members falling prey to such manipulation while the country is faced by much more severe problems ranging from healthcare to the war in Iraq.

Moreover, the intellectuals are raising their opposition to the one-sided story of the so-called genocide. In his article titled "Tawdry genocide tale," *The Washington Times* columnist Bruce Fein disputes the alleged analogy between the Holocaust and the Turkish-Armenian atrocities which took place during World War I by pointing at the real causes of those atrocities:

> As Bernard Lewis has observed, an analogy would have been if Adolf Hitler had left Jews in Berlin, Frankfurt and Vienna exempt from the Final Solution. For more than three centuries, under the Ottoman millet system, Armenians enjoyed religious, cultural and social harmony. Conflict with the Ottoman Empire was largely provoked by Armenian terrorism and plotting secession comparable to the Confederate States of America, not by a late-blooming desire to destroy Armenians as a group.

Similarly, *Jerusalem Post* columnist Lenny Ben-David notes that not only did Armenians massacre 2.5 million of the Muslim population of Armenia between 1914 and 1920, but also that some contemporary Armenians hold Jews to be accountable for the killings of Armenians in 1915.

The bottom line is that there is already great suspicion within the political and intellectual communities about the Armenian allegations of genocide. Yet the third parties, be they intellectuals or members of the US Congress, have either preferred to remain silent about it, or seemed to have supported it mainly to get rid of the Armenian lobby's pressure. The absence of the Turkish grassroots within the whole genocide debate has only made it easier for US Congress members to rightly justify their support by asking this simple question, "If there was no genocide and the passage of this genocide bill is so detrimental to the Turkish interests, why does no single Turkish-American call our office to express his or her objection while we are overwhelmed with letters, emails, faxes and telephone calls from Armenian-Americans?" It is time for the Turkish grassroots to take over the task of tackling the Armenian allegations, and it takes only a few dedicated nongovernmental organizations to help the American public realize how they are being manipulated. Once the Americans realize it, they would certainly deliver justice.

A ROSE (GÜL) REVOLUTION

The Military-Civilian Relations in President Abdullah Gül's Turkey[4]

Turkey's last five months of political uncertainty and tensions have ended with the election of the ruling Justice and Development Party (AK Party) nominee Abdullah Gül as the new president of the Republic of Turkey. Mr. Gül received 339 votes out of 448 cast in the third round of the parliamentary ballot.

His presidency will bring the headscarf back into Çankaya Palace long after Atatürk, whose wife also wore a headscarf. Besides losing yet another post to the AK Party, it was Mrs. Hayrunnisa Gül's headscarf that stirred reactions to Mr. Gül's nomination from the secularists. Mr. Gül laughed at the allegations of him plotting to "Islamize" Çankaya Palace and reacted to the criticisms on his wife's choice to wear a headscarf by defending her individual freedom of conscience. Similarly, some marginal secularist commentators viewed the election of Mr. Gül as the fall of the last castle, meaning the loss of the presidency to the ruling AK Party after the Prime Ministry and Parliament Speaker's Office. Prime Minister Recep Tayyip Erdoğan brushed aside these comments by asking whose castle was falling to whom. After all, did the presidency not belong to the Turkish public and was Mr. Gül not the very representation of that public? Mr. Gül's presidency attracted varying and interesting responses from abroad as well. *New York Times* Radio Editor Jane Bornemeier said, "For the first time, a 'Muslim' has become a president of Turkey," which should be quite a surprise to Turks if hers is not just a slip of the tongue.

---

[4]   First appeared in *Today's Zaman* daily on August 31, 2007.

Amid these reactions, the question of the military's response to all this has long been the matter of deep curiosity both inside and out of Turkey. How will the army generals react to President Gül, allegedly a former Islamist, becoming their commander-in-chief? How will they reconcile their self-appointed guardianship of the secular state regime with the headscarf in "the" government office while it is banned in all other government offices? Will the army officers' uneasiness with the outcome of the presidential election lead to a crisis in Turkey's military-civilian relations? Given the unmatched weight of secularism in the Turkish political sphere, these are questions whose answers are to shape not only Turkey's domestic politics but also its foreign policy in the following years.

Military-civilian relations in the shade of secularism and Kemalism

Secularism has long been the buzzword in civilian-military relations in Turkey, where the armed forces consider themselves the natural guardians of the country's secular regime and the Kemalist ideology. With this perception, the Turkish military has not shied away from disrupting the political process either directly or indirectly.

The tradition started in 1960 with a group of young officers' overthrowing of the government of Prime Minister Adnan Menderes. The ensuing suspicious court process resulted in the execution of the ousted prime minister as well as his finance and foreign ministers. The second military intervention took place in a form of a memorandum almost a decade later in March 1971. Amid the ongoing bloody leftist-rightist conflict in the country, army officers sent a letter to the government warning that political factions were developing within the army and that the regime would fall if precautions were not taken. The military came back into politics in Sept. 1980, this time not only to warn the civilians but to take over the administration. The takeover, which aimed to end the political violence between the leftists and rightists, was welcomed by the majority of the public. It was seen as a blockade to the spread of communism and the leftist political violence. Turkish politics once again sensed the heavy hand of the armed forces in

Feb. 1997 when army generals forced Islamist Prime Minister Necmettin Erbakan's resignation along with a series of layoffs in the Turkish military, removing officers alleged to be Islamist.

Most recently Mr. Gül's first presidential candidacy in late April sparked fierce debates on the fate of Turkey's secular regime. Arguably the secularists took to the streets to protest the ruling AK Party's decision to nominate Mr. Gül for president. Amid the organized street protests in the major cities, a memorandum was posted on the Turkish Armed Forces (TSK) Web site close to midnight on April 27. The memorandum allegedly expressed the army's unease with the ongoing polarization of the country over the presidential debate and warned that the military was ready to take the necessary precautions to protect the secular nature of the state regime. Despite the fact that Chief of General Staff Gen. Yaşar Büyükanıt reportedly said that he too read the "unfortunate" statement posted on the TSK Web site the following morning, implying that he was not aware of the "e-memorandum," the secularist media was quick to portray the statement as a memorandum to the government. The ruling AK Party's taking the initiative in calling early parliamentary elections initiated a political process that consolidated the AK Party government's power in office, bringing it 47 percent of the popular vote in the July 22 parliamentary elections, and eventually enabling it to complete the aborted election of its deputy prime minister and foreign minister as the country's president.

If it was partially Mr. Gül's Islamist background that disturbed the secularists; his wife's headscarf was another reason—probably the real reason—behind the uneasiness of the secularists. Mrs. Gül will be the second first lady after Atatürk's wife, Latife Hanım, to wear a headscarf. She will be the "headscarf wearing" host of the balls and receptions held in Çankaya Palace, the presidential residence, for the next seven years. Will the ongoing tradition of not inviting the headscarf-wearing wives of government officials and deputies to Çankaya events continue? How comfortable will the military officers feel as they host the headscarf-wearing first lady at their events and ceremonies? Will the very fact that the top woman in the country is wearing a headscarf do anything to ease the ban on wearing a headscarf in public spaces such as government offices and schools? And finally, will the Turkish Army somehow react to Mr. Gül's presidency? These are the questions awaiting answers nowadays.

Media reaction

According to dailies such as *Hürriyet* and *Milliyet*, known for a pro-establishment stance, the military has already shown its dissidence with the outcome of the presidential election. Referring to Gen. Büyükanıt's Aug. 30 National Victory Day message (released several day's early on Monday of that week), in which he notes, "Our nation has been watching the behavior of those separatists who can't embrace Turkey's unitary nature, and centers of evil that systematically try to corrode the secular nature of the Turkish Republic," some media outlets sought to portray the army as antagonistic to both the ruling AK Party and its recently elected presidential nominee, Mr. Gül. A *Milliyet* headline read, "Commanders did not show up at the commander-in-chief's oath-taking ceremony," portraying the absence of the commanders as their reaction to Mr. Gül's presidency. Yet *Milliyet* viewed former Islamist Gül's election as Turkey's new president as a step forward toward Turkey's democratic maturity.

Contrary to the Turkish secularist media's somewhat uneasy attitude, foreign observers welcomed Mr. Gül's presidency, suggesting that his foreign policy experience and good relations with Western leaders will energize Turkey's EU membership bid. The BBC reported that "the European Union welcomed Mr. Gül's election, calling it a positive step in the country's campaign to join the bloc." According to the BBC report, European Commission Chief Jose Manuel Barroso said the election was "an opportunity to give fresh, immediate and positive impetus to the accession process to the European Union through progress in a number of key areas." *The New York Times* reported that the US Ambassador to Turkey Ross Wilson welcomed Mr. Gül's presidency by noting, "Once again, Turkey's commitment to democratic institutions and the rule of law has proven durable and strong." Similarly US State Department spokesman Tom Casey said, "We welcome this exercise in Turkish democracy. It continues the course of democratic development in that country."

Prospects for a possible military intervention

The historical behavioral pattern of the Turkish military and the recent institutional transformation in the military mindset suggest that the prospects for a possible military intervention into the political process are at an all-time low. In addition, Mr. Gül's close relations with army generals, especially with Chief of General Staff Gen. Büyükanıt, which he developed during his tenure as foreign minister, diminish the possibility of a crisis in civilian-military relations in the years to come, even though the possibility of tension in the relations may not remain as low.

Firstly, the common characteristic of the four military interventions which took place in 1960, 1971, 1980, and 1997 was the presence of popular and elite support for the army's stepping in. In 1960 and 1997 the military intervened against the backdrop of a threat posed by the ruling governments to the secular regime of the state, Menderes' Democrat Party (DP) and Necmettin Erbakan's Welfare Party (RP), respectively. In both cases the army had strong elite support along with relatively lower, but present, popular support. Similarly, in 1971 and 1980 the army stepped in as a long-expected solution to the ongoing political polarization within the institutions and the following bloody violence between the leftists and rightists. In these two cases, too, the army had the support of the elite along with the relatively stronger support of the masses.

At the current point in time neither the elite nor the masses are likely to tolerate any kind of military intervention into politics, because both are sensitive to the damage to the political and economic stability achieved by the ruling AK Party government over the last five years. Popular opposition to a military intervention was proven during the street protests in the spring as the secularists cheered, "No Shariah, no coup d'état." On the question of a possible military intervention, Soli Özel of Bilgi University notes, "Quite frankly, unless the world goes totally upside down, I don't see how [the army officers] could find a context in which they could legitimately intervene."

Secondly, the Turkish military mindset has gone through a democratic transformation regarding the civilian-military relationship in the last decade. The transformation started with chiefs of General Staff Gen. Hüseyin Kıvrıkoğlu and Gen. Hilmi Özkök, both of whom approved the increased civilian authority over the military and supported the legal and political reforms toward Turkey's EU membership, which aims to eventually bring the military under civilian subordination, as it should be in any democracy. To the dismay of the militant secularists, Gen. Büyükanıt followed the democratic course and even furthered the democratic transformation by not acting unilaterally without the authorization of the civilian administration on the most pressing issues, such as the possible cross-border operation into northern Iraq in order to root out the Kurdistan Workers' Party (PKK). During his last year in office, Gen. Büyükanıt is unlikely to act radically different than the way to which he is accustomed. What about current Land Forces Commander Gen. İlker Başbuğ, who is to succeed Gen. Büyükanıt in 2008? His past behavioral pattern indicates that he will not resort to antidemocratic means to undermine civilian rule either.

Finally, Mr. Gül seems to be prepared to prevent possible tensions between the ruling AK Party government, his presidential office and the army from turning into a crisis. In his first presidential speech after taking his oath in Parliament, Mr. Gül signaled that civilians will strengthen relations with the generals. He emphasized the crucial role in regional stability of strong and modernized Turkish armed forces with an increased deterrence capability and affirmed his dedication to fighting terrorist activities threatening the national integrity of the country. In the same speech, Mr. Gül promised to maintain his impartiality, embracing all factions of society, and to protect the secular nature of the regime.

Nevertheless, First Lady Gül's headscarf is likely to be a matter of contention for some army officers who consider the headscarf a symbol of defiance of the secular system, even if they may not necessarily be able to do much about it. According to a survey conducted by the Konda poll agency for *Milliyet*, a majority of Turks—72.6 percent—regarded it as "normal" for the first lady to wear a headscarf, while

19.8 percent said they would be uncomfortable. In addition to general public acceptance of the headscarf in Çankaya Palace, the likelihood of the first lady becoming an iconic public figure like the late Princess Diana further diminishes the possibility of extreme tension between civilians and the army over the headscarf issue.

ANKARA'S GROWING IMPORTANCE FOR ISRAEL IN THE POST AMERICAN MIDDLE EAST[5]

Several developments are concurrently taking place in and around the Middle East, both national and regional ones, which are likely to have wider implications. First, the United States is reluctantly starting to realize that the mission "Operation Iraqi Freedom" is failing, and that fairly soon the withdrawal of troops from Iraq will be no longer an option, but a necessity.

Second, Turkey voted for its future with the parliamentary elections on July 22. The AK Party of PM Erdoğan won a landslide victory, receiving 46.6 percent of the votes and thus becoming the only party in the past 57 years to increase its votes in the second term. As such, the electoral victory has not only given the AK Party another five year in office, but also a strong popular mandate for its policy course in both domestic and foreign affairs. However, although Erdoğan's AK Party has indeed won the right to form the new government, questions remain over whether it will be able to govern.

Finally, despite all the international pressure and UN sanctions, Tehran is continuing its nuclear program. At the same time, its regional influence has grown, first through supporting the Shiite insurgents in Iraq and second through boosting its diplomatic relations with both Damascus and Riyadh.

What are the possible implications of these concurrent developments for Israel? One may be inclined to ask why for Israel but not for others. Certainly the same question may be raised for other states in the

---

[5]   This article first appeared in www.balkananalysis.com.

region, but what the implications will be for Israel is particularly important due to the particular position of Israel in the region. After all, the state of Israel has right to survive and to protect its citizens against potential threats. Yet it is not the only state which preserves those rights in the region. As such, with its unspecified but apparently immense military capabilities, Israel has a potential to trigger volatile events that are likely to affect both regional and international balance of power. Therefore, how would the outcome of the second development influence Israel, provided that the US withdraws from Iraq due to both its inability to maintain the costly war, and consequently is discouraged to confront Iran afterwards, and that Iran continues to become an ever more influential regional power as well as ever more antagonistic to Israel? These gradually materializing conditions put two options in front of Tel Aviv to choose. It will have to either resort to military options against multiplied regional threats, or return back to its tradition of diplomacy, seeking to revitalize the old alliances, especially the one with Turkey.

The bell tolls for American withdrawal, as Tehran becomes a regional leader

A growing number of Democrat, and even Republican senators want to set a date for the withdrawal of the US troops from Iraq; their concerns have once again been ignored by the rejection of the Levin-Reed Amendment on US Policy on Iraq. However, the very fact that there is a demand for a phased redeployment of US forces from Iraq by the end of the year and growing public unrest over the failure of President Bush's "new" strategy in Iraq, does suggest that the date for the withdrawal is soon, albeit not specified. The war in Iraq has cost the United States over 3,600 casualties, with an unspecified number of troops maimed or otherwise injured (believed to be around 30,000), and nearly $1 trillion in expenditures. This is expected to reach $2 trillion, provided troops remain in Iraq until 2010. Accepting the growing dissent over his Iraq policy, President Bush recently signaled "that he might be open to shifting toward a smaller, more limited mission in Iraq in the future."

In the meantime, Iran has sought and to a great extent been successful in increasing its political influence in the region through supporting the Shiite insurgency in Iraq. Similarly, Palestine has provided a fertile ground for Tehran to boost its popularity among the Sunni Arabs as well. According to a recent ISNA (Iranian Student News Agency) report, Iran's foreign minister in a phone conversation with his Saudi counterpart, Prince Saud al Faisal, discussed and talked about conditions in Lebanon, Palestine and bilateral ties. Minister Mottaki in this phone conversation stressed the importance of cooperation between all Islamic and Arab countries so as to aid the nation of Palestine and to free it from its current state.

Similarly, Iran's President Mahmoud Ahmadinejad recently paid a day-long visit to Syria in order to congratulate President Bashar al-Assad on the beginning of his second seven-year term as Syria's president, and to review expansion of Tehran-Damascus political and economic cooperation.

Tehran's engagement with the Arab governments in the region has started to yield tangible outcomes for its own ends. According to the ISNA report, President Ahmadinejad and his Syrian counterpart Bashar al-Assad issued a joint statement calling for unity in Lebanon, Palestine and Iraq. The report quotes the Iranian president, saying "cooperation between Tehran and Damascus is to the benefit of the region and both sides will stand strong against all regional enemies." Drawing the international community's attention to the effect and dangers of Israeli's nuclear weapons on international and regional peace and security, notes the report, both sides asserted the necessity for swift steps to be taken in order to face this threat.

Further, the statement reportedly condemned the continued actions of the Israeli regime, perceived as aggressive. In addition, *Sharq al-Awsat* newspaper reported that Iranian President Ahmedinejad offered his Syrian counterpart $1 billion in the form of military aid if the latter cuts off its recently developing relations with Israel, and if the latter considers using the aid for military purchases from Russia.

Reviving Ben-Gurion's peripheral alliance in the new era

The course of regional and international developments makes it necessary for Tel Aviv to reconsider, modify and re-implement the peripheral alliance initiative of Israel's first Prime Minister, David Ben-Gurion. In order to break the isolation imposed onto it by the surrounding Arab states and to gain their respect, Israel sought to establish an alliance with the countries in the periphery of the Middle East, which also outnumbered the Arab population in the region. The alliance was so crucial to the Israeli interests, argues Ofra Bengio, that in order to secure US support for forming the alliance, Ben-Gurion portrayed it as if it was crucial to US interests in the region as well, "[Ben-Gurion] sought to use American involvement or support for the agreement as an incentive to the countries in question to join in. In other words, Israel sought to use the United States to galvanize the pact, and use the pact to consolidate U.S. support for itself." The alliance ironically involved Sudan, Ethiopia, Iran, and Turkey.

Bengio further suggests that according to the CIA report captured by Iran [revolutionaries] in 1979 from the American Embassy in Tehran, at the end of 1958 Israel, Turkey, and Iran signed an agreement to form an organization called Trident, aiming to exchange intelligence information among the three's respective intelligence services. The immediate threats that necessitated the peripheral alliance in the late 1950s have not disappeared but multiplied over time.

The state of the alliance

Today out of those erstwhile allies, Iran has turned into a staunch enemy whose president-elect vowed to wipe Israel off of the map; similarly, upon one allegation after another on carrying out genocide in Darfur, Sudan is waiting to be invaded by the very mediator and guarantor of that alliance, while the United States has not only diminished its soft power and popularity to engage any government, but also is rapidly depleting its hard power capabilities to deter any government in the region. Once the United States withdraws from Iraq before fulfilling its goals, which seems to be inevitable, the withdrawal will, to the dismay of those who believe in the necessity of US leadership in global affairs, also shake the invincible image of the United States. From that point on, the dynamics of the power struggle are likely to change forever in the region.

What else remains from the old peripheral alliance? Turkey. Can Turkey play any constructive role in preventing a regional or international conflict which would dramatically risk the survival of Israel?

The answer is certainly not as long as the new government is unable to engage the Middle Eastern states. Even if the AK Party government would like to continue its multi-faceted diplomacy with regional powers such as Iran, Syria, and Israel, its ability to do so will be hindered by the domestic political instability likely to stem from, respectively, the debate over presidential election, the Kurdish issue, and cross-border operation into Iraq. The very fact that the new parliament will consist of deputies from the left-leaning CHP, the ultra-nationalistic, right-wing MHP, and ethnic-Kurdish independent deputies, promises no easy solution on either of those issues. In that case, it is nothing but unrealistic to expect politically unstable Ankara, even with the AK Party government's apparently clear win, to play any effective role in the Middle East.

What kind of Ankara in the post-American Middle East?

Two possibilities lie ahead of Ankara in the second term of the AK Party government. Ankara will either continue its multi-faceted engagement with the Middle East, or it will be bogged down in a series of political turmoil, and as such will not only be alienated from the region where Tehran is rapidly gaining prominence, but also from the West falling short of fulfilling the EU accession requirements. The political atmosphere in Ankara in the AK Party's second term will pretty much determine Turkey's diplomatic capabilities in the post-American Middle East as well. Soner Cagaptay of the Washington Institute for Near East Policy has prophesized political instability in the aftermath of the July 22 parliamentary election. Based on his assumption that the public rallies in spring were indeed against the AK Party instead of its presidential nominee, Cagaptay argues that the lifestyle issues, more specifically headscarf issue, will mobilize masses against the AK Party after July 22. In addition, he suggests that the new parliament's failure to elect a new president in thirty days after July 22 will lead to its dissolution and open the way for new parliamentary elections. Given the fact that the AK Party avoided the hot-button issue of the headscarf and sought to embrace all ways of life in its first term, and promises to continue this course by not mentioning the headscarf issue even in its party program, it is unlikely to cause instability during the AK Party's second term.

However, the political faultlines, which Cagaptay implies are likely to emerge in the new parliament consisting of leftist, Turkish nationalist and Kurdish nationalist deputies, are likely to cause instability in the parliament unless the parties recognize the country's interest in reconciliation over the presidential debate. The ensuing political instability would not only diminish Ankara's ability to continue reforms, but also its ability to be diplomatically as active in the regional affairs. Yet, the ongoing transformation in the regional balance of power and formation of new alliances necessitate Ankara to be even more active than before.

During the last four and a half years, the first-term AK Party government has proven to be the only one able to communicate with all the parties in the Middle East. While Ankara mediated talks between Damascus and Jerusalem, it also sought to use its influence on the Hamas leadership for moderation. In a geographical area where almost every Muslim individual grows up being taught that they should take revenge on Israel, which is perceived as far from credible in the quest for peace, the latter needs an ally capable of deflecting anti-Semitic frustration and articulating the view to Arabs that Israel has a right to survive.

CIVIL SOCIETY VERSUS KURDISH SEPARATISM

How to Deal with the Neo-Kurdish Separatism[6]

The long-awaited meeting between US President George W. Bush and Turkish Prime Minister Recep Tayyip Erdoğan took place on Nov. 5, 2007 in Washington.

The meeting Erdoğan attended, with a parliamentary mandate to carry out a military incursion into northern Iraq, marked a turning point in Ankara's plans after President Bush declared the Kurdistan Workers' Party (PKK) an enemy of the United States as well as of Iraq and Turkey, and accordingly pledged his full support to Turkey in fighting against the PKK terrorism. During a press conference in Arbil following the Bush-Erdoğan meeting in Washington, the Kurdish regional administration's Prime Minister Nechirvan Barzani declared that his government would no longer let the PKK use its territories to continue attacks against Turkey. Even though Barzani did not publicly declare the PKK a terrorist organization, he stressed that it is the Kurdish people who suffer most from the PKK's activities. Prior to the Bush-Erdoğan meeting, the Expanded Neighboring Countries of Iraq Foreign Ministers Meeting in Istanbul emerged with an agreement of the participating states, including the United States, to root PKK terrorism out of northern Iraq.

If all these recent developments mean something, it is the end of the PKK's armed struggle, which does not necessarily mean the end of its Kurdish-separatism through non-violent channels. Throughout the

---

6   First appeared in *Today's Zaman* daily on November 19, 2007.

last 23 years since its first civilian killings in 1984, the PKK has not only cost some 40,000 deaths in Turkey, but also acted as an agent of Kurdish solidarity formation abroad. Most notably in Europe, the PKK has been able to garner popular support among the ethnic-Kurdish immigrants either through persuasion or coercion. In the meantime, it has found allies within the political, intellectual and media circles who arguably advocate Kurdish emancipation, if not self-determination. Unlike before, from now on, the idea of Kurdish self-determination has its solid and living symbol, the Kurdistan regional administration, with which it is to be associated. Therefore, all those who hinder the regional administration's ability to become a full-fledged state in the absence of any credible security threat associated with that state are likely to be demonized nationally, regionally and internationally for being the oppressor of the "largest nation without a state."

The end of the PKK's armed struggle, which belonged to the last century, leads to a whole new phase in the play of Kurdish-separatism in the new century. What Turkey makes out of this transition and how it prepares itself to counter the neo Kurdish-separatism will mark Turkey's relationship with its Kurds as well as with the Western states. The only viable and durable solution for Ankara lies in fostering civil society in the country, reviving its southeastern region and dramatically reforming its representations in the Western capitals.

The end of the PKK's armed struggle: What is next?

The unfolding developments in northern Iraq and on the PKK front signal the end of the PKK's armed operations. It was Jalal Talabani, president of Iraq, who first hinted in December 2005 that the armed struggle of the PKK was over when he uttered, "The time of Mao, Ho Chi Min and Che Guevera is over," and called upon PKK members to take advantage of the positive approach of the Justice and Development Party (AK Party) government. During a recent interview with the German ARD TV, Murat Karayilan, the top leader of the terrorist PKK, expressed his wish that the Turkish Armed Forces (TSK) would fall into the PKK's trap by crossing into northern Iraq. The ARD TV reporter rightly interpreted what Karayilan had indeed referred to: "The latest crisis over the cross-border operation into northern Iraq is the last chance for the PKK, which has not accomplished anything substantial for the last 23 years and is doomed to be forgotten." Finally, after their meeting in the Oval Office, both President Bush and Prime Minister Erdoğan promised a joint effort to bring an end to the PKK. The fact that President Bush described the PKK as an enemy not only of Turkey but also of Iraq and the United States implies that Washington has already dismissed the PKK.

The end of the armed conflict does not necessarily mean that Ankara will suffer less in the coming decades unless it manages to tackle the growing hostility of the growing Kurdish diaspora and its satellites inside Turkey. The new ways of the pursuit of the Kurdish separatism seem to have already been deliberated as the PKK's infamous armed conflict has to a great extent lost its popularity among the Kurds of southeast Turkey, especially after the capture of the terrorist leader Abdullah Öcalan in 1998 and more so after the ruling AK Party government's success to address the long-ignored problems of the Kurds. According to an Economist article titled "Turkey's Kurds: Dreams and Reality," in the province of Hakkari, the dominantly Kurdish-populated and socio-economically much deprived city in Turkey's southeast corner, members of a group inspired by the Kurdistan Democratic Party (KDP) of Massoud Barzani whisper of a new plan to unite the Kurds of Turkey, Syria, Iran and Iraq. Such a shift in the pursuit of Kurdish self-determination comes at a time when Barzani, the de-facto leader of the Kurdish regional administration, is also seeking to convince Ankara to recognize himself as the sole representative of the Kurds in the region. According to the same report, Barzani suggests that he would be happy to mediate (between Ankara and the PKK) but insists that the Turks should first recognize him as the Kurd's legitimate representative.

Similarly, in a recent op-ed piece published by *The Washington Post*, Prime Minister Barzani uttered that the only solution to the PKK terrorism problem lies in diplomacy, referring to their desire to be recognized by Ankara as a legitimate counterpart. Interestingly enough, the developments leading to the release of the eight Turkish soldiers earlier captured by the PKK have unraveled almost in tandem with the regional administration's quest to be acknowledged as an able actor. According to a report by *The Independent*, the release was "arranged by the Kurdish regional government, which is eager to avert a Turkish cross-border campaign. Fuad Hussain, the chief of staff of the regional president, said, "This issue proved one thing, the Iraqi Kurds and Iraqi leadership are part of the solution. They are working to have a good relationship with the Turkish people." In the meantime, not only the Iraqi Kurds but also the Democratic Society Party (DTP), the ethnic-Kurdish party within Turkish Parliament often criticized for not publicly condemning the PKK, seemed arguably useful in the release of the soldiers. DTP leader Ahmet Turk took credit for his party by suggesting that his fellow party members had undertaken a crucial role in the release of the Turkish soldiers by traveling to northern Iraq. Both the Kurdish regional administration and DTP officials may have indeed been instrumental in the release of the eight Turkish soldiers. However, the question still remains in the minds of the general public—did the PKK release the eight Turkish soldiers because the regional administration and DTP officials had been able to convince it to do so? Or, did the PKK capture the eight Turkish soldiers as it had never done before in order to make the regional administration and DTP officials seem able to convince the PKK to do what the Turkish government is not able to do?

An inconvenient truth: gathering storm of the anti-Turkey lobby

After the recent turbulence in US-Turkish relations caused by the Armenian diaspora, this is probably the last thing that Ankara would like to come to grips with, but the fact is that once the PKK ceases its terrorist activities, the Kurdish diaspora's anti-Turkey lobbying is likely to take off with great momentum. No doubt the Kurdish diaspora will receive the know-how and logistical support it needs from the other diasporas Turkey has long been dealing with, thereby mobilizing relatively rapidly in both the United States and the European capitals.

The initial examples of such mobility were seen during the Prime Minister Erdoğan's recent visit to Washington. Throughout the week of his visit, the Kurdish-American communities had organized protests in such major cities as Atlanta, Los Angeles, Dallas, Nashville, Phoenix, San Francisco, New York and Washington, allegedly to "express a unified opposition to the recent developments in Turkey and the Turkish government's decision to invade Iraqi Kurdistan." Besides the Kurdish-American diaspora, which is receiving know-how and logistical support from the other more established anti-Turkey diaspora, the Kurdish regional administration's Washington representation is likely to be effective in the near future, as some may rightly argue, to the detriment of the Turkish interests in Washington.

In February 2007, British-educated Qubad Talabani, US representative of the Kurdish regional administration and son of Iraqi President Jalal Talabani, officially opened the Kurdish regional administration's Washington lobbying office. Talabani admirably stated that his goal was to organize grass roots to support the Kurdish interests, promote Kurdish cultural and educational ties with the US and establish a Kurdish congressional caucus and a Kurdish-American business council. Earlier in June 2006, during his speech at the Center for Strategic and International Studies, Talabani called for amnesty for the PKK, the outlawed organization which both the US and the EU lists as a terrorist organization. In addition, another Washington-based NGO allegedly is striving to bring together Turks, Kurds and Arabs in southeastern Turkey via providing professional training to groups of individuals who happen to be predominantly of Kurdish origin. One wonders when, if ever, Turks, Kurds and Arabs were not together for the last millennia.

No shortage to Western allies

Moreover, the recent foreign media coverage of the stand-off between Ankara and northern Iraq over the PKK issue has hinted that the foreign media are unlikely to remain completely unbiased throughout the prospective soft war between Turkey and the non-violent separatist Kurdish formations in northern Iraq and in the Western capitals. The foreign media reported on Ankara's plan to carry out targeted operations against the PKK bases in northern Iraq in such a way that it was hardly possible to tell whether Ankara was targeting the terrorist PKK, which recently killed 48 Turkish soldiers and captured eight, or actually flexing its muscles to invade all of northern Iraq. It seems like a meaningful coincidence that during the same period the Kurdish diaspora organizations close to the PKK were also seeking to garner popular support against Ankara's possible military incursion into northern Iraq, arguing that the latter is indeed planning to invade all of northern Iraq.

In addition to European media, which have generally refused to call the PKK a terrorist organization, certain European governments have not shied away from openly assisting the terrorist organization. The most notable of those include the Danish government, which repeatedly ignored Ankara's demands to shut down the Denmark-based Roj TV, the main media outlet of the PKK used for propaganda; and the French government, which refuses to deliver PKK leaders to Turkish authorities. In 1998, the then socialist French government passed a parliamentary resolution banning the delivery of the PKK members to Turkey. The premise of the resolution was the practice of capital punishment in Turkey and of torture in Turkish prisons. However, despite the ban on the former practice and radical improvements on the latter, French authorities still refuse to cooperate with their Turkish counterparts in capturing the PKK members.

Civil society in southeastern Turkey

Under normal circumstances, it is quite unlikely that Turkey's Kurds, especially those who have long been established in Western cities, would turn against the authority in Ankara and demand secession to the Kurdish regional administration in northern Iraq no matter how prosperous the latter becomes. However, it is not outside the realm of possibility that some may seek to create a non-Kurdish public opinion against Turkey's Kurds, which would expedite the rapprochement between Turkey's Kurds, Kurds abroad and the Kurdish regional administration. Unfortunately, making all this happen is not that difficult given the endowments of digital media and telecommunications as well as the creativity of psychological warfare. Countering it, though, is difficult and requires a deliberate effort on the Turkish side.

More than the official Ankara, it is Turkish civil society in general and the non-separatist Kurdish civil society within Turkey in particular that are able to counter such an existential threat to Turkey's national unity. Any sustainable solution to the threat posed by Kurdish separatism is possible with the socio-economic revival of southeastern Turkey. Accordingly, such revival is dependent on the proliferation of local business associations, volunteer private civic organizations and media outlets which would provide the local people with balanced information, thereby preventing them from being exposed to the Kurdish-separatist propaganda.

The traditional form of social organization called *aşiret*, which has long been viewed as an impediment to the modernization of the southeastern region, can in fact serve as a catalyst to modernization and to the formation of civil society in southeastern Turkey. During our interview, one of the local tribal leaders proudly noted that he has a "block vote" of 4,000 individuals in his tribe (aşiret) and was able to determine what party those votes would go to in the upcoming elections. Given the fact that this is only the number of those who are eligible to vote, and that the traditional size of a family in southeastern Turkey, one can conclude that this young modern tribal leader, aşiret reisi, wearing blue jeans has influence over some 20-30,000 individuals. In addition to the aşirets and the ability to mass mobilize, their allegiance to Turkey is another important factor which makes them critical to any effort addressing problems in southeastern Turkey. A leader of a more established aşiret noted, "I have refused to remove the Turkish flag from the top of my house even during the height of the PKK's raids because removing the Turkish flag would feel like I am stripping off my faith." The question is, why not use this potential to tackle the threat of Kurdish-separatism in the region and, though may seem rather ironic, to foster civil society in southeastern Turkey as a long-term solution to such a threat? Unlike before when the tribal leaders served as protector and provider to the members of their tribes, thereby coercing the members to abide by the aşiret rules, today their role has more of a symbolic nature, and yet influential. Therefore, their influence could be used to

mobilize the local masses to partake in proliferating civil society organizations in the region.

Reforming Turkey's representation abroad

Ankara should mirror similar proliferation of its private civic organizations abroad as well. That is, not only should the number of the Turkish diaspora NGOs in the Western capitals, most notably in Washington, increase, but also the existing ones must be dramatically reformed.
One of the biggest mistakes in Turkey's previous representation abroad
was the absence of the Armenian component of Turkish society. Such
absence has given the Armenian diaspora a lucrative opportunity to
exploit and nurture the "us vs. them" notion. The intellectually shallow
but ideologically deep nationalism present in Turkey's foreign representations, be they official or non-official, has only bolstered that notion.
That mistake should be avoided by making the Kurdish component
of Turkey's identity more visible simply by hiring ethnic-Kurdish citizens of Turkey. Similarly, staffing these organizations should be based
on meritocracy, not ideology. That is, the second generation of Turkish
immigrants as well as new immigrants with sufficient educational and
professional qualifications should be given more opportunity to represent Turkey abroad.

US FOREIGN POLICY
AFTER NOVEMBER 2008 - 1

Prospect for Increased
Turkish-American Cooperation[7]

The recent aerial strikes by Turkish fighter jets on Kurdistan Workers' Party (PKK) camps in the Kandil Mountains, where the terrorists have long found a safe haven, signify the substantial assistance given by Washington to Ankara in the latter's fight against terrorism.

Chief of General Staff Gen. Yaşar Büyükanıt noted that the operation became possible after Washington provided air clearance in northern Iraq and supplied real-time intelligence. This Washington-Ankara cooperation has been viewed as an immediate benefit of the President Bush-Prime Minister Erdoğan meeting on Nov. 5 in Washington. What does this cooperation mean then for US-Turkish relations? Is it just a simple accommodation of Ankara's continuous demands from Washington to finish off the PKK? Has the Justice and Development Party (AK Party) government promised anything in return, in particular to the Bush administration, as the ultranationalist opposition leader Devlet Bahçeli alleged recently? Or, is the so-called US-Turkish strategic partnership really gaining a strategic depth?

Whether the next American president is a Democrat or a Republican, the challenges for US foreign policy are pretty much the same—most notably, stabilizing Iraq and leaving it as soon as possible before the American economy falls into a recession and the country's credibility across the world is lost; securing an able Afghan government even

[7] First appeared in *Today's Zaman* daily on January 03, 2008.

if Osama bin Laden is still at large; balancing Chinese domination of global trade and of the energy resources from Latin America and Africa, thereby securing the US energy needs; containing Russia's revival as a global power; securing a smooth transition to a civilian administration in Pakistan and making sure that control of the country's nuclear weapons remains in the hands of the moderates, which seems less likely after the assassination of opposition leader Benazir Bhutto and the looming chaos; eliminating the Iranian nuclear threat in such a way that the world no longer thinks that Washington is simply a puppet of another regional actor; and finally tackling more general problems such as global warming, pandemic disease and the proliferation of terrorist networks and nuclear weapons.

Both the lessons learned from the mistakes of the Bush administration and the continuing challenges to American interests across the globe require policy makers and scholars to redefine American foreign policy. While the situation at hand is taken advantage of by the liberals to bash neoconservatives and to influence the US president's foreign policy, the mistakes made in the last seven years have forced conservatives to moderate their rhetoric. The conviction on both sides that the US can no longer go it alone assures an emphasis on multilateralism in US foreign policy after the Bush administration. In addition to such a paradigm shift in US foreign policy, converging regional and global interests of Turkey and the US are likely to bring about increased cooperation between the two so long as the former is able to draft long term foreign policy goals driven purely by national interests.

Differing foreign policy approaches of Democrats and Republicans

While the foreign policy approaches of the Democratic candidates of the 2008 US presidential race dramatically differ from that of the current Bush administration and promise multilateralism, relying more on diplomacy than on military power, that of the Republican candidates hardly differs from what has been in place during the last seven years. The Republican candidates, from the frontrunner Rudy Giuliani, former mayor of New York, to Arizona Senator John McCain, whose chance for the office seems quite low, more or less think the same way. That is, the Iraq war was necessary and the US should not refrain from using its military power again in order to protect the free world.

In either case, whether Washington continues to rely on its hard power or shifts to using its soft power in the new term, the prospective foreign policy challenges necessitate that the United States have not only reliable but also able and affable allies in the Muslim world in general and in the Middle East in particular. However, reaching out to such allies seems to be one of the biggest challenges facing the next American president. The discourse of the Republican presidential candidates such as Giuliani, McCain and Mitt Romney reveal their conviction that the United States will regain its global supremacy and be able to lead the international community on matters ranging from the war on terror to global warming. Though such a possibility may not necessarily be a complete delusion, fulfilling such a vision would require improving bilateral relations with Muslim nations. This is especially so given the fact that the current administration and its affiliates in Washington's policy circles have unabashedly associated the religion of those nations with fascism, thereby creating a pseudo-concept of Islamofascism, which may be viewed as an outright insult to the masses—whose hearts and minds are supposed to be won over. Thankfully though, on the other side of the political spectrum is an almost antithetical approach. Recently addressing a Turkish-American group in New York, former US President Bill Clinton, most likely a role model of the next Democratic US president, noted that Islam has been the fastest growing religion in the United States and that he has never felt threatened by that. Nevertheless, no matter how benign the leader in the Oval Office is, what determines the tone of his or her foreign policy is the paradigm or the set of ideas that the administration's policy makers and implementers subscribe to.

Neoconservatism's disastrous legacy

It is probably for this very reason that while running for office, the current president, George W. Bush, seemed quite friendly toward the Muslim world, and yet his foreign policy turned out to be the worst in US history, alienating both Muslim and non-Muslim nations alike across the globe as frequently admitted by both Republicans and Democrats. In his book *America at the Crossroads*, former neoconservative and one of the early advocates of the US invasion of Iraq, Francis Fukuyama, explains the simplistic view of the neoconservatives who have essentially shaped world politics over the last seven years. "Neoconservative theorists saw America exercising a benevolent hegemony over the world, using its enormous power wisely and decisively to fix problems like terrorism, proliferation, rogue states and human rights abuses. The message to the rest of the world was, in effect, 'Trust us, we know what's best for you, and even if you don't agree with our policies at the moment you will come to see that we are right in the end'." With this mindset guiding the advisors of the Bush administration in policy circles and academia, Fukuyama notes, US foreign policy has become associated with regime change, benevolent hegemony, monopolarity, pre-emption and American exceptionalism.

One wishes that the neoconservatives were as naïve as Fukuyama portrays them to be and that the disastrous results of their policies could easily be undone. The controversial question of whether they have been naïve or well-intentioned aside, some may claim almost a complete parallel between the mindset of the neoconservatives and that of authoritarian leaders such as Joseph Stalin and Saddam Hussein, who had considered themselves benevolent and believed that the masses would eventually understand the merits of their policies. Certainly, this is not to say there is a parallel between the Bush administration and the authoritarian regimes of Stalin or Saddam Hussein.

US FOREIGN POLICY
AFTER NOVEMBER 2008 - 2

What's next: Realism, liberal institutionalism or something in between like realistic Wilsonianism?[8]

The students of international relations in American academia are pondering the question of what paradigm should guide US foreign policy after the Bush administration, a period deemed the "post-post-Sept. 11 era."

Should the United States preserve its military presence around the globe at the present level? Should it directly or indirectly interfere with the internal affairs of other states for the sake of protecting the interests of its own and of the free world? How should it handle the national security threats such as nuclear proliferation, emergence of terrorist networks and the regional conflicts such as the Israeli-Palestinian conflict?

The co-authors of *The Israel Lobby and US Foreign Policy*, John Mearsheimer and former Harvard Professor Stephen Walt, propose "off-shore balancing" as a main US foreign policy approach, which recognizes, "the United States does not need to control other parts of the world or tell other societies how to govern their own internal processes." A neorealist who takes the world as it is and does not aspire to create a world in the image of the US, Walt suggests that the United States should instead "maintain local balances of power to ensure that key areas of the world are not dominated by hostile powers." That is, for instance, the oil resources in the Middle East or Africa should not fall under the control of a hostile power or of a group of such powers.

---

[8] First appeared in *Today's Zaman* daily on January 04, 2008.

Walt acknowledges that the US has a limit to its power and that it cannot run other societies. Therefore the US should not interfere with other nations' internal affairs and should reduce its global military presence since the high level of military presence generates resentment and fuels terrorism. The neorealist approach, Walt laments, has not been adopted by many US presidents because it is viewed as a method that would move the United States to isolationism.

An alternative to the "off-shore balancing" strategy of neorealism is liberal institutionalism, spearheaded by John Ikenberry of Princeton University. Ikenberry argues that the biggest challenge of the next US president will be to "rebuild US authority, respect and credibility and regain the ready support of its allies and other states." Therefore, he suggests, the US foreign policy in the post-post-Sept. 11 era should be based on multilateralism and exercise the US influence through international organizations and alliances. That is, instead of taking unilateral military actions and interfering with the internal affairs of other states, Washington should ensure economic and political interdependence among states by creating international frameworks for cooperation and by strengthening the existing ones such as the United Nations.

Another foreign policy approach comes from Francis Fukuyama of SAIS (School of Advanced International Studies) who seems to have come to grips with the perils of neoconservatism, which he had subscribed to previously. Though he had initially supported the US invasion of Iraq, Fukuyama admits that the invasion has turned Iraq into a training base for al-Qaeda and its affiliate terrorist networks, thereby helping the Bush administration fulfill its own prophecy that the Islamist terrorists pose the greatest danger to the US not only abroad but also at home. Parallel to the neorealists, Fukuyama agrees that the overwhelming military presence of the US in other countries, especially in the Middle East, has become counterproductive and breeds resentment toward the United States. With his alternative foreign policy strategy, "realistic Wilsonianism," Fukuyama suggests that with preventive wars and regime change via military intervention never off the table completely, the US should care about what goes on inside the countries, promote democratic ends via non-military means and exercise its power through international organizations. As such, he concurs with those who think the future of US foreign policy lies in multilateralism, international institutions and alliances.

If the last seven years of the Bush administration has taught any lesson to Americans, it is that the US can no longer go it alone in dealing with the regional and global challenges it faces. It is highly likely that with the new president, whether Republican or Democrat, Washington will still pursue a foreign policy driven by the present fears and concerns, such as transnational terrorism, the spiraling effects of the Israeli-Palestinian conflict, democratization of the Middle East, energy security and maintaining its dominance in world trade; however, it will do so more through multilateral channels and international institutions than on its own. At this point, the prospects for an increased Turkish-American cooperation in the years to come lie in Turkey's ability to shape itself as a regional power motivated more by its national interests than by national emotions.

Turkey: From passive partnership to active partnership

Turkey's ready compliance with the US ever since the strategic partnership agreement signed between the two earned the former continuous criticism from both Turkish and foreign observers that it has been giving priority to the US strategic interests over its own regional interests. While the subsequent Turkish governments were blamed for their inability to draft and execute a conclusive policy on the Kurdistan Workers' Party (PKK) terrorism, they have also been blamed for their inability to do anything in the region, let alone in the oil-rich northern Iraq populated with Kurds, without the approval of Washington. Not to mention Ankara's immediate support to the US during the first Gulf War, which in a way helped the PKK terrorists to infiltrate Turkish soil among the fleeing Iraqi Kurds and caused dramatic economic repercussions since it ended the sizeable trade between Turkey and Iraq almost overnight. With these lessons learned from the past experiences and under the closer scrutiny of the public, the new generation of Turkish political and military strata tends to be more cautious when it comes to cooperating with the US or accommodating the US interests in the region, especially when it comes to any Kurdish formation near Turkey's southeastern border.

Certainly Turkey would be better off engaging with and shaping the developments next to its border than simply blocking them because such an engagement would provide Ankara with the opportunity and ability to control the actual outcome of that formation. Those who argue that a truly democratic formation near Turkey's southeastern border with a predictable and rational government not under the grip of a particular clan or a well-connected leader but elected through free and fair elections would benefit Turkey's geostrategic and economic interests in the region may not necessarily be wrong. Nor does such a possible formation deserve outright opposition without any deep thought given to it just because it may also benefit the US interests in the region as well. It appears that from now on Ankara and Washington will share more common interests and as such will need more cooperation. After all, it is well known inside the beltway that Washington would also be better off having Ankara, its long time ally and compliant partner, instead of the soon-to-be nuclearized rogue state or a state having difficulty getting along with its Arab neighbors, in charge of the region where it can no longer sustain its military presence.

Last but not the least is the need for further and continuous intelligence sharing between the Turkish and American security services as the weakening PKK increases urban disturbance within Turkey's western cities. At the end of the day, nobody should expect Turkey's terrorism problem to come to an end after a series of successful operations on the PKK camps in northern Iraq, which may certainly finish off the PKK in the mountains.

ETHNIC CHALLENGES IN
POST-AK PARTY TURKISH POLITICS[9]

T urks tend to be cynical about the European Union's intentions when it comes to dealing with the Kurdish issue. That is to say, they view European attempts to make Turkey more liberal and respectful of the fundamental rights of its ethnic Kurdish community as a heinous attempt to create an independent Kurdish state. Instead, Turks could reciprocate their European counterparts' goodwill to promote ethnic and cultural pluralism in Turkey by simply promoting the Flemish and Walloon cultures of Belgium; the Scottish, Welsh and Northern Irish cultures of the United Kingdom; the Breton and North African cultures of France; the Albanian and Sicilian cultures of Italy; Spain's Basque and Catalan cultures; and the Turkish culture of Germany. No need to mention that Ankara could and should have used its diplomatic clout to convince Athens to recognize its ethnic Turkish and Muslim minorities, which it has so far not even included in the national census. Skeptics would argue that Athens indeed intends to let these minorities diminish either through migration to Turkey or assimilation into the orthodox Greek identity.

Regardless of any external meddling, Turkey's Kurdish issue seems already on the way to becoming a major source of instability for Turkey in the coming months. Though the Kurds have enjoyed unprecedented political expansion during the rule of the Justice and Development Party (AK Party) government and 20 pro-Kurdish representatives won seats in Parliament, enabling them to later form a parliamentary group, it is dubious whether they will enjoy the same political space in the absence of a unifying party like the AK Party. As a matter of fact,

---

[9]   First appeared in *Today's Zaman* daily on April 24, 2008.

even the current situation may be unsatisfactory for the Kurds. Sezgin Tanrıkulu, head of the Diyarbakır Bar Association, notes that a sizeable segment of the Kurdish population sees armed struggle as legitimate because they think they are excluded from the democratic process. Given the course of developments in Turkey, a real exclusion of Kurds from the political process will likely take place when and if the AK Party is shut down, literally leaving the Kurdish deputies alone in Parliament with the Republican People's Party (CHP) and the Nationalist Movement Party (MHP).

The other scenario is the following: Neither opposition party cooperates with the ruling AK Party to amend the Constitution to prevent the AK Party's closure, and then the government calls for an early election on June 29, 2008, combining parliamentary and local elections, and the AK Party gains a landslide electoral victory on both ballots, either severely marginalizing the opposition in Parliament or even leaving them out of Parliament due to the 10 percent entry threshold. The new parliamentary arithmetic, which would seem crushingly in favor of the AK Party and relatively in favor of the pro-Kurdish politicians, would mobilize ultranationalist groups against the Kurdish presence in Parliament while their representation is either marginalized or democratically left out of Parliament. Theoretically, the presence of pro-Kurdish politicians in Parliament and the political mobilization of Turkey's ethnic-Kurdish citizens along with it should create a peaceful cultural plurality. Practically, however, in the absence of two or more parties in Parliament at the same time balancing each other out on the Kurdish issue, a Turkish-versus-Kurdish struggle for political gain is likely to be the main source of conflict in Turkish politics.

Ethnic plurality or ethnic conflict?

Under purely secular circumstances where two or more ethnic groups view one another distinct as opposed to similar, the expansion of politics enables these ethnic groups' political mobilization and relative economic well-being, which in turn sustains their political mobilization. Therefore, political and economic expansion of the ethnic groups strengthens ethnic mobilization in general, which in turn increases prospects for conflict among various ethnic groups.

Subscribing to the constructivist approach, prominent American sociologist Joane Nagel argues that ethnicity is not a primordial identity but a way of self-definition: an identity constructed and reconstructed parallel to changing political and economic circumstances and the desire of reaping the benefits of those changing circumstances. Nagel further explains that parallel to political and economic modernization and to the extent that resources are available, ethnic identities diffuse from smaller to larger scale in order to seize emerging political and economic opportunities. Therefore, the concurrent diminishing and emergence of ethnic boundaries takes place as small ethnic groups join together to create a larger and stronger political unit under an overarching ethnic identity, or they dissolve themselves into a larger and stronger ethnic group to achieve their particular goals within and through that larger ethnic group. Once the small ethnic groups achieve their intended goals, they may reclaim their original ethnic identity.

The emergence and development of the ethnic Kurdish identity in Turkey illustrates such a political construction of ethnic identities. Ankara faced the Kurdish ethnicity challenge for the first time when the Allied Powers of World War I dictated at the Treaty of Sèvres in 1920 that the Kurds should be given autonomy after the division of the Ottoman Empire. Nevertheless, the treaty was not ratified by the Turkish Parliament, and three years later, in the Lausanne Treaty, Britain withdrew its earlier support for Kurdish autonomy to gain Turkish support to isolate Russia. Neither then nor later—at least so far—has the variety within the ethnic Kurdish identity been recognized. That is to say, the ethnic Kurdish identity has been viewed as monolithic for political reasons and its sub-categories—such as Kurmanji-speaking Kurds, Sorani-speaking Kurds, Zaza-speaking Kurds, Alevi Kurds, Sunni Kurds and Assyrian Kurds—have not been mentioned. It would only be reasonable for both Kurdish leaders and the external actors who have historically shown great interest in Kurdish autonomy to sustain an overarching Kurdish identity to achieve certain political and economic goals. However, once the Kurds achieve a political and economic autonomy, one can expect the fault lines among those sub-Kurdish identities to re-emerge and further ethnic division to take place. Then, one can even expect an Armenian claim over the Kurdish entity on the basis that a sizeable number of Armenians had converted to Islam and joined the Kurds to avoid the forced displacement imposed by the Ottoman state during World War I.

However the causes that led to the emergence and development of a seemingly monolithic Kurdish identity cannot be limited to the instrumental calculations of both Kurdish leaders and their foreign allies. As a matter of fact, the Turkish state's repressive policies, or fascist policies, as some may put it, against Kurdish locals during the course of the fight against the outlawed Kurdistan Workers' Party (PKK) have also greatly contributed to the construction of a unified ethnic Kurdish identity. Not only the poorly managed displacement of the Kurdish population from village to city, but the mistreatment and torture of Kurdish individuals due to alleged ties to the PKK have solidified the ethnic Kurdish identity against the state. So the Kurdish people's ever-increasing grievances were most effective in the political formation of the distinct Kurdish identity. After all, as Aliza Marcus notes in her *Blood and Belief*, how would Abdullah Öcalan manipulate Kurds to take up arms against the Turkish state without even firing one bullet himself throughout the 17 years in which he managed to administer the PKK from Damascus?

From mountain to Parliament: happily ever after?

Öcalan's 1999 capture and the subsequent dispersion of the PKK's leadership increased hopes for a non-violent resolution to Turkey's so-called Kurdish problem. With the CIA's assistance, the Turkish secret service took Öcalan into custody right after he left the Greek Embassy in Kenya hoping to flee to Holland. The first video images of Öcalan, in which he pleaded, "I love my country. My mother is a Turk. If I can be of service, I will," were probably more disappointing and devastating to the pro-PKK Kurds than anything else up until that point. No matter how regretful the Kurdish nationalists have been for years and the comrades lost to the PKK's armed struggle, they are unlikely to give up pursuit of their ethno-nationalist goals.

Turkey's recent political and legal reforms to accommodate ethnic and cultural plurality in the political space provide a fertile ground for the non-violent pursuit of ethnic Kurdish nationalism. The very fact that the pro-Kurdish Democratic Society Party (DTP) has so far peacefully coexisted with the Turkish nationalist MHP in Parliament illustrates a significant change in Turkish politics. The predecessors of the DTP, the pro-Kurdish People's Democracy Party (HADEP) and Democracy Party (DEP), were both shut down and their members banned from party politics while serving jail time. The question is whether this change is to stay or is just contingent on the ruling AK Party's parliamentary majority. If it is due to the AK Party, then the post-AK Party Parliament would be too small for the pro-Kurdish DTP to survive. The shrinking political space for Kurds would eventually lead to increased PKK violence. If the change is because Turkish nationalists have indeed liberalized, then the ethnic fault lines between Turks and Kurds are likely to deepen because the DTP and the emerging pro-Kurdish civic organizations would want to maximize their ethnic interests, which is quite normal and acceptable.

What will happen, then? Will Kurds be able to pursue their goals through politics happily ever after? Quite unlikely... In the absence of a majority center-right party in Parliament such as the AK Party, the military will inevitably step in to eliminate rising ethnic tensions between Turkish and Kurdish nationalists. Likely attacks by ultranationalists on Turkish citizens of Kurdish origin would only increase nationwide instability and insecurity, thereby making a regulative military interference amenable to the public.

What if the AK Party is not shut down? In other words, what if the ruling AK Party avoids being shut down by going for an early election on June 29, as has been proposed by a senior party member? According to AK Party deputy Salih Kapusuz, the AK Party will first seek to convince the CHP and MHP to support the government's constitutional amendment plan to toughen political party closure. If the two do not cooperate, the AK Party will alternatively resort to its earlier strategy of early elections to overcome the closure case against it by increasing its public support, just like it did to overcome the chaos sparked by the AK Party's nomination of Abdullah Gül for president in 2007. According to various recent polls, if there were an election today, the AK Party would be likely to get in excess of 51 percent of the popular vote, while the CHP and the MHP are likely to garner 12 and 9 percent or less, respectively. Given that political parties must receive at least 10 percent of the popular vote to enter Parliament, there is even a possibility of an electoral outcome that would make the AK Party the only party in Parliament, along with the independently elected pro-Kurdish DTP deputies. Such an overwhelming electoral victory by the AK Party would only exacerbate the political instability, instigating a possible civil unrest of which the citizens of Kurdish origin would likely be the prime target.

FETHULLAH GÜLEN

Threat, Benefactor, or Both?[10]

T urkey is a country where there is seemingly no end to oddities. As the majority of Turks (and foreign observers of Turkey) ponder how it is possible to shut down a ruling political
party that has been more pro-European, reformist and economically
successful than any other party in the history of the republic, the case
of Fethullah Gülen adds another to many such oddities. Gülen has been
prosecuted in his own country for alleged attempts to destroy the current state system and replace it with a government centered on religion. Yet Gülen is widely revered both home and abroad for his ideas
and the work that inspired a world-wide civic movement focused on
education and intercultural dialogue.

The Economist magazine has recently drawn attention to Gülen and
the schools across the world that his vision has inspired. A New York
Times article suggested that these Turkish schools inspired by Gülen
offer such countries as Pakistan a gentler vision of Islam. Various Western scholars have argued that Gülen is a bridge between Islam and the
West. Foreign Policy Magazine considers him one of the world's top 100
public intellectuals. Few marginal commentators view him as a grave
threat. Finally, a Reuters report described Gülen as an advocate of moderate Islam rooted in modern life and asked whether he is a threat or
benefactor.

What is he really? Is he a threat or benefactor? As a matter of fact,
Fethullah Gülen—and the world-wide movement he has inspired—is
neither a threat nor a benefactor, but both. After all, both descriptions
are relative and depend on where one stands.

---

[10] This article first appeared in Balkanalysis on June 16, 2008.

Why Gülen May Look Like a Threat to Status-quo Protectionists

Fethullah Gülen enjoys unprecedented popularity in Turkey, and increasingly abroad. He has touched the lives of the last three generations of Turks and continues to do so through writings and speeches broadcast through mass media and the Internet. The Gülen phenomenon, later developing into a broad non-contentious civic movement, had its origins in the early 1960s when Gülen began preaching at mosques and delivering open-to-the-public conferences throughout Turkey. His audience consisted primarily of middle-aged conservatives and older teenagers (both high school and university students). The former of these two groups later opened and financed university preparatory courses and private secondary-high schools, and the latter ran and taught at these schools. These courses met with unparalleled success in preparing students both for national university entrance exams and for successful competition in international science contests, thus attracting more and more pupils to schools and more and more volunteers to the movement's service projects. Though none of Gülen's teachings have literally been taught at these institutions, the morals of the teachers were telling all about who has inspired them and these schools.

Gülen's early teachings are generally characterized by his emphasis on religion and science as complementary, not contradictory. In addition to the extensive number of books he authored directly, many more have been compiled from his lectures and made available to public. Audio and video cassettes, CDs and DVDs of his lectures have reached an even wider audience. Through putting into practice what Gülen has preached, the schools have achieved national and international success. This has convinced the majority Turkish public that while preserving their Islamic values they can aim high. Those of the majority Turkish public who have been stuck in the periphery ever since the induction of a strictly secularist regime have realized that people can indeed remain observant Muslims and simultaneously become bureaucrats, judges, diplomats, or even generals, prime ministers and presidents.

It would certainly be an overestimation of Gülen's influence to attribute the entire social transformation in Turkey to the Gülen movement.

Nevertheless, its impact cannot be denied. Michael Rubin of the American Enterprise Institute argues that so-called "Gulen members dominate the Turkish police and divisions within the interior ministry. Under the stewardship of Prime Minister Recep Tayyip Erdoğan, one of Gülen's most prominent sympathizers, tens of thousands of other Gülen supporters have entered the Turkish bureaucracy." It may be a real challenge for thousands (or millions) of Turks to prove that they are not foot-soldiers of Gülen just because they admire him. In the meantime, they continue to pose a threat to both Turkey's exclusivist elite—who have traditionally occupied political, economic and judicial space—and to the vested interest abroad who have enjoyed the freedom of influencing, if not manipulating, Turkey through that elite.

Why Gülen May Look Like a Benefactor

Given the operation of schools all across the globe and the ongoing interfaith-intercultural dialogue he has inspired, Gülen may well be seen as a benefactor. He is seen so mostly by those who have benefited from his work and inspiration one way or another. For example, Kerim Balci of Turkey, a prominent columnist at Turkish newspaper *Zaman*, notes that the movement took him from his village and made him what he could not even dream of becoming then. Muid Rasul of Kenya, graduate of Nairobi's Light Academy (founded by Gülen movement volunteers), mentions the role of his dedicated teachers in his success, when he proudly notes that he has accepted a full-scholarship from Harvard University while declining the same offer from Yale. A Ugandan businessman in Kampala thanks his Gülen-inspired Turkish counterparts for setting an example for him and his Ugandan colleagues of how to open schools with their own resources and without expecting help from the state or other donors. Similarly, an ethnic Kurdish mother from a distant village in southeastern Turkey who cannot even speak Turkish expresses her gratitude to Gülen because his admirers helped her teenaged daughter go to school: "I did not have any say even during my marriage arrangement, let alone my childhood. But, my husband asks my daughter's opinion frequently on issues and she is able to influence his decisions."

Moreover, Gülen has touched lives through the massive interfaith dialogue that, initiated in Turkey, now spans through continents. An Assyrian Christian man from Mardin in southeastern Turkey says, "Up until Fethullah Gülen and the Journalists and Writers Foundation (GYV) started the interfaith dialogue process in the mid 1990s, people around us used to merely view us as 'unbelievers'. After Gülen initiated dialogue with the Christian and Jewish leaders, people started to respect us as 'People of the Book.'" Gülen may seem like a benefactor to this Christian man and many others who have had a similar experience. In addition, Gülen may seem a benefactor to a Jew who heard him publicly denouncing suicide bombings.

On the question of power, it is hard to make a convincing argument that Gülen is after political power given the fact that there does not seem to be any tangible attempt in his seventy-odd year lifetime to establish a political organization or take over the government. However, one can reasonably argue that Gülen may be seeking influence, for he advocates moderate Islam rooted in modern life, freedom of speech, and freedom of individual practice of faiths. In the final analysis, it is only normal that Gülen may be seen as a threat by some while a benefactor by others. What matters really is where one stands and how he or she perceives Gülen and the world-wide civic movement he has inspired.

A PLANNED MILITARY COUP IN TURKEY

How to Stage a Coup D'état in Turkey, or How to Prevent One[11]

Turks have been shaken by yet another "action plan" for military intervention in politics. The so-called action plan, drafted in September 2007 and recently leaked from within the military, outlines how the Turkish Armed Forces (TSK) was planning to intervene in politics and the civilian sphere.

According to the *Taraf* daily, the action allegedly intended to attract public attention onto matters the TSK "felt sensitive about." Accordingly, the action plan included a series of steps to change public opinion to regard the current Justice and Development Party (AK Party) government as "the focal point of anti-secular activities," the new constitutional reform package as "adversarial to the nation state" and the pro-Kurdish Democratic Society Party (DTP) in Parliament as "terrorist." Under the guiding principles section, the action plan cautioned its perpetrators not to come into conflict with other state institutions and not to look like they were interfering in daily politics. In addition, the plan underlined the importance of maintaining constant contact with the rectors of the universities capable of influencing public opinion, senior judges, influential journalists and artists, and of making sure that these people worked in tandem with the TSK.

Assuming that the current AK Party government and/or the civilian initiatives associated with it are not so cunning as to feed a fake "action plan" to the media in order to pre-empt a possible military coup d'état, and that what was leaked to the media was indeed an authentic "action plan" for a military coup against the civilian government, two

---

[11]   First appeared in *Today's Zaman* daily on June 23, 2008.

questions arise in a skeptical mind. First, would the perpetrators have succeeded in staging their intended military coup had the action plan not been leaked? Second, would the ruling AK Party government be able to prevent the coup if the action plan was enacted as intended? The answers to these two critical questions combined should also give an idea not only about whether Turkish democracy is now mature enough to counter its existential threats, but also on how to counter an action plan for a military intervention in Turkish politics.

Coups 101 and the "action plan"

The action plan seems to have missed the most essential aspect of a successful military coup: popular support. Thus it was already risking failure. David Hebditch and Ken Connor's survey of military coups in the 20th century, "How to Stage a Military Coup: From Planning to Execution," indicates that a successful military coup is possible only if it comes, or at least seems like it comes, as a panacea to prolonged public grievances. For instance, the first military coup of the century, the Wuchang Uprising of 1911, was carried out to end the Manchu (Qing) Dynasty in China by Western-educated army officers who thought an emperor was no longer needed. The underlying discourse of the coup was "democracy and liberty" against the brutal emperor. Another successful military coup was carried out in 1952 by Gen. Gamal Abdel Nasser and his "Free Officers" against King Farouk, who had long been resented by the public for his negligence of popular concerns and for his failure as commander-in-chief, which brought about Egypt's embarrassing defeat by Israel in 1948. In addition to King Farouk's unpopularity, Nasser's discourse of Arab nationalism and calls for an end to British imperialism in the Arab world made it relatively easier for the Free Officers to garner popular support for the coming military coup. Similarly, in 1959 when Fidel Castro and his armed comrades stormed Havana, the purpose was seemingly to overthrow the US-backed dictatorship of Fulgencio Batista, who allegedly allowed nearly 75 percent of Cuba's agricultural lands to fall into the hands of American sugar producers. Again the underlying discourse of the coup was to end US imperialism first in Cuba and then throughout Latin America.

Turkey's own record of military coups also indicates that strong popular support is necessary for a successful military coup. The infamous series of military coups in Turkey started with the one on May 27, 1960, when Gen. Cemal Gursel removed President Celal Bayar, Prime Minister Adnan Menderes and the Cabinet from power and dissolved Parliament. Gen. Gursel announced that "the purpose of the coup was to bring the country with all speed to a fair, clean and solid democracy." Though the discourse looks ironic, the junta could easily get away with it because the majority of the Turkish population was hardly familiar with the concept of democracy, let alone able to defend it against army generals and their civilian status quo protectionists. An even more ironic and yet successful military intervention in politics took place on March 12, 1971, when the government of Süleyman Demirel resigned at the military high command's order. The justification for the intervention was the need for a stronger government able to tackle the ongoing anarchical situation in the country and suppress civilian violence. The majority of the public welcomed the military intervention, hoping that it would bring security. Ten years later, on Sept. 12, 1980, history repeated itself and this time Gen. Kenan Evren overthrew Demirel's government, proclaiming that the army itself would tackle the ongoing anarchical situation in the country. The public welcomed the intervention again, hoping that it would end the daily carnage between leftists and rightists.

So, as seen in both foreign and local examples, popular support is essential to success in any military intervention. This became obvious once again in April 2007, when unknown members of the Turkish military posted a politically motivated statement on the TSK Web site. Yet even such a limited and abstract attempt to intervene in politics was met by the public with a harsh critique of the TSK.

Nevertheless, the authors of the action plan seem to have thought about it. The action plan advises increasing Turkish nationalism by provoking the ethnic Kurds in the Southeast with continuous military operations and village raids, as well as by creating civilian casualties among northern Iraq's Kurds as a result of a series of heavy bombings. It is technically wise to increase Turkish nationalism to garner popular support before any military intervention. However, the strategy advised in the action plan would only undermine the credibility of the TSK, because Turks already think that the brutal military operations in Turkey's Kurdish-dominated regions are partially responsible for prolonging Turkey's terror problem. So the more draconian the military becomes, as the government tries to revive Turkey's southeast, the further its credibility will be undermined. Any constructed rhetoric of Turkish patriotism by the coup perpetrators would likely be dwarfed by the patriotism that seems to be exhibited by the government's economic performance and political successes over the last six years and by the success of civilian initiatives in promoting Turkey and Turkish culture across the globe. Last but not the least, compared to the discourse of the previous successful military interventions, the discourse of removing a government because it has become a "focal point of anti-secular activities" while that very government is supported by half the voters in the country seems a little awkward, if not absurd.

Is the AK Party government sophisticated and strong enough?

So what would have happened if the action plan had not been leaked, and was indeed carried out? Would the AK Party government be able to counter its gradual and destructive impact? The action plan seems to have aimed at portraying the ruling AK Party government as a focal point of anti-secular activities. Given the priorities of the AK Party government in its second term, it would not be so difficult to do so. Fantasizing about solving Turkey's headscarf-ban problem overnight after receiving 47 percent of the popular vote was probably the biggest mistake the government has made so far. Starting the second term with the obvious goal of lifting the infamous headscarf-ban, the AK Party government has only irritated the status quo protectionists further and made the moderate seculars revisit their thoughts on Prime Minister Recep Tayyip Erdoğan and his team. The fact that the government has lost its momentum in negotiating for Turkey's EU membership also decreased the overarching popular support for the AK Party government.

Another mistake made by the government was not to embrace the pro-Kurdish DTP deputies and to remain silent when the Constitutional Court filed a closure case against the DTP. Therefore, once the coup perpetrators launched a smear campaign against the pro-Kurdish DTP as instructed by the action plan, the AK Party government would not be in a position to defend the freely elected DTP deputies' constitutional rights to remain in Parliament because Prime Minister Erdoğan himself had already acquiesced, if not paved the road to, viewing the DTP as a sort of political extension of the outlawed Kurdistan Workers' Party (PKK) terrorist organization. These two major mistakes of the government diminished the likelihood of the public standing behind it as a unified force.

Try another time?

Even though the AK Party government still has weaknesses that would make some rogue members of the military fantasize about intervening in politics, thankfully Turkey now has a burgeoning civil society with media outlets and nongovernmental organizations that are quite vigilant against any sort of military intervention. A day after the action plan leaked to the media, some 20 civil society organizations organized public protests, in which thousands of civilians chanted "Raise your voice against military intervention!" Certainly, the ability of civilians to stand firm in the face of any threat of military intervention has something to do with the country's six consecutive years of economic growth, the AK Party government's unprecedented success in Turkey's EU accession process and political-legal reforms, the opposition of the US and the EU to any sort of military intervention in Turkish politics and the generation shift that consolidated the idea that in democracies the military's place is the barracks, not Parliament. So long as these conditions are intact, it would probably not be wise to attempt another military coup in Turkey because it would only undermine the credibility of the TSK.

GÜLEN AND THE AK PARTY

A Common Quest for Democracy
or Something More?[12]

Given the variety of opinions on the subject, it is obvious that the question of what kind of relationship exists between the Gülen movement and the Justice and Development Party (AK Party) intrigues not only foreign observers of Turkey but also some Turks. While foreign observers categorically associate the Gülen movement and the AK Party with one another, most Turks see the two as natural allies in promoting democracy and liberties in the country and some marginal commentators speculate that the two pose a threat to the secular regime of the state.

An article in *The Economist* magazine ("A Religious Revival," Jan. 31, 2008) wrote: "Turkey's richest Islamic fraternity is helping the AK [Party] to win more Kurdish votes. [The Gülen-admirers] distributed meat to some 60,000 families during the Muslim Feast of Sacrifice in December." Another one ("A farm boy on the world stage," March 6, 2008) explained, "The [Gülen-admirers] have lots in common with the ruling Justice and Development Party, and they cooperate, but their interests are not identical." One report in *The Guardian* daily ("Islamic scholar voted world's No. 1 thinker," June 23, 2008) refers to an alliance between the AK Party and the Gülen movement: "The AKP, which is allied to Gülen, is contesting a case brought by Turkey's chief prosecutor to shut it down and ban it from politics for allegedly…[breaching] the country's secular constitution."

Many Turkish intellectuals and academics point rather at the common values that bring the Gülen movement and the AK Party togeth-

---

[12] First appeared in *Today's Zaman* daily on July 02, 2008.

er. Muhammed Çetin argues that Fethullah Gülen has always favored democratic institutions and free elections while opposing the use of Islam as a political ideology and a party philosophy. Ahmet Kuru suggests that Gülen gradually brought about change in the Turkish attitude toward the European Union, which was previously perceived as a "Christian club" and a threat to Turkish national and Muslim identity. According to Nevval Sevindi, Gülen struggles to promote a democratic, pluralistic and free society. Along similar lines, Şahin Alpay contends that Gülen's efforts to build bridges of dialogue within the society have put the religion in its rightful place and prevented the society from polarizing into believers and nonbelievers. Therefore, these and many other intellectuals have perceived the Gülen movement's interaction with political parties, most notably with the AK Party, as an attempt to consolidate democracy in Turkey.

Deeper than it seems?

However, the controversy over the relationship between the ruling AK Party and the diffused social network, which happens to be called—for brevity—the Gülen movement, goes beyond the issue of merely exchanging opinions on policy matters and promoting democracy and liberties. Though so far has no solid evidence surfaced regarding the existence of a possibly deeper relationship between the AK Party and the Gülen movement, certain marginal groups and media commentators have frequently alleged that bureaucratic positions, especially within the judiciary and police force, are filled with "Gülen followers" and that the AK Party government has been complicit, if not instrumental, in this happening. In addition, it has been alleged that those "Gülen followers" in the judiciary and the police are behind the two most critical organized-crime operation in republican history. One is the Şemdinli case, following which a court case extended in 2005 against Chief of General Staff Gen. Yaşar Büyükanıt, then the land forces commander, for his alleged role in a plot that seemed to aim at instigating the ethnic-Kurds in Şemdinli, a southeastern province in Turkey.

The other is the Ergenekon operation, which is technically ongoing, and yet pretty much stalled due to the closure case against the AK

Party. It is a police operation against the so-called "deep state," an organized criminal network of corrupt judges, military and police officials,
senior bureaucrats, diplomats, politicians and the mafia, which is believed
to have perpetrated a number of political assassinations and frequently obstructed the democratization process in the country. As a matter
of fact, the Şemdinli case was thought to be the first attempt to crack
down on the "deep state." Yet it was suddenly aborted and the prosecutor, Ferhat Sarıkaya, was banned from practicing law by the Supreme
Board of Prosecutors and Judges (HSYK) due to his allegedly having
insulted the Turkish military by opening the case. No need to mention that the same marginal groups and commentators labeled liberal
prosecutor Sarıkaya a "Gülen follower" in the due process leading to
the revoking of his law credentials.

The Şemdinli case is not the only one that saw its investigation
and prosecution processes stalled. The investigations into the assassinations of Catholic priest Andrea Santoro, Turkish-Armenian journalist Hrant Dink and Council of State Judge M. Yücel Özbilgin have
also been subject to stalling attempts through the bringing of issues
related to Gülen into the picture and diverting attention from the real
suspects. From the status quo protectionists' perspective, the name
"Fethullah Gülen" is certainly quite a lucrative one to exploit. Gülen
has such a wide public recognition in the country that whenever his
name is involved in any discussion, at least for a while, the topic shifts
from the main point. As the record hitherto indicates, Gülen prefers not
to get involved in such day-to-day debates and scandals and, hence, not
to respond to his accusers with attacks. This makes it even more tempt-
ing for the status quo protectionists to exploit his name on every likely and unlikely occasion.

Based on this unfair treatment of Gülen and the Gülen movement
by the status quo protectionists, one may be tempted to conclude that
these very same status quo protectionists are making up allegations
one after another about an instrumental or symbiotic relationship
between the Gülen movement and the AK Party. However, such a quick
conclusion may also hinder one's ability to explore the true nature of
the relationship between the Gülen movement and the AK Party.

Similarities, differences, obligations:
possible interpretations of the relationship

There are similarities and differences between the Gülen movement and the AK Party's positions on various social, economic and political matters, and hence multiple ways of interpreting the relationship between the Gülen movement and the AK Party. Also, there are contextual obligations that bring the two together. On the one hand, the Gülen movement and the AK Party seem like they share a similar vision for Turkey.

First of all, having bitter experiences with the status quo protectionists' strict interpretation and practice of secularism, both the Gülen movement and the AK Party have interest in promoting participatory democracy and civil liberties at all levels, and hence in creating a vibrant civil society. According to Jill Carroll of the University of Houston, Gülen envisions a society in which freedom of thought and conscience is guaranteed, which is tolerant in matters of religious belief and practice and which allows vigorous inquiry and debate on all issues. The initial steps in search of such a society were taken in the mid-1990s by the Gülen-inspired Journalists and Writers' Foundation's Abant Platform, in which Turkish intellectuals from all camps (leftist, rightist, liberal, conservative and atheist) gathered together and contested their opinions. Among those intellectuals were politicians who later on took part in the formation of the AK Party. One may speculate that the "conservative democracy" discourse of the AK Party was inspired by those series of intellectual gatherings. It is hard to know for sure whether or to what extent the founders of the AK Party were inspired by the ideas presented at the platform. They may well have benefited from the Abant Platform or from the other idea platforms in the media initiated by Gülen-admirers, as these platforms have been quite active in fostering debate in the public sphere and in creating knowledge. However, one thing is certain: Today the status-quo protectionists accuse some of the government ministers and senior members of being "Gülen-followers" just because they participated in the Abant Platform and the like.

Second, both the Gülen movement and the AK Party commonly share Mustafa Kemal Atatürk's vision of bringing Turkey up to the level of the modern civilizations, namely creating a new Turkey that is politically and economically capable of competing in the global arena. In his public speeches and writings, Gülen often notes that he had very much resented the fact that Turkey's opinion is not regarded in any international platform. Accordingly, both the Gülen movement and the AK Party seem to agree that creating a strong Turkey regarded by other international actors is possible only through full integration with the West via EU membership and a strong alliance with the United States. At the same time, they both recognize Turkey's potential in Central Asia, the Caucasus and the Middle East. Unlike the status quo protectionists' one-dimensional foreign policy, which was based on an unconditional attachment to the West only, the AK Party's multi-dimensional foreign policy is guided by the belief that Turkey can and should develop strong relations not only with the West but also with the East, the North and the South. Guided with the same belief, but long before the AK Party, the Gülen movement seems to have been working toward that goal. One can hardly deny the contribution of the Gülen-inspired Turkish schools in making Turkey a point of attraction in more than 100 countries across the globe and of the movement's some 9,000-member Turkish Confederation of Industrialists and Businessmen (TUSKON) in boosting Turkey's export rates in recent years. Founded in 2006, TUSKON has already brought Turkish industrialists together with their counterparts in Eurasia, the Pacific and Africa in several business summits where the parties signed billion-dollar business contracts.

Third, both the Gülen movement and the ruling Justice and Development Party (AK Party) seem to believe that military operations alone cannot solve Turkey's terrorism problem. Because of this shared understanding, the movement's civil society organizations and government agencies have been working hand-in-hand in the Southeast to revive the region socially and economically. However, one should remember that, as the historical record indicates, the movement has been conducting its educational and aid projects in the region since the early 1980s, when the AK Party was not yet even an idea.

On the other hand, there are differences between the approaches of the Gülen movement and the AK Party to some of Turkey's chronic problems. Most notable among these is the headscarf ban, which has traumatized Turkish society time and again over the last few decades. From the very beginning, Fethullah Gülen has made his position clear on the issue by saying that he would choose education if he had to choose between the two and that such an undemocratic ban would be naturally lifted only when true democracy is achieved in Turkey. Therefore, from his perspective, there is no need to confront the secularist establishment and raise social tension. The AK Party government, however, has managed to turn its insistence on lifting the ban overnight into an existential threat to itself by meddling with the issue. For this very reason, the Gülen movement may have felt obliged to work closely, at the inspirational level, with the AK Party in order to help it stay away from policies that would eventually revoke the democratic rights already gained.

Finally, there are obligations that may explain the affinity between the Gülen movement and the AK Party. "The worst government is better than the absence of a government," notes Gülen, "Because the absence of a government would lead to anarchy and insecurity." So, by this token, the AK Party government (note the difference between the AK Party government and the AK Party) automatically secures the Gülen movement's basic support, just like other previous governments, even social democrat ones. Moreover, maybe for the Gülen movement and many others in Turkish society, it is not that the AK Party is so likeable, but that the Republican People's Party (CHP) is so dislikeable. After all, the political record of the CHP and its attitude toward Turkish society for the last couple of years have intimidated even the staunchest secularists, not to mention those center-right majority voters who would not necessarily rule out the possibility of voting for the CHP if it behaved well. So, given the record of the CHP and the fact that it is the only other major party in Parliament, with the exception of the ultra-nationalist Nationalist Movement Party (MHP), it is hardly possible to discern whether the Gülen movement supports the AK Party government, if indeed it does, for the sake of the AK Party, or simply because there is no other viable choice available. If the latter is true, one can expect that in the next elections the Gülen movement would favor a political party that was more dedicated to the rule of law, Turkey's democratization and EU accession than the AK Party.

Last, but not least, one can never ignore the possibility that there may be individuals within both the Gülen movement and the AK Party—or outside both—who may proclaim a deeper relationship between the two than really exists for their own purposes. For such individuals within the AK Party, the movement seemingly presents a fertile base for political support during the elections. Similarly, for those individuals within the Gülen movement with political aspirations but without much practical success, developing close ties with the AK Party by using the resources of the movement may have seemed appealing, since it would help them reach their unfulfilled political goals. The bottom line is that the relationship between the Gülen movement and the AK Party has multiple dimensions characterized by common objectives, differences and contextual obligations. To view the Gülen movement and the AK Party simply as a continuum basically means not knowing either of the two.

IN THE AFTERMATH OF
THE RUSSIAN INVASION

How to Counter Resurrected
Russian Expansionism[13]

Georgian President Mikhail Saakashvili's move to ensure Tbilisi's control over the separatist province of South Ossetia was an appropriate action at the intentional level, but a poorly calculated one in practice. Nevertheless, his intention was seemingly to maintain his country's sovereignty over its territory and, more importantly, to assert his country's independence from the regional wannabe hegemon. Though it could have been avoided, the recent conflict reminds one of Russia's expansionist heritage and encourages us to draw lessons for today. It puts not only the Georgians in the difficult position of making a critical decision for the future of their country, but also the international community for the future of democracy within the former Soviet republics. Finally, it is a reminder of the necessity of revitalizing dormant regional cooperation initiatives.

Traditional Russian expansionism and the ghost of serfdom in the Caucasus

If there is one lesson that every concerned state within neighborhood of Central Asia, the Caucasus, and the Black Sea should learn, it is that they will always have to account for Russia's revisionist heritage, which may occasionally be resurrected in its international affairs. According to Olivier Roy, Russian expansionism is characterized by two distinc-

---

[13] First appeared in *Today's Zaman* daily on August 18, 2008.

tive features that have always differentiated it from European colonialism. The first is that Russian expansion has occurred continuously over time; it has slowed down at times, but it hardly ever stopped. Similarly, Russian expansionism has maintained the territorial unity of the empire's grand land mass. The second is that the Russians accommodated the local political systems and cultural identities, which in turn enabled the Russian center to effectively control the non-Russian periphery.

On the other hand, Roy notes, European colonialism was characterized by a discontinuity in regard to both time and territorial unity. That is, the expansion of the European colonial powers occurred with territory acquired on different continents. This was probably because the European colonialists, unlike imperial Russia, which was driven by security concerns and pursuit of glory, were interested more in quenching their thirst for the raw materials required for their industrial revolution by simply exploiting the natural resources of other regions than in building up the territorial-based grandeur of their nations.

The distinction between the two forms of expansionism hints that Russian expansionism could well be continuing, though at a much slower pace and at a lower profile, while European expansionism ended with decolonization in the latter half of the twentieth century. By this token, Moscow's policy of granting citizenship to the Abkhazians and the South Ossetians so as to be able to claim Russian sovereignty over Abkhazia and South Ossetia on the pretext of protecting its own citizens becomes more significant. In addition, Moscow's slightly different policy of making Russia's Western neighbors—such as Belarus and Ukraine, both former Soviet republics—more and more dependent on Russian energy sources resonates well with Russia's traditional style of expansionism. As such, Moscow may see alternative energy pipeline projects, such as Baku-Tbilisi-Ceyhan (BTC), Baku-Tbilisi-Erzurum (BTE) and Nabucco, which are likely to undermine Russia's energy monopoly, as an existential threat to its influence in the Russian periphery.

Moscow's energy policies in general and its attitude during the course of the South Ossetia conflict strongly signal that Russia's expansionist aspirations in political, if not territorial, form are still intact. If that is not the case, it is Moscow's responsibility to prove it. Otherwise, the ghost of serfdom to Moscow, a la the "ghost of freedom" coined by Georgetown University's Charles King, will always haunt the former Soviet republics, more so in the Caucasus.

Ousting Saakashvili, Georgians would lose twice

It seems like Georgian President Saakashvili's move toward South Ossetia was driven by a desire to break the curse of this ghost of serfdom as much as to protect his country's territorial integrity. Running his election campaign on this fundamental discourse of ensuring Georgia's territorial unity, Saakashvili asserted Tbilisi's sovereignty over the Adjara region after taking office. This relative success encouraged him to try doing the same for South Ossetia and Abkhazia, only to run up against the Russian factor behind the two at a very high cost. During his recent meeting with the two separatist leaders, Eduard Kokoity of South Ossetia and Sergei Bagapsh of Abkhazia, Russian President Dmitry Medvedev pledged his country's open support for both Abkhazian and South Ossetian secession from Georgia, and promised to rebuild the South Ossetian capital of Tskhinvali, having already sent some 1,700 construction workers there. Similarly, Russian Foreign Minister Sergey Lavrov responded to the Western insistence on protecting Georgia's territorial integrity by simply saying that the notion of Georgia's territorial integrity was dead and that nobody could force Abkhazia and South Ossetia to remain within the Georgian state.

Interestingly enough, the political pundits seem to hold the Georgian president completely responsible for the plight of the Georgian refugees and those killed in the conflict while ignoring, and almost condoning, Moscow's explicitly stated revisionist intentions. Included in this group of commentators are some Georgians who see the recent blunder of Tbilisi as an opportunity to oust the Georgian president. The current circumstances make this quite a difficult decision for the Georgians. Should they keep the current president or not? Was he responsible for the deaths of about 2,000 Georgians and the plight of some 100,000 displaced people? Although President Saakashvili's poor calculation of the negative consequences of military action against South

Ossetia would legitimize ousting him, doing so at this point would simply mean a surrender of sovereignty to the regional wannabe hegemon. As such, Georgians will have lost their sovereignty in addition to the lives lost during the conflict.

Ousting Saakashvili would not serve Russian interests, either. As a matter of fact, it would be counterproductive when the peoples of the former Soviet countries are convinced that Moscow will never be their rational and equal partner, no matter how advanced their countries become, but will always act with its historically revisionist reflexes. The ousting of Saakashvili would only cast that opinion of Russia on the psyche of every single individual living within the commonwealth of [in]dependent states.

BSEC: Boosting regional cooperation to undo the damage

The recent conflict over South Ossetia, which brought two sovereign states to the brink of war, and the imperatives of the post-conflict rehabilitation make it necessary to consider revitalizing the long-dormant cooperative structures in the Black Sea region and to strengthen new partnerships in the south Caucasus. While these economic partnerships would make the regional states economically and politically interdependent, thereby less prone to conflict, they would also give Moscow an opportunity to behave and demonstrate to its neighbors that it can manage to be a rational partner.

The Organization of the Black Sea Economic Cooperation (BSEC) is one such partnership. Bringing together the Black Sea littoral states, such as Russia, Ukraine, Romania, Bulgaria, Turkey and Georgia, the BSEC provided a window of opportunity for countries formerly pressed under Soviet socialism to rapidly integrate into the global economy through economic cooperation. With Moldova, Albania, Greece, Azerbaijan and Armenia on its side the BSEC attracted non-Black Sea littoral countries such as Tunisia, Egypt, Slovakia, Poland and Israel. This rapid overstretch probably paralyzed the union in the absence of credible leadership.

According to Ahmet Davutoğlu, the EU's France-Germany type of leadership is what was missing within the BSEC and, if managed properly, a similar Turkey-Russia leadership could have been the moving force behind the BSEC. Occupied with their own projects—EU membership for Turkey and the domination of the CIS for Russia—both countries failed to utilize the potential of the BSEC. However, it is never too late to revitalize the organization. As a matter of fact, the recent incident in the Caucasus presents a credible motivation to boost economic, as well as political, cooperation among the BSEC member states. The BSEC also presents an opportunity for countries like Georgia to join in on regional affairs instead of falling back into isolation and to recover from conflict. Keen on playing a mediator role in the region, Ankara could help revitalize the long-dormant BSEC, instead of coming up with new ideas for a "Caucasus Stability Forum."

AFRICA AND THE TURKS

Reconstructing the Perceptions and
Whispering Hope to Africa[14]

Turkey recently hosted the first Turkey-Africa Cooperation Summit, which brought together political, business and NGO leaders of some 50 countries from Africa with their Turkish counterparts to discuss possible avenues of cooperation for a common and prosperous future.

The Istanbul Declaration and Cooperation Outline for Africa-Turkey Partnership, which has come out of the deliberations of the four-day conference, set out the practical framework of the prospective partnership, which was also described as "solidarity and partnership for a common future." The document identified a range of areas of cooperation between African countries and Turkey, which included intergovernmental cooperation, peace and security, trade and investment, agriculture, small and medium-sized enterprises, health, infrastructure, energy, transportation, telecommunications, culture, education, media and communications.

The summit is one of the latest efforts by Ankara to boost relations with African countries. Previously, in 2005, Ankara succeeded in gaining observer status within the African Union and signed a strategic partnership agreement with the union; more recently, on various occasions it appealed to African states for their support in Turkey's bid for a non-permanent seat on the UN Security Council for 2009-2010, and finally pledged to open 15 more embassies throughout Africa in addi-

---

[14] First appeared in *Today's Zaman* daily on August 24, 2008.

tion to the 12 existing ones. Ankara's efforts to strengthen relations with Africa were preceded by a leading Turkish business NGO, the Turkish Confederation of Businessmen and Industrialists (TUSKON), which brought together some 950 African business leaders with 2,500 of their Turkish counterparts at the Turkey-Africa Foreign Trade Bridge business summit in May 2008. The summit resulted in securing some $3 billion worth of business contracts between African and Turkish companies. In years to come, Turkey's relationship with African countries is only expected to become stronger thanks to such intergovernmental and nongovernmental initiatives.

Turkey's evolving relations with Africa

As articulated in the language of the recent cooperation summit and implied in Ankara's overall efforts to boost Turkey's long-ignored relations with many African states on the basis of equal and rational partnership, Turkey's approach to Africa seems to be slightly different from that of other developed or developing countries. For so many years, the first world has considered—and probably to some extent still does—Africa as a burden which it has to bear. Conscious of their responsibilities to help Africa prosper or as some would argue, ashamed by their historical role in the underdevelopment of the continent, the notable Western European countries, which also happen to be the leading colonizers of Africa in the nineteenth century, allocated their resources partially to aid Africa. Whether the aid to Africa is working or not is a major question in the contemporary development studies that is yet to be answered.

Why would Turkey's evolving relations with African countries be considered any different from those of Western European countries? One reason could be that in the psyche of the African leaders or the Africans in general, Turkey, as opposed to the Western European countries, is not viewed as a former colonizer that exploited their respective countries' resources. The second factor could be that the African leaders consider Turkey as not so different from their own countries as Turkey is still a developing country, and thus easier to work with.

Macro transformations rooted at the micro level

It seems like the answer to this question lies at the micro level. After all, the intergovernmental affairs are pretty much influenced, if not solely determined, by the individual perceptions of the leaders of their mutual history and culture. Individuals' perceptions of a given country or culture—whether those of the man on the street or the state leader—are determined by their first encounter with the individuals or the group of individuals representing that particular country and culture. In that regard, Turkey enjoys not only the advantage of not having any colonial experience with the African countries, but also that of being well-represented in these countries from the very beginning. In the last decade of the last century, a number of Turkish teachers and businessmen inspired by the contemporary thinker and scholar Fethullah Gülen set out to open schools in Africa's most impoverished corners, leaving everything, including their personal aspirations, back in Turkey.

One of many such examples is that of Ömer Kutlu. Graduating from a prominent law school in Turkey his early 20s, instead of pursuing his law career for an affluent life, Kutlu decided to move to Kenya—the location of which he couldn't even point out on a map at the time—when he encountered the opportunity to initiate a school project in that country. Hardly speaking English, let alone the local Kiswahili language, Kutlu and his companions first tried to become acquainted with the country and its people with whom he had had no contact whatsoever previously, and sought local partners who could possibly help them establish the school they had in mind. A former Kenyan supreme court justice of Pakistani origin notes that from the very beginning he had known that Kutlu and his friends were quite different from the other Turks he had come across: "I used to meet many Turks either in Europe where I was educated or at the international conferences elsewhere. The problem with them was that they did not seem to have any sense of identity, but an identity dilemma, not sure of where they belonged." However, the former justice noted, "There was something totally different about Mr. Kutlu and his friends. They knew exactly who they were, and they were very resolute to start a school here in Nairobi where they could provide modern education to Kenya's children. Then I said to myself that I had to be with these young Turks and help them start the school."

Another example is that of Ilhan Erdoğan. Having participated in several school projects in Central Asia in the 1990s, Erdoğan set forth with his wife and a toddler to start a school in Kampala, Uganda, after spending a year or two in Kenya. He recalls the hardships he and his wife had to endure in the beginning just to be able to settle in Uganda, where not many other Turks lived. "The several hours we had to wait at the customs before entering Uganda were probably the most difficult hours in my life." The difficulty was essentially because Turkey had not had any diplomatic representation in Uganda, and only last week—a decade later—did Ankara announce that it will open an embassy in this country. Like his colleague Kutlu, Erdoğan spent his early years in Uganda trying to get to know the local people and encouraging them to be part of the education project he had in mind. Today, the school he and his colleagues started educates some 200 students, who compete with their counterparts in international contests, be it math, sciences, humanities or computer technology.

A local businesswoman who runs several hardware stores in Kampala notes that she had been to Turkey on a trip organized by Erdoğan, during which she visited the schools established by the Turkish businessmen. "We saw the school in Nazilli. It was a very good school. We, the Ugandan business leaders, will do the same here in our country." She notes that she and her husband, along with the other Ugandan business owners, frequently come together with the teachers of the Turkish Light Academy to discuss ways to improve the school facilities and hopefully open another school. For the record, both Erdoğan and his fellow Turkish teachers still live with their families in the small houses which they themselves constructed near the school campus.

The late Erkan Çağıl from Turkey's eastern city of Erzurum was one of the businessmen engaging in commercial enterprise in Tanzania. His dedication to sponsoring schools in Tanzania illustrated clearly that there are many other businessmen who sold their businesses in Turkey to start from scratch in various countries of Africa in order to sponsor school projects in these countries and help African peoples change their bitter fate. Amid the criticisms from his friends and relatives, Çağıl closed his business in Istanbul and moved to Darussalam, Tanzania, in 2005, where he had visited the Turkish schools for the first time in 2001. Reportedly, his dream was to build a university in Darussalam, which would surpass any other university in Africa in terms of both quality of facilities and the education it offered. Yet he passed away in a car accident, leaving his colleagues behind to fulfill his dream, and has already become a symbol of the friendship between the Tanzanians and the Turks.

Turkish Light Academy: the light of Africa

The impact of such individual accounts of dedication and sacrifice likely have gone far beyond the individuals involved and have started to influence the perceptions at the national and international level in Africa-Turkey relations.

Recently graduated from the Turkish Light Academy in Nairobi, Richard Otolo is a devout Christian who regularly attends church services and sings in the church choir. His father was killed by the al-Qaeda bombing of the US Embassy in Nairobi in 1998 while he was working as an engineer in the building next door. When asked about how he feels about Muslims after what happened to his father, and how he felt attending a school run by Kenyan as well as Turkish teachers who happened to all be Muslim, Otolo noted:

> The Turkish teachers are Muslim. But religion was not an issue here. There is a freedom here. The Light Academy is quite different from other schools. […] The teachers stay on campus after classes and help us with our studies. We ended up being really good friends with our teachers. In other schools, it is different. There is this barrier between teacher and student. That is not the case here at the Light Academy. They are not only my teachers but also friends. Even after graduation, we are still in touch. In other schools, once you graduate, you do not remain in touch with your teachers. Sometimes when you see your teacher on the street, you try to avoid having him see you.

Mr. Verre teaches business studies at the Turkish Light Academy. After growing up and being educated in an impoverished eastern province of Kenya, Verre joined his Turkish colleagues in the early years of the school. "I have been working here now for some seven years. I have good relations with my students and colleagues. They are from a different culture, which creates a multicultural environment on the campus. The school has exchange programs with Turkey though I have never been to Turkey so far. So it has been quite a good experience for me." Verre takes a rightful pride in the Light Academy's accomplishments.

> I remember, when it started about 10 years ago, our school's space was very limited and in an impoverished building. Now, when I look around, I see a modern and huge campus with different facilities. This is the most important accomplishment of the school, I believe. Secondly, when we did our first national KCSE [Kenya Certificate of Secondary Education] exam in 2002, we were nowhere on the map of Kenya. However, when we look at it today, we can say that the Light Academy is likely to be the light of this country, because the success graphic is always showing a positive trend. We ranked tenth, then eighth and then seventh. Finally this year [2007], we ranked second among some 5,000 private schools in Kenya.

Verre's words explain the general characteristics of Turkish-Africa relations. That is, neither African peoples nor Turks see one another as different, but as equal partners who are dedicated to changing the bitter fate of Africa and are looking forward to rejoicing in the better future together.

GETTING REALISTIC ABOUT IRAN

Why, When and How Turkey
Becomes a Nuclear Power[15]

The trendy rhetoric regarding Turkish-Iranian relations is that the two have enjoyed friendly relations ever since the Qasr-i Shirin Treaty of 1639, which more or less determined today's border between the two countries. It is also fashionable to wish that the Middle East be cleared of nuclear weapons. Whether or not it is true about Turkish-Iranian relations, the real question is whether it is justifiable in terms of Turkish national security interests to have a nuclear power next door while Turkey itself does not have the same capabilities. Another question is what Ankara's plan B is if Iran eventually becomes able to develop its own nuclear weapons. Wishing for the region to be free of nuclear weapons is one thing, and failing to counter the shift in the regional balance of power is another, even if Iran arguably does not pose a direct military threat to Turkey.

Furthermore, the German Marshall Fund's recent report *Transatlantic Trends 2008* signals that Turkey's becoming a nuclear power may not necessarily be up to the political leadership in Ankara, but rather to the Turkish public, which is becoming increasingly confident and nationalistic. According to the report, 48 percent of the Turks who participated in the poll want Turkey to act unilaterally in its international affairs while only 8 percent view US global leadership as desirable and only 22 percent the EU's. The numbers of Turks who view Iran and the EU positively are almost tied, with the first group at 32 percent and the second at 33 percent. The numbers are not so favorable for the US and Israel. Only 14 percent of Turks view the US positively while only 8

---

[15] First appeared in *Today's Zaman* daily on September 18–19, 2008.

percent see Israel in a positive light. Another poll recently conducted by WorldPublicOpinion.org indicates that 36 percent of the Turkish respondents believe that Sept. 11 was an insider job, and 39 percent believes that al-Qaeda was behind it. While, as some may argue, these two are not necessarily mutually exclusive possibilities, the evolving trends in Turkish public opinion suggest that the question of whether Turks would favor the idea of Turkey having its own nuclear capabilities seems irrelevant.

So the real question is why, when and how Turkey would become a nuclear power. What are the underlying and governing assumptions? And finally, what are the possible scenarios that could lead Turkey to become a nuclear power?

In the retrospect: Turkey acquires nuclear weapons technology

I- Underlying assumptions

Anchored in the Western hemisphere and encouraged by the recently improved prospects of Turkey's EU membership, Ankara is unlikely to proactively adopt a policy toward acquiring nuclear weapon capabilities. Any signs of such policy would irritate Turkey's Western allies, most notably the United States and the EU, and put the present government's political survival at risk. That is, the government in Ankara with little or no Western support would be vulnerable to the continuous interference of the Turkish military, though the military may seem relatively silent at the moment. In addition, such an orientation would dramatically weaken Ankara's diplomatic capabilities with regards to its major foreign policy and security issues, which include EU membership, the Cyprus issue, the so-called Armenian genocide issue, the Kurdish formation in northern Iraq and fighting the Kurdistan Workers' Party (PKK), which has been launching attacks on Turkey from northern Iraq. Although all these foreign policy and security matters seem to have been handled relatively well and hence lie dormant thanks to the Justice and Development Party (AK Party) government's diplomatic skills, they can easily be used against Ankara at any given time.

Therefore, Ankara, be it under the current AK Party government or another one in the near future, would first be inclined to seek the protection of the security alliances such as NATO instead of itself becoming a self-reliant military power.

However, Iran's emergence as a nuclear power in the region changes the regional balance of power, puts Israel's survival at risk and bolsters the extremists around the Muslim world. Therefore, it becomes a moral and strategic imperative for Turkey to seek nuclear weapon capabilities to counterbalance nuclear Iran and offset its possible radicalizing impact on the Muslim world. Once Iran declares its nuclear weapon capabilities, the Turkish public will force the standing government to make Turkey a nuclear power as well. As a matter of fact, the *2008 Transatlantic Trends* report indicates that 48 percent of Turks already want Turkey to act unilaterally in its international affairs, which requires it to be fully capable of doing so. Moreover, in recent years an increasing number of Turks have criticized the AK Party government for not being as bold as Iran in pursuing a nuclear program independently from the West.

II- Governing assumptions

1. The EU accession process is directly related to the political survival of the current AK Party government and likely to be so for the following government(s) given the importance attached to Turkey's Western orientation and secular-democratic regime. Therefore, Ankara refrains from any move within the realm of nuclear energy that would harm its EU accession negotiations.

2. Turkey and Iran have been inherent rivals, with both aspiring to become the regional leader. Turkey aspires to do so via becoming de-facto leader of the Sunni world, while Iran seeks to do the same through reviving the Shiite populations not only in Iraq but also within Saudi Arabia and even in Yemen.

3. Iran is likely to continue its financial and military support of the Shiites inside Iraq for the duration of the US occupation and after the number of US troops are substantially reduced. Iran does so in order to make sure that in Iraq, whether it is governed under a repre-

sentative central government or under a federal system, the Shiites dominate Iraqi politics, especially policies and international agreements governing the country's energy resources.

4. Saudi Arabia, Egypt and Syria are cautious about Iran's prospects of acquiring nuclear weapon capabilities. They would seek to acquire the same capabilities in order to counterbalance nuclear Iran. For Saudi Arabia, it seems also a moral and, as they would put it, divine imperative to do so because it perceives itself as the natural leader of the Sunni Muslims vis-à-vis the Shiite Iran.

5. Compared to Saudi Arabia, Egypt and Syria, with their authoritarian regimes and lack of checks and balances, Turkey, with its secular and democratic regime and modern military closely cooperating with the US and Israel, would seem more amenable to become a nuclear counterbalance to nuclear Iran.

Likely scenario

Parallel to the decline of the US military presence in Iraq, the current multi-ethnic Iraqi government in Baghdad has stagnated due to the conflict between the Sunni and the Shiite members of the government. The Kurds in the north and in the central government refrain from becoming involved in the conflict and prefer rapprochement with Ankara. Once the ethnic conflict in Iraq turns into a civil war primarily between the Sunnis and the Shiites, Iran will continue to clandestinely support the Shiites militarily and politically. In the meantime, in order to divert the Muslims' growing criticism of it for being the force behind the Shiite upheaval, Tehran will become increasingly hostile and confrontational with Israel. That is, Tehran will become more vocal about the "Israeli occupation of the holy Muslim land." In order to back up its confrontational position, Tehran will also declare publicly that it is continuing with its nuclear program and that soon Iran will be a nuclear power. Alarmed with Iran's threats, Israel and the US will carry out air strikes on Iran's nuclear sites. The White House, if occupied by John McCain-Sarah Palin, would stand firmly behind and pledge its continuous military support to Israel. At this juncture, it may be useful to remember that, according to the projections of the US

National Intelligence Council, a series of terrorist attacks in various European capitals of no lesser scale than the Sept. 11 attacks may take place between the years 2010 and 2012. Such likely terrorist attacks would naturally increase the overall European support for the so-called war on terror. This time, Iran would be legitimized as the main target.

In turn, Iran seeks to further exploit the situation in Iraq in order to turn it into a hell for US troops. The ongoing conflict between the Sunnis and Shiites in Iraq is triggering similar conflicts in neighboring Arab countries, most notably in Saudi Arabia. Tehran's likely exploitation of those conflicts irritates Riyadh, Damascus and Cairo, forcing them to find ways to counterbalance Tehran. Acquiring nuclear weapons or the capability to build nuclear weapons would seemingly be the only means to counterbalance the emerging nuclear hegemon.

In the meantime, Turkish public opinion is increasing pressure on the Ankara government, be it an AK Party government or any other, to assert itself against Iran, which is constantly increasing its power in the region. The marginal leftist groups known as the *ulusalcılar* (neo-nationalists) and the center-left parties take advantage of the situation and criticize the AK Party government for its sluggishness in responding to national security challenges. In addition, the extremist groups on both the left and the right criticize the government for relying on Western security alliances such as NATO and not being able to even develop defense capabilities to protect the nation without permission from the US and the EU. In the meantime, as a major nuclear power, Russia is becoming increasingly assertive in its international relations in general and in its relations with its neighbors in particular, giving more salience to the idea that Turkey must have its own nuclear weapon capabilities.

Consequently, Ankara is intensifying its lobbying in Western capitals, most notably in Washington, to get the green light to develop nuclear weapons. Ankara presents itself as the most viable nuclear power in the region to counterbalance the nuclear Iran, pointing out that the other likely candidates, such as Saudi Arabia, Egypt and Syria, which lack democratic institutions, checks and balances and transparency, cannot be trusted with such military capabilities. Furthermore, Ankara is seeking to justify its quest for nuclear weapons by arguing that with or without the approval of its Western allies Turkey has to develop such capabilities because a nuclear Iran next to its border puts Turkish national security under threat. Accordingly, Ankara is seeking assistance from the major material and know-how suppliers, such as the United States, Canada, France, the United Kingdom and Israel. Finally, the United States tacitly approves Turkey's acquisition of nuclear weapon capabilities in order to both counterbalance a nuclear Iran in the Middle East and to prevent another rogue state in the region besides Iran from becoming a nuclear power. Consequently, the US is competing with the other suppliers to seize the lion share in Turkey's emerging nuclear market.

Alternative scenario

Any possible reluctance on the side of Turkey's Western allies to provide Turkey with the necessary material and know-how to develop nuclear weapons will encourage Ankara to seek other possible partners, which are quite numerous, including Iran itself. The most likely scenarios and the alternative scenarios of Turkey acquiring nuclear weapons or the capability of building nuclear weapons differ from each other not in terms of Turkey's driving motivations but in terms of the acquisition process.

It is possible that the United States and the European Union will not give the green light to Turkey to acquire nuclear weapon capabilities, and will at the same time try to deter Saudi Arabia, Egypt, Syria and/or another nuclear aspirant from acquiring or developing nuclear weapons. However, the two cannot succeed in doing so, as is the case with Iran. In addition, the US and the EU may not provide a credible and reliable guarantee to Turkey that they will protect Turkey against a nuclear threat. Actually, no such guarantee, including the NATO membership, may suffice to convince Turkey to stop its quest for nuclear weapon capabilities given the destructive capability of a nuclear attack and the fact that its very national security is at stake. Worried with the risk of remaining weak and vulnerable in its region and being threatened by a rogue nuclear power, Turkey would then seek nuclear weapon capabilities, risking confrontation with both the United States and the European Union. After all, then the domestic public opinion wouldn't just condone Turkey acquiring nuclear weapons, but demand it from the government.

Given that Turkey's Western allies do not condone Turkey becoming a nuclear power, Ankara is forced to seek non-Western partners and suppliers for its nuclear program. Turkey does not have difficulty in finding them. Actually, most likely, they would find Turkey anyway. Respectively, Pakistan, Russia, Israel and finally Iran are among the possible partners in Turkey's nuclear endeavor. Historically, Pakistan has always been supportive of the idea of Turkey becoming a nuclear power. Islamabad first approached Ankara to offer Pakistan's assistance to Turkey in developing nuclear weapons during the rule of Gen. Zia Ul-Haq in the 1960s and then during the rule of Nawaz Sharif in the late 1990s. However, Ankara had to disregard both offers because of concerns about alienating its Western allies. However, under the current circumstances, the national security threat Turkey faces and the Western allies' refusal to address Turkey's concerns make it imperative for Ankara to seek Pakistan's help in developing a nuclear weapons program.

Once Turkey comes out as a possible buyer of nuclear material and technology, Israel, Turkey's long-time ally in the Middle East, would also want to help Turkey by selling it the necessary material, equipment and know-how. Similarly, Russia is likely to reap the benefits of this emerging market for its nuclear technology before the US or the EU does. Finally, though reluctantly, Tehran would also be willing to assist Ankara, calculating that Turkey's becoming a nuclear power would only further legitimize Iran having nuclear weapons, even if it would eliminate Iran's chances of becoming the sole regional leader.

A CRITICAL DECISION

Turkey's Chief EU Negotiator and the AK Party Government's Fate[16]

A number of items occupy the Justice and Development Party (AK Party) government's foreign policy agenda. Not least among these is Turkey's European Union membership and eradicating the never-ending terrorism perpetrated by the Kurdistan Workers' Party (PKK). As part of this fight, Turkey must monitor the Kurdish formation in northern Iraq, coordinate efforts with countries neighboring Iraq and the major parties involved to ensure the country's territorial integrity and counter the shift in the regional balance of power likely to be caused by a nuclear Iran.

Turkey must also focus on maintaining the success of the Caucasus Stability Platform as well as normalize relations with Armenia in parallel to Armenia's withdrawal from Azerbaijani territories it has occupied and to its cooperation in bringing about a reasonable end to the so-called genocide allegations.

Additionally, priority will also be given to the issues of rendering a sustainable solution to the Cyprus issue, mediating indirect or possibly direct talks between Syria and Israel, contributing to the infrastructural development of Palestine, assisting the rapprochement between Pakistan and Afghanistan while contributing to the post-conflict rehabilitation and development of the latter and contributing to the global fighting against terror.

Furthermore, assisting the maintenance of peace and stability in the Balkans in general and Kosovo's survival as a sovereign state in particu-

---

16 First appeared in *Today's Zaman* daily on October 10, 2008.

lar as well as revitalizing Turkey's long-ignored relations with the African countries, minimizing Turkey's energy dependency and possibly ensuring its energy independence via developing a civilian nuclear program and securing a non-permanent seat on the UN Security Council for 2009-2010 rank high in importance.

Finally, maintaining friendly relations with the US and preparing for the post-American Middle East must also be addressed by the AK Party.

While they are all critical on their own, the consistency and success in the pursuit of the first item on the agenda is pretty much decisive on Ankara's ability to consistently and successfully pursue the rest. Yet, the consistent and successful pursuit of Turkey's EU membership depends on the political stability of the AK Party government.

As Parliament begins its new legislative year, the AK Party leadership is preparing to undertake a major reshuffling of the Cabinet. In addition to its relatively successful foreign policy and sustained economic growth for several years in a row, the AK Party leadership proved successful in reshuffling the Cabinet at the start of its second term in office, reducing the number of former Islamist Welfare Party (RP) members in it and replacing them with social democrats. These days, Prime Minister Recep Tayyip Erdoğan is preparing to do the same with one difference: He is planning to appoint a "chief EU negotiator."

A critical decision

Certainly one of the critical decisions the prime minister has to make is choosing who is to lead Turkey's negotiations with the European Union. The position has so far been held by Foreign Minister Ali Babacan because acquiring EU membership has long been the main pillar of Turkish foreign policy. However, lately, probably as a result Turkey's increased involvement in regional and international affairs, it appears the government believes that the responsibility for EU negotiations should be taken off the foreign minister's shoulders to ease his burden.

Some would argue that creating a separate "chief EU negotiator" position is just a cunning attempt to train a potential contender to the

AK Party leadership. In a way, Erdoğan by himself will bring about his and his government's own end, depending on who is chosen to be the prospective chief. After all, given the importance Turkish foreign policy attaches to full EU membership and the public's increasing involvement in debates regarding the EU accession process, there is no doubt that the prospective chief EU negotiator will be one of the most popular political figures and a person who will make headlines every day. He may well be the most popular person—depending on the dominant media groups' tendency to promote him as a potential contender to Erdoğan's political leadership either within or without the AK Party. As such, depending on who he is, the prospective chief EU negotiator may well be manipulated to clash with the prime minister as his popularity grows. It goes without saying that a political figure that clashes with the prime minister would certainly fail, if not purposefully resist, to work with the country's foreign minister and seek to exclude the latter by all means from deliberations and decisions regarding Turkey's EU accession.

A recent row between Prime Minister Erdoğan and media mogul Aydın Doğan, who owns more than 50 percent of the Turkish media as well as a substantial part of the country's banking and energy sector, guarantees gigantic media and capital support for any possible contender to Erdoğan.

Last month Turks witnessed a fierce row between Erdoğan and Doğan, a row that allegedly erupted when newspapers and TV stations owned by the Doğan Media Group (DMG), in what seemed to be a concerted effort, argued that Erdoğan was involved in a major corruption scandal. According to an article published by the *Turkish Daily News*, a Doğan Media Group newspaper, the German prosecutor's indictment—part of a court case against the Germany-based charity organization Lighthouse e.V., accused of embezzling some 42 million euros worth of donations—included evidence of one of the suspects saying that he had received an unspecified amount of money to be given to Prime Minister Erdoğan.

Although this allegation has been disputed by the German prosecutor, while the trial was pending major DMG newspapers, such as

Hürriyet and *Milliyet*, headlined with the allegation as if it was already a proven fact, which in turn led to Erdoğan arguing that it was merely a smear campaign against him and his government because he did not respond to multi-billion dollar favors Doğan had asked of him earlier.

Given the DMG's previous record on matters concerning the AK Party, argues columnist Bülent Keneş, what seemed like a personal clash between Doğan and Erdoğan has deeper roots in the inherent power struggle between a secularist minority and a democratic majority of Turkey. Keneş further notes as follows:

> The Doğan group lent support to all anti-democratic campaigns and even to an absurd claim concerning a quorum of 367 deputies in the presidential election. [Doğan Media Group] newspapers and TV stations engaged in provocative and antidemocratic publications and broadcasting during the presidential election. They supported the military memorandum of April 27. They lent support to the republican rallies, which called on the army to overthrow the government. But they failed to prevent Abdullah Gül from being elected president. Still they did not give in. The headline '411 hands raised to chaos,' which the *Hürriyet* newspaper ran after Parliament passed constitutional amendments lifting the headscarf ban at universities, will never be forgotten by Erdoğan, just like a majority of the nation. All these things have accumulated and have eventually caused Erdoğan to burst...

Given the personal and ideological stakes involved in the infamous power struggle, whether it is a chief EU negotiator, ranking member of the AK Party, or even a close aide to Erdoğan, whoever possesses leadership aspirations within or without the AK Party will be a perfect candidate to be manipulated against Erdoğan.

Chief EU negotiator: surrogate foreign minister to replace prime minister?

Unlike any other political position within the government, the chief EU negotiator position provides such a contender with a unique opportunity to show himself off and garner popular support for his future campaign for leadership. After all, he will be negotiating for a prize that has long been the only common goal which could bring together the otherwise differing segments of Turkish society, be they secularists, seculars, moderates, conservatives, nationalists, liberals, and so on. If the negotiations with the EU go well, as intended and expected, it is not the prime minister or the foreign minister who will be given credit for the success, but the chief EU negotiator. It will be more so if the prospective chief is bent on taking the credit himself instead of giving it to the entire Foreign Ministry or the government. In that regard, he will be much easier to manipulate than not.

Moreover, given the relative importance of the EU membership vis-à-vis the other items on Turkey's foreign policy agenda, institutionalizing the pursuit of the EU accession negotiations under the supervision of a chief EU negotiator would naturally entail staffing and/or re-staffing within the relevant units in line with the preferences of the chief negotiator, which may pave the road to further cronyism in the Foreign Ministry. In addition, there is also a possibility of a constant conflict between the chief EU negotiator and the foreign minister on issues regarding, but not limited to, Turkey's policies directly or indirectly related to the EU accession process. The prospects for such a conflict increase if the prospective chief is someone who has so far directly reported to and developed a personal relationship with the prime minister.

At least as important as what he should not be is what the chief EU negotiator should be. The ideal candidate for the job should have a keen understanding of not only EU-Turkey relations but also a wide range of issues—from US-Turkish relations to Turkey's evolving foreign policy toward the Middle East in general and Iraq in particular, Central Asia and the Caucasus, and the major regional powers, such as Russia and Iran. Moreover, he should be able write on these issues and speak to a foreign audience knowing what he is talking about. In order to do that, he should come from an academic and professional background in international relations, be acquainted with Western media and think tank circles, have experience in publishing op-ed articles in major Western media outlets such as *The New York Times*, *The Washington Post*, the *International Herald Tribune*, the *Financial Times* and the like. All this is necessary for the chief to successfully negotiate Turkey's EU membership.

These days, two names are being tossed around to be considered for the position: one is Egemen Bağış, deputy chairman of the AK Party for external affairs; the other is Lütfi Elvan, a deputy for Karaman who served as deputy undersecretary in the State Planning Organization (DPT). If the AK Party leadership is incapable of seeing that there are candidates in the party much better suited for the job than these two, it should at least realize that the candidate who has allegedly been claiming to have been the "shadow foreign minister" of Turkey, should be the last person to be considered for the chief EU negotiator position.

SEEKING A SEAT FOR TURKEY AT THE UN SECURITY COUNCIL[17]

On Oct. 17, the UN General Assembly will vote to determine which member states will be holding the non-permanent seats on the UN Security Council for the 2009-2010 term. As the critical date draws closer, Turks are holding their breath to see the result of the four-year national campaign for Turkey's candidacy for one of the two non-permanent seats allocated to the Western European region, which will be emptied by Belgium and Italy this year. Turkey was last represented on the UN Security Council in 1961. As he recently pointed out, Turkish Foreign Minister Ali Babacan has had bilateral meetings with the foreign ministers of about 150 countries over the last year and is currently in New York in the midst of the final efforts to secure Turkey a seat on the council.

Even if non-permanent, membership in the 15-member UN Security Council is a prestigious status and has its own advantages for UN member states. Every member, permanent or non-permanent, has one vote on the council. On procedural matters, an affirmative vote of any nine of the 15 members is required, while on substantive matters nine affirmative votes, including the concurring votes of all five permanent members, are required for a motion to pass. Also, unlike the resolutions passed by other bodies of the UN, which have advisory status, the resolutions passed by the Security Council are binding for all of the UN member states and they are supposed to comply with the resolutions passed. Practically, it means that if the Security Council's five permanent members agree on something such as applying political or economic sanctions to a state or carrying out a military intervention, Tur-

---

[17] First appeared in *Today's Zaman* daily on October 17, 2008.

key will be one of the four non-permanent members that they will have to convince for that agreement to materialize. Certainly, this will not only increase Ankara's bargaining power, but also force it to take sides on pressing issues, such as Iran's nuclear program.

There are two fundamental questions regarding Turkey's candidacy for a non-permanent seat on the UN Security Council: What does Turkey to offer the Security Council? And what kind of resistance does it face?

Not much competition after all, so why not?

The second question is relatively easier to address, as it relates to the current context of the UN and Turkey's ability to utilize the available opportunities present within that context. Turkey is competing for one of the two non-permanent seats on the Security Council designated for the Western European regional quota, and its only rivals in this contest are Austria and Iceland. Compared to Turkey, both states have been much less involved, at least for the last six years, in international diplomacy. Furthermore, they are much smaller in size and population, lack the strategic depth Turkey enjoys and are not even close to providing what Turkey can in terms of contributing to the peace-building process in the Middle East, Balkans, Caucasus or other important conflict zones. So, if at the end of the day that seat is going to be taken by a state, and if the other two candidates are only Austria and Iceland, why shouldn't Turkey take that seat?

Turkey should also be enjoying a much greater advantage compared to the other two candidates in terms of securing the UN member states' votes, given that Turkey shares cultural, historical, economic and political ties with a substantial percentage of the member states, and that Turkey has been contributing to a majority of them at both the governmental and nongovernmental levels. In his recent address at the sixty-third session of the UN General Assembly, Turkish President Abdullah Gül recalled that Turkey has deservedly been recognized by the international community as an emerging donor country, as its development aid has amounted to $1 billion. Similarly, Turkish nongovernmental initiatives have been actively contributing to more than 100 developing and underdeveloped countries around the globe by founding and running educational, charity and relief organizations in these countries.

President Gül also stressed Turkey's increased contribution to the peace-building process in the Middle East and in the Caucasus, refer- ring to Turkey's mediation of talks between Syria and Israel and Anka- ra's proposal for the formation of a Caucasus Stability and Coopera- tion Platform. In addition, he reminded the UN member states that Turkey has become a major hub for energy lines and, as such, is criti- cal to global energy security. Similarly, referring to the Turkish mili- tary's leadership of the international peacekeeping forces in Afghani- stan, Gül emphasized that Turkey is one of the major contributors to international peace-keeping efforts.

So Turkey's UN representation, led by experienced Ambassador Baki Ilkin, should have no problems acquiring a non-permanent seat on the UN Security Council. This is especially so given the fact that the voting will be cast through secret ballots and, as such, no member state will be discouraged from voting in favor of Turkey due to possible psychological pressure from other member states. Nor is Turkey com- peting with other such strong Security Council membership contes- tants as Brazil, India, Germany or Japan, which could understandably exert immense influence on member states that would otherwise vote for Turkey. Therefore, given the clearly favorable conditions Turkey is enjoying in this contest, losing a non-permanent seat to either Aus- tria or Iceland would be a surprise, and a rather shameful one at that.

If Turkey loses the bid, there will be those who claim to have done everything they could, that the competition was tough and that it will not affect Turkey's diplomatic dynamism. Certainly, it will not and should not affect Turkey's dynamic foreign policy. However, they should at least show enough responsibility to answer the following questions: Was the competition tough because Turkey's rivals were too strong or because the Turkish campaign was too weak? And did those individu- als who were primarily responsible for leading Turkey's campaign for Security Council membership, including the civil society organizations in Turkey, the US and the countries who were to vote in the Security Council election, utilize all means available to them?

What does Turkey's UN performance say?

The first question is relatively difficult to address, however, as why Turkey should be on the UN Security Council requires an analysis of what Turkey has contributed to the resolution of the security-related issues on the UN's agenda so far. It is common sense that what can be done in the future may be predicted by merely looking at what has been done so far. But this common sense may not necessarily be applicable to Turkish foreign policy. The arrival of the current Justice and Development Party (AK Party) government in 2002 and a multidimensional foreign policy orientation formulated by Ahmet Davutoğlu constituted a break with the old-school, one-dimensional (meaning unconscious attachment to the West) and strictly exclusivist foreign policy of the past. Up until the 2000s, not only was Turkish foreign policy one-dimensional and passive, but the Turkish diplomatic corps was formed of those individuals, with a few exceptions, who would best carry out such a foreign policy. In his book *Cenevre Yılları* (Geneva Years), Kamuran Inan, Turkey's former permanent representative to the UN in Geneva, laments that the Turkish foreign ministry was long filled with the cronies of the senior bureaucrats or politicians who considered their appointments to the UN and other intergovernmental organizations a personal vacation on the state's funds, did not attend to their routine duties as diplomats and even lacked sufficient language skills to follow the debates in the UN, much less contribute to them.

Turkey's performance in the UN headquarters in New York so far has not defied Turkish foreign policy's generally passive nature. In the pursuit of the UN General Assembly's agenda, Turkey's approach can at best be described as that of a "follower" rather than a "leader." The General Assembly's agenda includes, among other things, such security-related issues as disarmament and non-proliferation of nuclear, chemical, biological and conventional weapons; the struggle against black-market trade of small arms and light weapons; drug control, crime prevention and combating international terrorism in all forms; and building regional zones free of nuclear weapons. UN records indicate that in drafting resolutions regarding these security issues and raising similar security issues, Turkey seems to have preferred to follow the course of other countries instead of taking a leadership role. Some of the very rare issues that Turkey has proactively raised seem to be related to regional issues that directly or indirectly affect Turkey. These include the Cyprus issue and Armenia's unlawful occupation of Azerbaijani territory.

Turkey's record hitherto hinders one's ability to make a convincing argument as to why Turkey should be on the UN Security Council or how much of a contribution Turkey may bring to the resolution of various contemporary security issues. However, one should not be deceived by such a poor performance, but instead should take Turkey's recently developed diplomatic clout into consideration while judging its possible contribution to the UN Security Council.

In the final analysis, if the question is whether Turkey deserves a seat on the UN Security Council or not, given its record of involvement in the general assembly and relevant committee debates regarding international security and peace building, it is difficult to give a convincingly favorable answer. Turkey's bid for a non-permanent seat on the UN Security Council should be judged on the basis of what Turkey is likely to accomplish, as opposed to how it failed to contribute to the UN's work. However, if the question is whether Turkey deserves a non-permanent seat on the UN Security Council, given that the other two candidates for that particular seat are Austria and Iceland, the answer is an easy one: Sure, why not?

ISRAEL'S INVASION OF GAZA

A Litmus Test for Turkey's New Foreign Policy[18]

N ow that the six-month cease-fire between Hamas and Israel has come to an end and the ensuing Israeli air assaults and ground operation have inflicted an unprecedented tragedy on the Palestinians, not only have the prospects for a sustainable peace in the Middle East been diminished, but Ankara's hope for becoming a formidable peace broker in the region has also been shattered.

Turkish Prime Minister Recep Tayyip Erdoğan reacted to the Israeli attack on Gaza by stating that the attack was an insult to Ankara, which had been working diligently to mediate peace talks between Syria and Israel for quite some time. Mr. Erdoğan said he had canceled his previously planned telephone call to Israeli Prime Minister Ehud Olmert because he deemed it useless to engage in any diplomatic dialogue with Israel at this point. As many would argue, Ankara is hardly in a position to change Israel's course of action so long as Washington condones Israel's uncompromising attitude vis-à-vis the Palestinians and even its disproportional use of force victimizing civilians, as manifested in the recent incidents. There is no need to mention that even Fatah leader Mahmoud Abbas, president of the Palestinian Authority, holds Hamas, as opposed to Israel, primarily responsible for the ensuing bloodshed. The UN Security Council failed to produce a resolution to stop Israel's military operation. Moreover, the unrelenting stance of the Israeli leaders in the face of widespread public protests, while Western leaders prefer to remain silent, only signals that the Israeli attack on Gaza may only be the first circle of the chain of bloody conflicts yet to unravel and spread throughout the region. As such, one won-

---

[18] First appeared in *Today's Zaman* daily on January 05, 2009.

ders how influential Ankara may actually be in reversing Israel's attitude toward the Palestinians in the future.

Ankara's motivations

However, aside from the question of how much Israel cares about
Ankara's reaction, if it even does, and of whether Ankara can actually
stop the unraveling violence in the Middle East, the way Ankara has
reacted to the Israeli attack on Gaza begs a series of broader questions: What makes Prime Minister Erdoğan think his government can
broker a sustainable peace among the parties of the so-called Middle
East peace process, while the very phenomenon is meant to be just a
process without a peaceful end? What inspires and motivates the Justice and Development Party (AK Party) leadership to aspire for a more
significant role in international politics in general and in the Middle
East, in particular? Is Turkey's new foreign policy orientation strategically deep enough to turn Turkey into an able power broker in its region
and in the broader international arena? Finally, is Turkey destined to
remain a secondary player in the international system; if not, how could
it possibly become a global actor capable of influencing the course of
action of other regional and global actors?

Prospects for a larger role in the Middle East

The way the AK Party has come into office and the extent of the popularity it has managed to garner in its Muslim neighborhood may have
given the party leaders an overly optimistic belief that the AK Party
government's Ankara can transform such popularity into an actual
mandate to penetrate the status quo in the Middle East and change
the traditional behavior of the states in the region. Although Turkey's
new foreign policy outlook seems likely to gain Turkey such an ability at some point in the future, it is premature to expect that to happen
now with the current leadership in the region. After all, almost all of
those leaders are remnants of an era against whose representatives in
Turkey the AK Party government came into being. As such, there is
and will always be differences between the AK Party's Ankara and the

other Muslims states' leaderships in the region in terms of how to approach the Israeli-Palestinian conflict and other regional matters.

That Egypt keeps the Rafah gate, the Gazans' only lifeline, closed due to fear of a refugee influx; that Palestinian Authority President Abbas is allegedly providing intelligence to the Israeli authorities to eliminate the Hamas leadership, Fatah's rival; and that Iranian President Mahmoud Ahmedinejad is seizing the opportunity to declare the so-called coming of the end of Israel are only three of examples of how Ankara may differ from the other actors in the region. That is to say, Ankara—with the AK Party government or any other—can hardly formulate or implement any sustainable policy in the region unless the current leaderships in the region also go through structural transformation similar to what Ankara has recently undergone with the AK Party. Nevertheless, this is not to say that Ankara can never be a formidable actor in the region and around the globe, but that it should actively wait until at least one generational shift takes place in the region and around the globe while it visibly contributes to the infrastructural and human development of the countries it is concerned with.

Turkey's new foreign policy: Is it strategically deep enough?

Is Turkey's new foreign policy strategically deep enough to make Turkey a formidable regional power capable of changing the other regional actors' patterns of behavior? With the AK Party's coming into office, an equally, if not more, revolutionary transformation occurred in Turkey's foreign policy orientation: Adviser to both the president and the prime minister, Professor Ahmet Davutoğlu, introduced his "multidimensional" foreign policy paradigm into Turkish foreign policy making. Pointing at its peculiar geographical, cultural and historical presence in the midst of the Afro-Eurasian landmass, Davutoğlu argues that Turkey is a central country not with a single static identity, but with multiple dynamic identities, each of which gains prominence over the others depending on the geopolitical context at hand. That is, depending on the geopolitical context, Turkey can be a Middle Eastern, Balkan, Caucasian, Central Asian, Caspian, Mediterranean, Gulf and Black Sea country variably or all at the same time. In this regard, Turkey is neither a "frontier" country, as it had been considered when it was a bulwark against the threat of communism throughout the Cold War, nor a "bridge" between the "free world" and the "yet-to-be-freed" world, as some argued after the end of the Cold War. But Turkey is a "central" country that has the potential to provide security and stability not only for itself but also for its neighbors and the wider region. Accordingly, he concludes, given Turkey's unique central geopolitical identity, a series of domestic initiatives such as deepening and enriching its democracy, accommodating differences within its society, and strengthening the coordination and balance among its institutions will eventually make Turkey a global power by the year 2023, the centennial anniversary of the republic's establishment.

While Davutoğlu's conclusion sounds like music to any and every patriotic Turkish ear, as it articulates every Turk's long-sought dream, it runs the risk of being hardly more than wishful thinking, as it looks to be based on the same contextual premises as the "frontier" and "bridge" identities, and as there is a causal void between the premises and the articulated conclusion. First of all, the conception of a "central" identity is functionally hardly different from those of "frontier" and "bridge" identities, although theoretically it signifies a departure from how Turkey has been defined in relation to its hitherto geopolitical environment. That is, while both the "frontier" and "bridge" identities were determined exclusively by the contemporary geopolitical conditions Turkey had found itself in, much less by its ability to influence those conditions, the "central" identity is too determined by the simplistic notion of "bridge," except that this time it looks more like a star-shaped bridge connecting multiple points, as opposed to a linear bridge connecting just two.

In a way, according to the "centrality" description, Turkey finds itself connected to multiple regions, such as the Middle East and the Balkans for historical and cultural reasons, the Caucasus, the Black Sea littoral region and Central Asia for economic and cultural reasons, and Europe for idealistic and economic reasons. Yet the majority of those regions, and certainly the Middle East, have remained unchanged in terms of leadership mentality since the Cold War, thereby diminishing the rejuvenated Ankara's ability to lead any structural change in the power politics of the region or in the great powers' approaches to the region. At the end of the day, the only clear lesson for Ankara may be that so long as the current authoritarian regimes remain intact in the Middle East, Ankara should not expect to be able to formulate and implement any sustainable policy in cooperation with the leaders of those authoritarian regimes. Organization of the Islamic Conference (OIC) Secretary-General Ekmeleddin İhsanoğlu's insistent calls to the international community in general and to Muslim leaders in particular to go beyond mere promises and verbal condemnations and to actually do something only confirms the presence of the rigid status quo vis-à-vis the Middle East and the Israeli-Palestinian conflict.

Active patience: contributing to human development and post-conflict rehabilitation

Nevertheless, there is quite a bit that Ankara, either with the AK Party government or with others, can accomplish within the present status quo, thereby expanding its sphere of influence. First of all, Ankara should not expect Israel to change its policies vis-à-vis the Palestinian territories or the current Arab leaders to give up their traditional reluctance to act, but should focus on what it can do for the Palestinians and for the region. As such, in the immediate term, Ankara should use its diplomatic clout to gain access to the occupied territories in order to provide humanitarian and post-conflict rehabilitation assistance to the Palestinians. In the long term, Ankara should finance the establishment of as many boarding schools as possible in southern Gaza. These schools, ranging from elementary school to vocational high schools and universities, should aim to get the Palestinian youth off the streets, thereby preventing them from falling prey to the provocations of both Hamas and Israeli aggression. While the vocational high schools train the Palestinian youth to become the human ingredient of Palestine's economic development, the universities should educate them in the social sciences to help them gain different outlooks on the fate of their region and on how to coexist with their unavoidable neighbor, Israel.

Ankara should pursue such an aid-oriented approach in its foreign policy vis-à-vis the other nations, as well. In this regard, Ankara should further strengthen its relations with major regional and international organizations, such as the OIC, the African Union, the League of Arab States, the Association of Southeast Asian Nations (ASEAN) and the Southern Common Market (MERCOSUR), and offer Turkey's assistance to their member states in such areas as education, culture and economic cooperation. Turkey's consistent assistance to and cooperation with developing nations would inevitably tilt the international balance in favor of Turkey in no longer than a generation. And finally, the AK Party leadership and its supporters should realize that the AK Party phenomenon is not "the" step, but "a" step for Turkey toward attaining its much-deserved grandeur in the international system, and possibly transforming that system for the better and forever.

THE BIG PICTURE IN ISRAEL'S INVASION OF GAZA[19]

Roughly three weeks after the Israeli invasion of Gaza started, the conflict seems more and more likely to boomerang back to Israel as a two-front war: one against Hamas in the south, and the other against Hezbullah in the north.

It has been reported that Israel has recently fired a number of rockets into southern Lebanon in retaliation against several rockets fired from the region into northern Israel.

Although neither Hezbullah nor any other organization has yet assumed responsibility for the rockets, the increasing number of rocket fire exchanges across the border raises the prospect for a military conflict between Hezbullah and Israel in addition to the ongoing conflict in Gaza. Consequently, the possibility of the Israeli-Palestinian conflict triggering a broader Israeli-Arab conflict gradually comes into the realm of possibility, thereby diminishing hopes for a sustainable peace in the region in the foreseeable future.

The so-called Israeli-Palestinian and Israeli-Arab conflicts have marred both regional and international peace so much and for so long that one is obliged to question the involved parties' commitment to finding a sustainable solution to the conflicts. The recent Israeli invasion of Gaza and the ensuing humanitarian crisis provide a unique case in this regard. A skeptical mind asks if the current tragedy that befell the Gazans might simply be the consequence of a mere political design to benefit not only the ruling Kadima government in Israel, but also some Arab leaders who are party to the Israeli-Palestinian conflict. A brief look at the way the developments have unraveled during the invasion

---

[19] First appeared in *Today's Zaman* daily on January 18, 2009.

and the positions of the parties involved after the UN Security Council's resolution for an immediate cease-fire may aid the skeptical mind to answer such questions, though it may not yield concrete answers.

Israel and the ruling Kadima government

Long before launching Israel's military operation into Gaza, Israeli leaders had frequently expressed their concern over the missiles fired by Hamas militants. They became increasingly vigilant once the missiles appeared to reach farther north into more crowded urban areas. Although the missiles fired from Gaza did not cause many fatalities and mostly ended up in the open fields of southern Israel, it left open the possibility that the Hamas militants could fire rockets with a longer range and a more destructive capability, and therefore the Israeli leadership was understandably urged to take action.

Appearing incapable of protecting their citizens, the ruling Kadima Party leaders have found themselves between a rock and a hard place in the face of parliamentary elections on Feb. 10. Seemingly their biggest failures were Israel's humiliating defeat by Hezbullah in the summer of 2006 and the continuation of the Hamas threat from the south. With these concerns and the goal of eliminating the Hamas threat in mind, Israel began its military operation into Gaza with a series of heavy air strikes and has continued with the ground operations. Israel certainly has the right to exist within its internationally recognized borders, and the Israeli government has a mandate to protect its citizens just like any other democratically elected government does. But following its extremely aggressive and unrelenting course, Israel diminished the international community's ability to sympathize with it in the event a similar disaster befalls its people in the future.

Interestingly enough, the current course of action is not unusual for Israel. In his book, titled *Treacherous Alliance: the Secret Dealings of Israel, Iran and the U.S.*, Trita Parsi recalls the Israeli invasion of southern Lebanon on June 6, 1982, under the supervision of then Prime Minister Menachem Begin, and states the following:

[This was] "ostensibly in response to an attempt by Palestinian militants to assassinate Shlomo Argov, Israel's ambassador to the United Kingdom. But Ariel Sharon, then Israel's defense minister, had been planning a Lebanon invasion to wipe out the Palestinian Liberation Organization (PLO) presence there for many months—at least as early as late 1981. Although the PLO had been observing a cease-fire with Israel since the summer of 1981, Sharon and Prime Minister Menachem Begin calculated that if they could destroy the PLO presence in Lebanon, they would both derail the PLO's growing diplomatic strength and quell the nationalist Palestinian ferment in the occupied territories.[20]

With apparently a similar mindset, Israeli Prime Minister Ehud Olmert remarked recently at a Knesset meeting that the operation had yielded impressive gains and that this was a time to translate Israel's achievements into the goals they had set. Olmert also noted, "Israel is nearing the goals which it set itself, but more patience, determination and effort are still demanded." Not only did he urge to his colleagues to be patient, but also Israel's blatant disregard of the UN Security Council's Resolution 1860, which called for an immediate cease-fire in Gaza, signaled that the violence in Gaza is likely to continue.

Meanwhile, the Israeli rhetoric regarding to the conflict has already started to shift in a way that tried to justify the military operation not only for the security of the Israeli civilians in southern Israel, but also oddly for the Palestinians. According to a *Haaretz* report, Israeli Foreign Minister Tzipi Livni argued that Israel's military operation served the interests of the Palestinian people as well as those of the Israelis. Soon after the influx of many other issues with more "news value," the most notable of which is the nearing inauguration of US President-elect Barack Obama, what happened in Gaza is likely to be forgotten, just as the infamous Sabra-Shatila massacre, which took place during the Israeli invasion of southern Lebanon in 1982 and caused a major outcry in Israel and internationally.

---

[20] Parsi, 2008, p. 110.

Fatah and Hamas

Under normal circumstances, meaning if there was no Israeli invasion of Gaza, Jan. 9, 2009 would be election day for Palestinians in the West Bank and Gaza. According to the Palestinian Authority's Basic Law, President Mahmoud Abbas' term in office, which began in January 2005, was supposed to end on Jan. 8, 2009. However, whether the presidential and the legislative elections were to be held at the same time had become the major source of conflict between the secular Fatah and the Islamist Hamas factions. According to a *Middle East Times* report, while Abbas announced on Dec. 16 that both elections were to be held in the West Bank and Gaza, the Hamas leadership vehemently opposed it, arguing that only the presidential election was to be held in January 2009 and that the legislative elections were not due until 2010. Moreover, Hamas leaders argued that the American and Israeli-backed Abbas' mandate as the Palestinian Authority's (PA) president would end on Jan. 8.

Amid the conflicts between Fatah and Hamas over the date of the presidential and legislative elections came Israel's invasion of Gaza. The ongoing war and the ensuing humanitarian crisis put the election debates on hold, at least for the time being. According to a *Jerusalem Post* report, Fatah legislator Hatem Abdel Qader defended Abbas' decision to stay in power, for the current war in Gaza would not allow the election to be held. Another Fatah legislator, Jihad Abu Zneid, reportedly remarked that raising the issue of election at the moment while the war in Gaza is continuing would work against the interests of the Palestinian people. In the meantime, Abbas engaged in seemingly intensive diplomacy with world leaders at the United Nations to bring an end to the ongoing violence.

Oddly enough, once the UN Security Council resolution for a cease-fire was passed, it was not only Israel that disregarded the resolution but also Hamas. According to a BBC report, Hamas spokesman Ayman Taha said that Hamas would not heed the resolution because it did not take into consideration the interests of the Palestinian people and that Hamas was not consulted about the resolution. As such,

Hamas put itself in the same position as Israel by defying the international call for cease-fire and continuing the bloodshed and violence.

Iran and Egypt

Despite Iranian President Mahmoud Ahmedinejad and other Iranian officials' inflammatory rhetoric against the state of Israel, Iran remained ineffective in ending the Gazans' plight. However, given the Islamic republic's overall approach to the Israeli-Palestinian conflict, Iran's rhetorical support to the Palestinians and reluctance to become practically involved with the ensuing conflict in Gaza was not unusual or unexpected by Israel and other parties involved in the conflict.

Analyzing Israeli-Iranian relations regarding the Israeli-Palestinian conflict after Iran's Islamic revolution in 1979, Parsi notes the following:

> According to the Father of the Iranian revolution [Ayatollah Khomeini], the person embodying its ideology, the Israeli-Palestinian conflict was primarily a Palestinian issue. At the second level, it should involve the Arab states neighboring Israel, and only at the third level should it involve Iran and other Islamic states. As a result, Iran should never be more involved in the conflict than the Palestinians themselves and their Arab neighbors, and Iran should not be a frontline state against Israel. Direct confrontation with the Jewish State should be left to the Palestinians themselves and their immediate Arab neighbors.[21]

It seems like Ali Larijani, speaker of the Iranian Majlis, followed this very approach of the Iranian regime when he warned in Tehran that Gaza would turn into a graveyard for Israeli forces.

Finally, though criticized for not opening the Rafah gate to allow international aid to reach Gazans, Egyptian President Hosni Mubarak is likely to be remembered as the peace broker who paved the road to ending the violence in Gaza. Mubarak and French President Nicolas Sarkozy engaged in a peace initiative to halt the Israeli invasion. In due course, while Iran has been excluded altogether, Turkey has been

---

[21] Parsi, 2008, p. 102.

invited to the peace talks only as an observer and represented at the ambassadorial level. In addition, the way the Egyptian initiative is carried out has pretty much "Arabized" the Gaza conflict, thereby hindering non-Arab Muslim states from engaging in the resolution of the humanitarian crisis in Gaza. As such, it is still unclear whether the so-called Egyptian peace initiative has expedited or slowed down the process to reach a sustainable cease-fire in Gaza.

At the end of the day, it is quite clear that the Palestinian civilians, children and women, are the ones who bear the absolute tragedy caused by the Israeli invasion of Gaza. But it may not be necessarily as clear whether the Israelis are the only ones who will benefit from that invasion.

TURKEY'S TURN FROM THE WEST, OR YET ANOTHER SMEAR CAMPAIGN?[22]

I n a recent *Washington Post* article titled "Turkey's Turn From the West," Soner Çağaptay argued that the shifts in Turkey's domestic and foreign policies under the current Justice and Development Party (AK Party) government and Turkey's strained relationship with Israel mark Turkey's turn away from the West.

He suggested that under the current government liberal political trends have been disappearing, EU accession talks have stalled and Turkey's relations with anti-Western states such as Iran have improved, while those with Israel have deteriorated. On the top of all this, notes Çağaptay, Turkish Prime Minister Recep Tayyip Erdoğan walked out of a Davos panel after chiding Israeli President Shimon Peres for "killing people." Then, somewhat redundantly, Çağaptay concludes that if Turkey fails in "these areas," or wavers in its commitment to transatlantic structures such as NATO, it cannot expect to be President Barack Obama's favorite Muslim country.

Senior fellow and director of the Turkish Research Program at the Washington Institute for Near East Policy (WINEP), Çağaptay has long been the most sought-after scholar on Turkey and US-Turkish relations in the United States. Not only has he taught at the most prominent institutions, such as Georgetown, Princeton and Yale, and chaired the Turkey Advanced Area Studies Program at the State Department's Foreign Service Institute, where he trains American diplomats to be deployed to Turkey, he has also testified before congressional committees, often on the most pressing issues pertaining to US-Turkish relations.

---

[22] First appeared in *Today's Zaman* daily on February 04, 2009.

In addition, Çağaptay is perhaps the most renowned political pundit in the United States on the same subject. He has published in scholarly journals and print media, including the *Wall Street Journal*, the *Middle East Quarterly*, *Middle Eastern Studies*, *Los Angeles Times*, *The Washington Post* and *Newsweek*. He has also appeared on Fox News, CNN, NPR, Voice of America, Al-Jazeera, BBC, CNN-Türk and al-Hurra. Therefore, what Çağaptay says about Turkey's contemporary direction should make sense, at least theoretically. Better yet, one should pay even more attention to what he says, if, as the rumor goes, it appears in *The Washington Post*, except for that it is the newspaper of columnist David Ignatius, the very man who allegedly caused the infamous scandal at the Davos panel on Gaza.

However, Çağaptay's apparent readiness and attempt to explain the AK Party government's each and every policy as a signal of Turkey's detachment from the West and the apparent logical gap between his premises and conclusions raises a question about the validity of his arguments in general and his most recent *Washington Post* op-ed piece in particular.

One man's crusade against the AK Party

Çağaptay certainly seems to be one of the most brilliant Turkish scholars given his popularity in Washington and his prolific publication record so far. No need to mention that without academic credentials such as his, it would be difficult for one to lead the Turkish Research Program at WINEP, an influential think tank known for its allegedly pro-Israeli tendencies. In their most debated book, *The Israel Lobby and US Foreign Policy*, two American scholars, John J. Mearsheimer and Stephen M. Walt, argued about the so-called Israel lobby as follows:

> [The lobby] dominates the think-tanks which play an important role in shaping public debate as well as actual policy. The lobby created its own think tank in 1985, when Martin Indyk [who would later become an influential Middle East adviser to President Clinton] helped to found the Washington Institute for Near East Policy. Although WINEP plays down its links to Israel, claiming instead to provide a "balanced and realistic" perspective on the Middle

East issues, it is funded by individuals deeply committed to advanc-
ing Israel's agenda.

One definitely cannot argue that WINEP is a mere instrument
for the pursuit of the Israeli interests just because it has been founded
and funded by individuals fond of or zealous about Israel. Nor can
one argue that Çağaptay is simply voicing WINEP's discontent with
Turkey's current AK Party government just because he is paid by the
organization. Maybe, he is; but that is not the point.

Rather, the point is that there seems to be a pattern of increasing
discontent with the AK Party government in Çağaptay's speeches and
writings. In July 2007, appearing before the US Commission on Security and Cooperation in Europe (the Helsinki Commission) right after
the parliamentary elections in Turkey, Çağaptay commented:

> While 47 percent of the population voted for the ruling [AK] party,
> 37 percent voted for opposition secular leftist nationalists. ... In this
> regard, with the country being split into two opposing political
> views, I think the election outcome is probably the best outcome in
> terms of political stability, because what we see is that the ruling
> party ... emerged with 340 seats in the 550-member parliament.

Accordingly, he goes on to acknowledge that during the first term
of the AK Party government in office, as a result of Turkey's EU drive,
reforms in the path of liberalization and further democratic consolida-
tion took place.

In addition, he stressed, with the lowered outlawed Kurdistan
Workers' Party (PKK) threat after the capture of its leader, Abdullah
Öcalan:

> Issues that would have been considered taboo became possible to
> discuss in Turkish media. In fact, as a result of that, no taboos
> remained in Turkish media. And finally, the much-publicized reforms
> [related to Kurds], including broadcasting in the Kurdish language,
> as well as education in Kurdish, became possible.

In May 2008 during his interview with the staunchly secularist
Cumhuriyet daily, Çağaptay argued that the AK Party government has
increasingly transformed from a pluralist party that sought political

alliances with opposition parties into a majoritarian party that prefers to rely solely on the 47 percent popular vote it received. What Çağaptay argued would very much make sense if out of the two opposition parties, the CHP did not appear to be the main political force behind the court case to close the AK Party, and the MHP did not appear to have caused the court case in the first place by luring the AK Party government to lift the infamous headscarf ban. Moreover, rather interestingly, he also argued that the AK Party government's appetite for Turkey's EU membership had diminished after the EU accession talks actually started in 2005 and, as such, the prospect of the EU membership turned from an idea into a reality.

Again, his argument would be convincing if after 2005 the AK Party government did not face one existential threat after another, was not occupied with increasing PKK terrorist attacks from northern Iraq and did not have to deal with the global economic crisis, which has affected Turkey, as well. If nothing else, the government's recent decision to create a "chief EU negotiator" position separate from the foreign minister should indicate its revitalized interest in pursuing the EU accession talks.

In the aftermath of the Davos scandal

Nevertheless, it seems Çağaptay is not convinced by the AK Party government's recent overtures toward re-boosting Turkey's EU accession process. In his *Washington Post* article, which coincided with the immediate aftermath of Prime Minister Erdoğan's public criticism of Israel in Davos, Çağaptay argued that Turkey's domestic situation and foreign policy signified the country's departure from the Western camp. According to Çağaptay, women in Turkey are politically, economically and socially less empowered and, as such, less free than their counterparts in Saudi Arabia. By that token, he implies, Turkey under the AK Party government has become less democratic than Saudi Arabia.

Furthermore, he suggests that Ankara's rapprochement with Tehran poses a grave danger to Turkey's Western orientation as well as its alliance with the United States. One wonders how that is possible given the fact that the Obama administration has stated that it would consider even open diplomatic relations with Iran, and that the European Union has never ceased its relations with Iran. No need to mention that, according to Trita Parsi of John Hopkins University's School of Advanced International Studies (SAIS), not even Israel has ever ceased its relations with Iran, despite all the inflammatory rhetoric between the two.

Çağaptay also seems concerned about the fate of the Turkish-Israeli relationship and the alleged emergence of anti-Semitism in Turkey. He stresses that anti-Semitism is not hard-wired into Turkish society—rather its seeds are being spread by the political leadership. Similarly, he stresses that the Israelis have long felt comfortable visiting, doing business and vacationing in Turkey. These are certainly legitimate concerns and should be addressed thoroughly. During the infamous Davos panel, Prime Minister Erdoğan stressed that anti-Semitism was a crime against humanity and should be eliminated by all means. Later, Mr. Erdoğan continued to announce that whoever wants to harm the Jews in Turkey must face him first.

In a similar fashion, Israeli officials, most prominently President Shimon Peres and Foreign Minister Tzipi Livni, announced that the Turkish-Israeli relationship was strong enough to endure occasional disagreements. Nevertheless, the AK Party government should not suffice with the current nature of Turkish-Israeli relations, and should boost social and cultural relations between the two countries, as well. However, in order for that to happen, it would be necessary for the Israeli authorities to make necessary arrangements to enable an equal number of Turks, some 500,000 of them, feel comfortable visiting, doing business and vacationing in Israel every year.

Finally, Çağaptay suggests, "If Turkish foreign policy is based on solidarity with Islamist regimes or causes, Ankara cannot hope to be considered a serious NATO ally. Likewise, if the AKP discriminates against women, forgoes normal relations with Israel, curbs media freedoms or loses interest in joining Europe, it will hardly endear itself to the United States." What he suggests is quite right indeed.

However, those suggestions seem quite hypothetical and far from reflecting the realities on the ground, at least at the moment. Unless Çağaptay himself says so, one cannot know for sure whether the op-ed piece genuinely reflects his own views on the AK Party government and the contemporary direction Turkey is heading in; however, unlike his fine scholarly work, Çağaptay's op-ed piece in *The Washington Post* seems more like a hastily-written diatribe against the AK Party government produced in retaliation for Israeli President Peres' humiliation at the Davos panel. It is sad to see that because of the special interests reigning in Washington, Turkey risks not only facing another smear campaign in the months to come, but also losing one of its finest scholars and most talented advocates.

HR.106 ALL OVER AGAIN

The Winners and Losers with the So-Called
Armenian Genocide Resolutions[23]

A rticle 2 of the United Nations Convention on the Prevention and Punishment of the Crime of Genocide defines "genocide" as "any of the following acts committed with intent to destroy, in whole or in part, a national, ethnical, and racial or religious group, as such:

(1) "killing members of the group"; (2) "causing serious bodily or mental harm to members of the group"; (3) "deliberately inflicting on the group conditions of life calculated to bring about its physical destruction in whole or in part"; (4) "imposing measures intended to prevent births within the group"; and (5) "forcibly transferring children of the group to another group." So, the key is the "intent to destroy, in whole or in part," or in other words, the intent to "annihilate, or put out of existence." Therefore, the committing of any or all of these acts constitutes genocide only if done with such intent. By this definition, the Holocaust obviously constitutes genocide because the very definition of the word "genocide" seems to almost perfectly describe the Nazis' horrendous treatment of the Jews during World War II.

However, describing what befell a portion of the Ottoman Armenians as genocide is tantamount to either refuting the credibility of the Holocaust, or paving the way to describing every kind of war casualty as genocide because "causing casualties within a group while internally displacing a portion of that group in the time of war, or causing unintentional civilian casualties within that group" is not a part of the

---

[23] First appeared in *Today's Zaman* daily on March 10, 2009.

"genocide" definition. Similarly, the exploitation of the UN convention on genocide to prosecute crimes retrospectively is contradictory to the very logic of law, if such a law had not been enacted with such a purpose in the first place, which, if it was, would jeopardize the credibility of all other international laws. Another matter of curiosity is the fact that then-Ottoman Minister of Interior Talat Pasha's controversial telegrams, which allegedly approved the annihilation of the Ottoman Armenians, are the only evidence to certify such intention and that the very authenticity of those telegrams is still questionable and has yet to be verified.

One wonders if Reps. George Radanovich (R-Calif.), Adam Schiff (D-Calif.), Frank Pallone (D-N.J.), and Joe Knollenberg (R-Mich.) paid attention to these nuances, or if they were even aware of these nuances, before they introduced the so-called Armenian genocide resolution, HR 106, in the House of Representatives. It would not be a surprise if they had not or were not because of what some would call the so-called Armenian genocide industry seems to have long been yielding lucrative profits for the resolution sponsors, the Armenian diaspora organizations and for Washington's lobbying establishment. Next month, the whole "Armenian genocide resolution" play is likely to be staged once again and to strain US-Turkish relations, thereby yielding lucrative profits for some while harming others.

Armenian diaspora and the so-called Jewish lobby

Within the Armenian diaspora, the proponents of the so-called genocide resolution think they simply have nothing to lose no matter how long they prolong their campaign against Turkey. After all, there are two likely outcomes. If the resolution does not pass Congress, and/or the US president does not mention the "g"-word in his annual speech commemorating the 1915 tragedies, then business continues as usual: The Armenian diaspora reaffirms its allegedly "underdog" status, portrays Turkey as an anti-democratic state incapable of facing its history and embarks on yet another year of intensive political campaigning, which in turn strengthens the diaspora's solidarity and creates lucrative lobbying opportunities.

If the resolution passes Congress and the US recognizes the so-called genocide, then the whole so-called genocide enterprise becomes an international business. Relying on the fact that the US government recognizes the so-called genocide, a US state or federal court or an international authority such as an International Criminal Court (ICC) prosecutor could take the issue to The Hague to prosecute the late Ottoman government for the alleged genocide and war crimes. Similarly, the proponents of the so-called genocide would try to convince one or more of the UN member states to take the issue to the International Court of Justice against Turkey. The ICC cannot rule for any reparations to be given to the Armenians because the ICC does not have jurisdiction over Turkey, as Turkey is not a signatory to the Rome Statute, which founded the ICC. However, the mere existence of the ICC prosecution would bring, the Armenian diaspora thinks, satisfactory damage to Turkey's image. No need to mention that such an outcome would materialize, if ever, only after several decades throughout which lucrative lobbying opportunities would emerge, and Turkey would be forced to a series of concessions to the Armenians—and not necessarily only to the Armenians.

The Armenian diaspora organizations' unrelenting defamation campaign against the Turks and Turkey is somewhat understandable given the fact that the hatred of the Ottoman Empire—if not of the Turks and contemporary Turkey—seems to be the only factor binding the different factions and generations within the Armenian diasporas, and that the so-called genocide resolutions seem to be the most effective means for the political mobilization of the Armenian diasporas. However, some Jewish-American organizations' pattern of shifting loyalties vis-à-vis the so-called Armenian genocide allegations is confusing at best.

In his *Backstabbing for Beginners*, Michael Soussan observes what used to be probably the most distinguishing characteristic of Jack Abramoff, Washington's legendary lobbyist who is currently serving a prison term for federal felony charges. Soussan suggests that potential clients would walk into Abramoff's office thinking that they had a tiny problem, and then walk out thinking that they were in huge trouble and that Abramoff was the only person who could help them out. From one perspective, what Abramoff used to do was just "business as usual," doing what any other Washington lobbyist would do. It also reflected general characteristics of the broader entity that Abramoff belonged to: what the two American scholars John Mearsheimer and Stephen Walt termed as the "Israel Lobby." From another perspective, what Abramoff used to do was not any different from what certain Jewish organizations do whenever a so-called Armenian genocide resolution is introduced in the House of Representatives. Simply stated, certain Jewish organizations in the US have taken advantage of these infamous resolutions to manipulate Ankara and make the Turks agree to what they might not otherwise vis-à-vis Turkish-Israeli relations. Although it would be unfair to assume that these Jewish-American organizations have simply been manipulating US-Turkish relations for the sake of Israel's interests, the continuous shift of these organizations' attitude toward Turkey that almost always occurs in parallel to the changes in the Turkish-Israeli relations makes one rethink the situation.

It seems like certain Jewish-American organizations—and Israel indirectly through them—have vastly benefited from the recurring waves of the so-called Armenian genocide resolutions popping up on the US House Committee on Foreign Affairs agenda every year around April. However, with the changing political and economic dynamics both in the US and Turkey, not only are such resolutions no longer profitable, but also what some may term "Jewish opportunism" may grow increasingly detrimental to the wellbeing of Jews in general.

One should be reminded of the fact that—no matter how hypothetical a situation it is—if the Americans turn cold on the Jews and Israel at some point in the future, the Turks are pretty much the likeliest, if not the only, people whose help the Jews can seek and possibly get. At least, that is what history teaches. With that thought in mind, the Jewish organizations in the West in particular and the world Jewry and Israel in general would be better off avoiding the shortsighted practices and policies that would alienate the Turks in the long run. Although seemingly a hypothetical situation at the moment, it has already been forecasted by many Jewish intellectuals in the US. Thankfully, despite the oscillating attitude of certain Jewish-American organizations, there have always been Jewish-Americans who have never wavered in their support for Turkey and for the improvement of the US-Turkish and Turkish-Israeli relations.

The US and the American people

Although the United States and the American people have always been victimized by the manipulation of the US Congress by certain interest groups, there have not been many—if any—scholarly studies that scrutinize the impact of the so-called Armenian genocide resolution on US interests. Some tend to make comparisons between the Ottoman Empire in its last century and the United States today. As the argument goes, in the late 19th century, the Ottoman Empire introduced a comprehensive series of democratic reforms that intended to improve the political environment so that the non-Muslim minorities, a prominent component of which was the Ottoman Armenians, could become more politically active and take a role in the Ottoman administration. However, it continues that certain militant Armenian groups such as the Tashnaks exploited this window of opportunity to pursue their own narrow interests, thereby contributing to the collapse of the empire. Similarly, as the argument goes, in the last several decades certain Armenian-American organizations such as the Armenian National Committee of America (ANCA), which itself originates in the Tashnak movement, have been exploiting American democracy to pursue their narrow group interests, even though it gravely damages the US's image and interests.

Whether such a similarity exists is certainly something that their fellow Americans are to decide. However, one difference is certain: While within the Ottoman Empire numerous militant Armenian groups engaged in armed conflict against the empire, massacred some 800,000 Muslims and defected to the invading Russian army, such is not the case today in the United States. The only similarity is that Armenian terrorists such as Murad Topalian and his accomplices in the Armenian Secret Army for the Liberation of Armenia (ASALA) inflicted terror on American soil long before the terrorist attacks of Sept. 11 by assassinating Turkish diplomats and attacking the American scholars who called for an objective investigation of the genocide allegations. While these terrorist acts deserve condemnation, they should not overshadow the fact that today there seems to be a sizeable peace-loving Armenian-American community that is as disturbed by the Armenian National Committee of America (ANCA) as many Americans and Turks are.

What should Turkey do?

Turkish Ambassador to the US Nabi Şensoy recently commented that "the Turkish nation is ready to struggle altogether [against a possible passage of the so-called genocide resolution in the Congress]," and hoped that the US administration would understand the importance of Turkey, the meaning of this issue to the Turkish people and the harm it would bring to Turkish-American relations. More important than the US administration's comprehension of this is the American people's understanding of how such resolution and its concomitant political intrigues harm their country.

In this regard, by reaching out to the American people via ads in the major newspapers, Ankara should express Turkey's respect for the rights of Americans and for their representatives in the Congress to do what is right and rational, and what they believe serves the US's national interests. The ad should point out that Turkey believes that passing a controversial resolution in Congress recognizing the so-called Armenian genocide is neither right nor rational, nor does it serve US national interests. Nevertheless, it should assert that Turkey would respect it no matter how wrong, irrational and detrimental to the US interests that resolution would be. Moreover, the Justice and Development Party (AK Party) government should say what it can guarantee is that it would do its best in the aftermath of such a resolution to counter the Turks' rising discontent with the US and everything related to it, because Turkey is committed to the US-Turkish partnership. However, the AK Party government should clarify that it cannot guarantee that Turkey will be able to maintain its responsiveness to cooperation with the United States. The American people would appreciate the fact that, just like any other democratic nation's government, the Turkish government is bound by the preferences of its citizens.

Finally, the Turks should remain calm and enjoy the blessings of the Armenian diaspora's defamation of Turkey, because there could literally be no better justification and reason for mobilization than this continuous defamation effort for the Turks to reach out to the US Congress and the American people, introducing Turkey and all it stands for.

FROM THE PERIPHERAL ALLIANCE TO GAZA AND THEREAFTER

Redefining the Turkish-Israeli Relationship[24]

Although Israel's recent aggression on Gaza, the infamous Davos incident and the subsequent exchange of bitter comments between Turkish and Israeli officials have stirred some anxiety in the Turkish-Israeli relationship, the relations between the two countries have almost always been stable and quite lucrative for some ever since 1948, the occasional scandals notwithstanding.

(Another one is yet to unravel as the second indictment in the Ergenekon case suggests that in 2004 Israel's Mossad planned to assassinate Turkish Prime Minister Recep Tayyip Erdoğan.)

The relationship dates back to the early 1950s, when it was first initiated as part of Israel's peripheral alliance strategy. Considering its Arab neighbors as an imminent threat, Israel under the leadership of Prime Minister David Ben Gurion sought to reach out to non-Arab countries like Turkey, Iran and Ethiopia. Seemingly, Israel's alliance with Iran ended with the so-called Islamic revolution in 1979, yet the alliance with Turkey has endured. The Turkish-Israeli relationship has grown so strong over time that even during the coalition government of the Islamist Welfare Party (RP) in 1997, under the auspices of the army generals, the relationship bore a free trade agreement between the two countries.

Nevertheless, the Turkish-Israeli relationship, which has suffered characteristic problems from the very beginning to the present by remaining exclusively within the military realm, is likely to be serious-

---

[24] First appeared in *Today's Zaman* daily on April 09, 2009.

ly threatened by the changing dynamics in Turkey and in Israel as well as in the region, and hence is certain to threaten regional stability in the years to come unless a series of structural policy changes are undertaken. The necessary changes in Turkish foreign policy toward Israel include promoting socio-economic and cultural ties with Israel in addition to the military ties, ensuring full transparency and taking initiatives in the resolution of the Israeli-Palestinian conflict by helping Hamas give up its armed struggle and remain committed to the peace negotiations.

Promoting the socio-economic and cultural aspects of the relationship

The non-Jewish Turks have traditionally failed to show an interest in Israel commensurate to the interest the Israelis have shown in Turkey. According to a report in the *Haaretz* daily dated Feb. 1, 2009, thirteen percent of all Israelis vacationing abroad prefer to travel to Turkey, and as such, Turkey is the second most popular destination— after the United States—the Israelis visit every year. The Turks should reciprocate the favor by visiting Israel every year in no fewer numbers. Better yet, they should compensate for the past by establishing the necessary permanent infrastructures both in Turkey and Israel to ensure the continuous flow of Turkish tourists into Israel throughout the year. Their encounter with Israel would give them the opportunity to comprehend the Israelis' perseverance and recognize not only that Israel is to remain on the map, but also that Israel is much more than what it seems on the map.

Developing the socio-economic and cultural aspects of the Turkish-Israeli relationship would have a moderating impact on Israel's security concerns as well. The Palestinians living in Israel have so far failed to integrate themselves into Israeli society, and there may be various reasons for that. The everyday fact that at any given time of the day there are dozens of Israeli Defense Forces (IDF) groups, both boys and girls, walking on the streets of Jerusalem with their fully automatic machine guns in hand while no Palestinian is allowed to posses weapons is crushingly humiliating and sufficient for the Palestinians living in Israel to feel dissociated from the Israeli state. Moreover, the dire socio-economic situation of the Palestinians living either in Israel, the West Bank or Gaza may have made the so-called "martyr's check" that the late Saddam Hussein and some other Arab states have paid to the families of the suicide bombers appealing. Given that the Palestinians have long been living on less than $2 a day, the martyr's check—reportedly varying between $500 and $10,000—may not seem, after all, to be a bad investment to trade one's life for.

Turkey's increased economic presence in Jerusalem and other Muslim-populated areas in Israel would help the Palestinians living in Israel prosper to a certain degree and to give an incentive to work with the authorities to maintain stability and security. The economic disparity between the Jews and the Muslims of Israel is perhaps most obvious in the Old City. While the Jewish Quarter overflows with Jewish tourists visiting from all around the world and the Jewish shopkeepers can hardly keep up with all the customers, the Muslim Quarter is like an abandoned city where the Palestinian shopkeepers feel fortunate if they make any sales during the day.

Therefore, boosting tourism between Turkey and Israel would have multiple benefits, although, based on the personal experience of a four-hour detention at Israel's Ben-Gurion airport and of the ensuing random interrogation by some eight different officers throughout, it is quite easy to argue that the current travel customs regulations in place do not really help Israel attract many tourists from around the world, especially from Muslim countries like Turkey. Faced with such mean treatment, one is tempted to have second thoughts about the widely held argument that Israelis do not want non-Jews to visit Israel, anyway. It would be unfair to accede to that argument, however, especially given that Israeli leaders have time and again urged people to visit Israel.

A Turkish approach: living for Palestine instead of dying for it

Understandably, the possibility of Israel opening itself up to the world and welcoming the Turks in particular, and Muslim tourists from all around the world in general, depends on the maintenance of security and stability within Israel, especially in tourist cities like Jerusalem and Ashkelon, which is near the Gazan border. And that in turn depends on the progress of the resolution of the Israeli-Palestinian conflict. As a prerequisite for helping Israel mend its relations with the Muslim world and become a legitimate entity and secure place in the region, Ankara should take an active role in the renewed peace process and use its rapport with the Hamas and the Fatah leaders to moderate their respective stands vis-à-vis Israel and each other in order to achieve a sustainable peace agreement with the Israelis.

As recently illustrated at the infamous Davos panel, the Turkish-Israeli relationship in the near future is almost certainly going to be greatly influenced by the Israeli-Palestinian conflict. The Turks have grown increasingly sensitive to the conflict because it lies beneath the never-ending regional instability, which has long threatened Turkey's economic and security interests. Additionally, the Turks—just like the rest of the world—have been outraged by Israel's armed aggressions on the Palestinians and the economic embargoes seemingly triggered by Hamas' terrorist attacks. Therefore, it will be imperative for Ankara, the only actor capable of talking to both the Israelis and Hamas, to take an active role in the resolution of the Israeli-Palestinian conflict.

Looking ahead to Palestine's January 2010 elections, which are likely to multiply Hamas' political power, and the right wing-dominated Israeli coalition government under the leadership of Prime Minister Benjamin Netanyahu, as well as US President Barack Obama's commitment to finding a sustainable solution to the Israeli-Palestinian conflict, one may expect the renewal of an Oslo-type peace process between the Israelis and the Palestinians next year. This time, however, Mr. Netanyahu may find a different Palestinian counterpart to negotiate with: the Hamas leader Khalid Mashaal. Prime Minister Netanyahu and the Hamas leader are not completely strangers to one another: The former sought to have the latter assassinated a decade ago. In *Kill Khalid*, Paul McGeough reports that on Sept. 25, 1997, Israel's Mossad tried to kill Mashaal in a failed assassination attempt in Amman, where he then resided with his family. The ensuing crisis brought Israel's relations with Jordan, one of its very rare Arab allies, to the brink of complete disruption.

Despite their rather odd encounter, Netanyahu and Mashaal may not necessarily be far from making substantial progress toward a sustainable peace. Provided that both Israel and Hamas cease their attacks on Palestinian and Israeli civilians, respectively, and heed President Obama's commitment to the solution on the basis of the land-for-peace agreement, there may be hope for peace. After all, it was the very same Mashaal who proposed a 30-year truce between Israel and the Palestinians before Mossad tried to assassinate him. Similarly, according to an *Associated Press* report, speaking at a conference in Jerusalem, Netanyahu vowed to push for Israeli-Palestinian peace. The way to peace may be a little bumpy though, because, as he hints in *A Durable Peace: Israel and Its Place among the Nations*, Mr. Netanyahu believes that a durable peace in the region is only attainable if Israel has complete military and economic dominance over its neighbors.

Of course, the peace talks may also completely collapse if the US, Turkey and the other parties do not stand by them. Netanyahu and Mashaal may prefer to settle old scores once they face each other as two opposing leaders. Once he took office in February 2001, McGeough argued, Prime Minister Ariel Sharon seemed to target the Palestine Liberation Organization (PLO) leader, Yasser Arafat, by all means possible, as if he intended to take revenge for the latter's narrow escape from Sharon's 1982 assault on the southern Lebanon, which was marked by the Sabra-Shatila camp massacre that left some 3,000 Palestinians dead.

Critical to the success of the Israeli-Palestinian peace talks is that the divided Palestinian factions—mainly Fatah and Hamas—unite, that Hamas stop its terrorist attacks on Israel and that both Fatah and Hamas remain committed to dialogue with the Israeli authorities. Philosophically speaking, the prospects are not good for those to happen. In *Leviathan*, Thomas Hobbes argues: "The passions that incline men to peace are: fear of death; desire of such things as are necessary to commodious living; and a hope by their industry to obtain them." By this token, given the socio-economic situation in Gaza and Israel's continuous embargoes, the Hamas leaders may be unable to recognize the advantages of engaging in peace negotiations with Israelis, which have thus far often collapsed.

However, Ankara's rapport with Hamas may prove instrumental to the continuation of the peace talks amid the absence of immediate gains. This has one downside, though: As Ankara becomes increasingly involved with the issue, the Arab leaders—and not necessarily the Arabs on the street—may grow uneasy because they deem it an exclusively Arab matter. Nonetheless, the very fact that both the Egyptian and Jordanian regimes, as well as the Fatah, have been as brutal to Hamas as Israel has diminished the ability of the Arab leaders to attract Hamas to a dialogue with Israel, and keep it on track thereafter. Moreover, the Turkish government has learned from experience that extremism is not the appropriate way forward to peace and prosperity. In this regard, it may convince the Hamas leaders that Palestinians would better serve their cause by living for Palestine instead of dying for it.

In the final analysis, Israel stays on the map and stays in close proximity to Turkey. Also, the two share vital interests in the region's stability, although both may have occasionally had leaders that perceived their best interests as being served by constant instability. Therefore, far from sentimentally charged rhetoric, Turkey and Israel should redefine their relationship on the basis of fostering socio-economic and cultural relations and cooperating closely toward a sustainable solution of the Israeli-Palestinian conflict. In the meantime, it would also be greatly helpful if the pertinent parties could clarify how one can criticize the policies of the state of Israel without being called either anti-Semitic or a self-hating Jew.

SONER CAGAPTAY'S FIGHT
AGAINST TURKEY[25]

S
oner Çağaptay of the Washington Institute for Near East Policy recently published yet another controversial piece in *Newsweek* magazine that appears to be seriously distorting the reality regarding the ongoing Ergenekon court case in Turkey and targeting the faith-based civil society movement inspired by Fethullah Gülen
by alleging that it is controlling the Turkish police.

In his piece, titled "Behind Turkey's Witch Hunt: The Ergenekon
case exposes the power of a shadowy Islamic brotherhood that controls
the Turkish police," Çağaptay alleges that the current Justice and Development Party (AK Party) government is using the Ergenekon court
case to suppress its opponents and that the so-called Gülen movement
manipulates the Turkish police force to assist the government.

Çağaptay poses a serious allegation in his article's title, and it should
certainly be thoroughly investigated. If what he alleges is true, then it
means Turkish democracy is under an imminent threat. However, as
one continues to read his article, it becomes all too clear that his purpose is to misinform *Newsweek* readers about the ongoing Ergenekon
court case and, at the same time defame the current AK Party government and the Gülen movement by associating them with various
unlawful acts.

Today, the readers of *Newsweek* should be open-minded enough not
to readily subscribe to Çağaptay's apparently baseless and conflicting
arguments, and hence take a deeper look into the various Turkish media
to gain a better understanding of the ongoing Ergenekon case. Similarly, the Gülen movement is not an obscure phenomenon that is hard

---

[25] First appeared in *Today's Zaman* daily on May 17, 2009.

to find out about. By now, there are perhaps countless academic studies and news reports on the movement. Moreover, the schools and other cultural initiatives inspired by the movement have been operating for more than a decade in more than a hundred countries. Surely, these countries' respective governments and security services would have continuously scrutinized the Gülen movement-inspired organizations with respect to whether they are Islamic or not. So, given the abundance of tools to study the Gülen movement, and given Çağaptay's increasingly biased and less scholarly writings, the more he writes, the less credible he will become.

However, the real problem is that despite his apparent distance from scholarly objectivity, Çağaptay is in a position to significantly influence US public and official opinion on Turkey. He is frequently given opportunities to publish articles and opinion pieces in well-known newspapers and magazines. (His latest article in *The Washington Post* titled "Turkey's turn from the West" and the above-mentioned article in *Newsweek* are the latest examples.) The lack of objectivity and scholarship in these published pieces raises questions about the editorial objectivity of the newspapers, journals and magazines in which these pieces are published. He is frequently asked to testify before the US Senate and House foreign relations committees. He seems to be directing the so-called Turkish research program at the Washington Institute for Near East Policy. Probably the gravest of all, at the Foreign Service Institute in Arlington, Virginia, Çağaptay is reportedly training the US diplomats and ranking military officers to be stationed in Turkey. One wonders with what kind of intellectual background about Turkey and Turkish society the US diplomats are starting their duties in their respective posts in Turkey and how this intellectual background is affecting their attitude toward the country's people.

Çağaptay's art of distorting reality

Anybody who is not even slightly informed about the issues that Çağaptay refers to throughout the piece would easily conclude that his purpose is not to objectively and intellectually address them, but to misinform *Newsweek* readers about the actors involved with the issues and about some others who are not even distantly related to those issues. Here, Çağaptay rightly reports as follows:

> In an early morning raid on April 13, Turkish police arrested more than a dozen middle-aged liberal women working for the Society for Contemporary Life (ÇYDD), a nongovernmental organization that provides educational scholarships to poor teenage girls. The arrests were part of the Ergenekon court case, in which police have arrested hundreds of people, including Army officers, opponents of the Justice and Development Party (AKP) government, renowned journalists, artists and now these women, charging them with plotting to overthrow the government.

However, Çağaptay fails to note that the independent prosecutors of the Turkish judiciary have not indicted—and consequently the Turkish police have not arrested—those women for doing charity work and providing scholarship to poor teenage girls, but for plotting with the retired army generals to overthrow Turkey's elected government via a military coup d'état. Therefore, not only those women but also all of the others indicted within the framework of the Ergenekon investigation are naturally the "opponents" of the current AK Party government. After all, they are charged with the crime of seeking to overthrow that government. For this reason, one can conclude that everybody indicted in the Ergenekon investigation are the opponents of the AK Party government, but not every opponent of the AK Party government is indicted due to the Ergenekon investigation.

The charges against the claimed Ergenekon terror network are not limited to plotting to overthrow a democratically elected government. It happens to be the latest alleged crime of the network. Retrospectively, the claimed Ergenekon terror network is charged with being responsible for carrying out kidnappings and assassinations, especially in heavily Kurdish-populated southeastern Turkey. Given the fact that in the last several decades a total of 17,000 individuals have vanished, mostly in this region, it is only reasonable and imperative for the prosecutors to indict for interrogation of the individuals who are likely to be involved.

Çağaptay somewhat abruptly tries to tie the Ergenekon investigation to the Gülen movement: "[The Ergenekon investigation] is a tool for the AKP to curb freedoms, and more than anything else illustrates the power of the Gülen *tarikat* (Islamic order) that now controls the Turkish police and, you guessed it, educational scholarships for the poor." Obviously, Çağaptay does not seem to feel obliged to provide a reasonable explanation either to how the AK Party government uses the investigation to curb the freedoms, or to how the investigation illustrates the alleged power of the Gülen movement to control the police and educational scholarships for the poor. Çağaptay rather wants readers to believe what he says. Or he could be simply aiming to produce written material that could later be used against the Gülen movement.

The first thing that strikes one is Çağaptay's description of the Gülen movement as a *tarikat* (Islamic order) and his allegation that the Turkish police are a part of that Islamic order simply because the police do their job by arresting the suspects as warranted by the prosecutors.

As a civil society movement that promotes interfaith and intercultural dialogue through a worldwide network of NGOs, which involves Muslims, Christians, Jews, Hindus, Buddhists, agnostics, atheists and others, and which mobilizes the philanthropists to open schools, hospitals and other charity organizations in more than a hundred countries, the Gülen movement looks somewhat different from a *tarikat*.

If not, then the late Pope John Paul II, who invited Gülen to the Vatican in 1997 as a gesture to promote interfaith dialogue, Chief Rabbi of Israel Eliyahu Bakshi-Doron, who became a champion of the interfaith dialogue initiated by Gülen, the Greek Orthodox Patriarch Bartholomew, who publicly joined Gülen in promoting interfaith dialogue, the late Turkish Jewish businessman and industrialist Uzeyir Garih, who reportedly vouched for Gülen-inspired school to be opened in Moscow, and many others who have not seemed quite of Muslim origin should also be the members of the Islamic order alleged by Çağaptay.

Çağaptay's art of labeling

Moreover, it is quite difficult, if not impossible, to discern how Çağaptay links the Turkish police to the Gülen movement. He does not provide a reasonable explanation for this argument, or better to say, "allegation." Nor does he seem interested in doing so. Throughout the piece, Çağaptay uses various key terms and tries to associate them with the Gülen movement, thereby bolstering the suspicion that his intention is merely to produce written material in the media, so that those who think along the same lines as him can manipulate those materials in the future in their persecution of Gülen and those who have been inspired by his thoughts and ideas.

"Most Turks have a sinister view of the spiritual message of this tarikat," says Çağaptay in an attempt to create a view that the Gülen movement is a controversial phenomenon that is not welcomed by the majority of the Turkish people. As a matter of fact, a recent survey by Akbar Ahmed of American University has demonstrated that 84 percent of Turkish society has a highly favorable opinion of Gülen and the civil society initiatives he has inspired. Similarly, "Thanks to missionary and volunteer work, the Gülen tarikat obtained social and political power globally over the decades," says Çağaptay in an attempt to create a view that the Gülen-inspired schools are doing missionary work and seeking political power in the respective countries where they operate. Finally, Çağaptay tries to associate the Ergenekon investigation with the Joseph McCarthy trials in the US, and thereby attempts to create a view that the current AK Party government has created a state of fear by exploiting the investigation.

Çağaptay's true intentions are implicit in his last statement: "There is a way out of this conundrum if the AKP turns Ergenekon into a case that targets only criminals." Çağaptay contradicts himself by acknowledging that the government can and should manipulate the legal investigation by asking the AK Party government to intervene in the Ergenekon investigation. He also appears ignorant of the fact that the prosecutors indict the suspects to find the true criminals.

IRAN'S PRESIDENTIAL ELECTIONS

The US-Iranian Relations after
Mahmoud Ahmadinejad[26]

O n June 12, a presidential election almost no less critical than the recent American one that brought "change" to America is set to take place in Iran.

The strongest contender against incumbent President Mahmoud Ahmadinejad is Mir Hussein Mousavi, who previously served as the prime minister and the foreign minister of Iran. Mousavi promises more reforms, better relations with the United States and the West, more freedom on private TV channels and less restriction on the way the Iranians dress. According to the latest polls, Mousavi leads the incumbent Ahmadinejad by 4 percentage points, thereby increasing his prospects to take over the presidential office. The lingering question is whether Mousavi's potential presidency would entail healthy US-Iranian relations given his relatively moderate stance and US President Barack Hussein Obama's opening of relations with Iran.

The Obama administration's opening of relations with Iran and willingness to give a chance to diplomacy is not an open-ended offer; it has a deadline. US Vice President Joe Biden recently asserted at the American Israel Public Affairs Committee (AIPAC) conference in Washington that if Iran does not cooperate (meaning dismantle its nuclear program), then the world can return to isolating this state with the moral authority of having tried to engage it. Hence, one may argue that then the world should be ready for tougher measures, and even for a US and/or Israeli military operation against Iran, because the latter will have arguably proven that it is not interested in peace and dialogue with

---

[26] First appeared in *Today's Zaman* daily on June 07, 2009.

the US, or with the "world," for that matter. There is no need to mention that the Obama administration asked Israel only not to attack Iran "unilaterally."

For the time being, the issue of whether there is going to be a military confrontation between the US and Iran is relatively easier to discern than whether such confrontation will take place because the two cannot get along, or the two cannot get along because there needs to be a military confrontation between them. The record hitherto suggests that even if Iran witnesses more reforms with potential President Mousavi as it once did with President Mohammad Khatami, US-Iranian relations are likely to remain sour, and Iran's image as a regional and global threat is likely to remain unchanged. The reasons for that are primarily that the two states possess continuously distorted views not only of each other but also of themselves, and that Iran will arguably continue to pose a threat to Israel's and the world's security, as Israeli President Shimon Peres and Prime Minister Benjamin Netanyahu reiterated during their recent visits to Washington, as they have in almost all of their media interviews and addresses since 2006.

'Iran the Islamic Republic, Iran the global threat,' they say...

There are two dominant sources of information influencing US policy toward Iran, and pretty much making it what it has been so far: first, the Iranian diaspora, the majority of whose members are predominantly secular and fled Iran immediately before and after the so-called Islamic Revolution in 1979; and second, the scholars, think tankers, journalists and policy-makers who prioritize the well being of the State of Israel relatively more than anything else in the region for understandable reasons.

The first group tends to see contemporary Iran through the image of 1979, just like the members of any other diaspora see their country of origin through the image of the year when they left it, unless they do travel back and forth. However, the Iranian diaspora differs from the other diasporas in the US in some critical ways. While the diasporas in general are formed of individuals who have chosen to migrate to the US for economic or other personal reasons, the Iranian diaspora consists of individuals who had been forced out of Iran, exiled, in a sense. Their subsequent generations were born and raised in the US knowing that the current Iranian regime is responsible for their parents' exile. Moreover, while the diaspora members in general are able to visit their country of origin and hence keep themselves updated with the socioeconomic and political developments there, the majority of the Iranian diaspora are barred from visiting Iran, and if they are not, they refrain from visiting it because they are afraid of being detained once they are in the country. In addition to that, the current Iranian regime's closed nature and tight grip on media makes it even more difficult for the Iranian diaspora to have an accurate perspective on contemporary Iran. Therefore, their views are much likely to be shaped by their old grievances and new speculations. For this reason, probably, many in the Iranian diaspora think that contemporary Iranians are deprived of all political and economic freedoms while they have to adhere strictly to religious lifestyle in the so-called Islamic Republic.

The second group consists of individuals and organizations such as think tanks and news networks that are deeply concerned about the well being of the State of Israel, and are capable of directly or indirectly, intellectually or financially influencing US policy-makers. For them, it seems, every kind of development taking place in the Middle East and likely to somehow risk Israel's security requires immediate attention and action of the United States, because the latter is allegedly committed to the well being of Israel. Like the two American scholars John Mearsheimer and Stephen Walt, some tend to simply describe this group of people as part of the so-called Israeli lobby.

However, it would be misleading to do so, because then one would have to consider a substantial number of members of the US Congress a part of that lobby, for they seem too often to equate the national interests of the US to those of Israel, and at times forego the former for the sake of the latter. It would be even more misleading to argue, as some do, that key congressional, White House or other governmental positions, such as the committee chairs, chiefs of staff and senior advisers, are held by the individuals of Jewish heritage just to secure Israel's interests. Nevertheless, the actual influence of such members may not be totally ineffective in shaping US foreign policy in general and its policy toward Iran in particular. After all, Iran is widely argued to pose a potential, if not active, threat to Israel and Iranian officials, most notably President Ahmadinejad, have not so far failed the holders of this argument by consistently targeting Israel in their speeches.

If one relies solely on these two sources of information, he or she may be excused for thinking that the contemporary Iranian regime is readying itself with a nuclear program for a standoff with the United States and Israel, and that contemporary Iranians are suffering at the hands of this clerical regime. However, traveling across the country and talking to the Iranians about the US and Israel as well as their expectations from life, one develops a somewhat different view on both the contemporary Iranian regime and what it may and can do.

Another Iran and the usual America

In Iran, the visible and the invisible, or the outside and the inside seem to be extremely different from each other. For instance, the streets, buildings, and to a great extent, automobiles look like they have not changed since the revolution. In a way, life in the cities of Iran, except for Tehran, seems as if it stopped in 1979. The view of the outside reflects the fact that Iran has been deprived of the benefits of globalization such as the import of new ideas, technologies and practices. Similarly, Iranians outside of Tehran do not generally show off their wealth. However, inside their houses, the lifestyle of Iranians suggests that they are following almost every contemporary trend, from fashion to the use of technology. The upper-middle and higher class Iranians seem to be obsessed with luxury, and as such, own mini-palaces, which from the outside look like just ordinary houses. Those who are economically able (and many of them are, thanks to government subsidies) travel occasionally to Turkey and other neighboring countries. The middle and lower classes seem heavily dependent on the government subsidies to pay their bills and put bread on the table. The Iranians—both the sec-

ularists and the supporters of the regime—seem to be pleased with
the performance of the Ahmadinejad administration and agree that
during his term Iran has developed its infrastructure more than the
previous administrations. The most striking of all the cities of Iran is
probably Tehran. The city "looks" quite rich and modern. The shopping
malls, cafes and restaurants run nearly until midnight, and after that it
becomes even more difficult to tell the difference between some parts
of Tehran and any European city.

Moreover, regardless of their political inclinations, Iranians note
that they do not have any problem with the US, but American politicians seem to be always against them. In this regard, President Obama's
Nevruz message to the Iranian people seemed to have somehow contributed to improving the Iranian opinion on the American politicians.
When it comes to Israel, again the ordinary Iranians seem proud of
Iran's seemingly unrelenting support for Palestine, and they think that
the inflammatory rhetoric of their leaders against Israel would never turn
into a military action unless the latter attacks Iran. If Israel does attack
Iran, though, they say, not only with its long-range missiles but also
with their countless youngsters ready to be martyrs, Iran would unleash
the hell onto Israel. The vast graveyards of the Iran-Iraq War martyrs
stretching across every Iranian city suggest that they may not be bluff-
ing at all. So, while the conventional view on the current Iranian regime
is that it would engage in a military standoff with Israel and possibly
with the US, a deeper look into the country suggests that it would not,
so long as neither of the latter two attacks Iran.

To be clear, Israel is unlikely to wage any military action against
Iran without the backing of the United States. Then, the question is
whether the US would directly or indirectly support a military operation against Iran. It may, actually. Not because the US is keen on destroying Iran, but because US policymakers seem to have an extremely
high opinion of what they are capable of doing. Their mesmerism with
US power is implicit with their oft-repeated statement: "We are the
most powerful nation on earth and in history." It would be wise for
them to remember that, as the old Turkish saying goes, one supposes
his own fist to be iron until the moment someone else punches him

in the face. Their apparent failure to distinguish between the power to construct and the power to destruct seems to be causing them to develop misleading assessments about the US power. It is the relative ease of destruction that makes policymakers believe that the US has an unparalleled power. While Iraq and Afghanistan have proven that the US may not necessarily be so powerful to construct, Iran may be that punch in the face that reminds the US of the others' power to destruct.

However, so far, the US policymakers and opinion leaders have generally not seemed mindful of that possibility. In his book *The Persian Puzzle*, Kenneth Pollack of the Brookings Institution suggests that the United States does not need to have a relationship with Iran:

> [W]e have been isolated from Iran for 25 years and in that time have experienced the most extraordinary economic prosperity in our history, coupled with strategic developments that have made the United States the most powerful nation the world has ever seen. Clearly, the lack of a warm relationship with Iran has not held us back.

The current US policymakers may be thinking along the same lines. Moreover, the US policymakers may indeed be thinking that Iran's ultimate target is the United States. Both Shimon Peres and Benjamin Netanyahu have frequently asserted during their interviews to the American media and most likely while talking to the policymakers that "Israel is targeted by Iran, only because it is viewed as an extension of America in the region, and because both Israel and the United States represent the same ideals of freedom, which the militant Islamists hate." Some, if not most, policymakers may be thinking along the same lines as well.

At the end of the day, the prospects for sustained improvement in US-Iranian relations seem low unless either the sources of information about Iran in the United States or the Iranian regime itself changes. The only change with Mousavi's presidency would be the following: The United States, whose last administration had defined its mission as a fight against a villain named Hussein, today has an administration headed by a president whose name is Hussein. Similarly, Iran, which is currently headed by a president who reportedly vowed to wipe Israel off the map, questioned the validity of the Holocaust and has allegedly become the number one enemy of the Jews—is most likely to be headed by a president whose name, "Mousavi," which literally means "Jewish." Finally, both the US and Iran will be governed by presidents named "Hussein." Isn't that an interesting change?

RETHINKING ANKARA'S RESPONSE
TO THE UIGHUR MASSACRE[27]

Turkish Prime Minister Recep Tayyip Erdoğan's historic stand off against Israeli President Shimon Peres was apparently a genuine expression of the world's collective frustration with Israeli practices against the Palestinians.

Mr. Erdoğan's reaction mesmerized Muslims from Morocco to Indonesia and was even admired by some Westerners. As such, his growing popularity gave him a unique opportunity to create awareness among the world's leaders about inhumane practices perpetrated by certain states. The unfortunate incidents that recently took place in Urumqi, the capital of China's Xinjiang autonomous region, presented yet another sad example of such practices, thereby stressing the gravity of the problem.

However, not only did Mr. Erdoğan's uncalculated sentimental rhetoric risk his role as an objective supporter of the oppressed, including his ability to help the Uighurs, but Ankara's presumptuous attitude, demanding an explanation from the Chinese government regarding what happened in Urumqi, is likely to have cost Turkey a historic opportunity to assume a mediating role between the Chinese government and one of its major minorities as well. Turkey's prospects for such a role will further lessen if the so-called Mother Uighur, Rabiya Kadeer, who is considered by the Chinese government as a main instigator of the protests in Urumqi, visits Turkey. It is not difficult to imagine how the ultranationalists in the country would manipulate her visit to organize a series of public protests denouncing the Chinese government.

---

[27] First appeared in *Today's Zaman* daily on July 15, 2009.

Nevertheless, according to recent news reports, during his lengthy telephone conversation with his Chinese counterpart, Turkish Foreign Minister Ahmet Davutoğlu expressed that Turkey respects China's territorial integrity and does not have any intention of meddling in its internal affairs, but from a human rights perspective is concerned with the deteriorating situation of the Uighurs. Should it manage to view the Uighur-Chinese conflict merely from a human rights perspective, not a nationalistic one, and act accordingly, Ankara may still seize the opportunity to mediate between the Chinese government and its Uighur minority. As such, Turkey would not only fortify its image as an international peacemaker, but also possibly become a sought-after mediator for the resolution of the other major conflicts. However, in order to become an able mediator, Ankara must refrain from sentimentally loaded rhetoric on the Uighur issue. In addition, the Turkish public should help their government do so by avoiding hateful protests against the Chinese government.

The Urumqi massacre: Internal Chinese matter

Ankara's initial position vis-à-vis the outbreak of violent clashes between the Uighurs and the Han Chinese, and the Chinese security forces' brutal suppression of the Uighur protests, could best be described as confusion followed by hesitation and a misguided reaction. There was confusion because the clashes between the Uighurs and the Han Chinese took place less than a week after Turkish President Abdullah Gül's visit to China's Xinjiang region, which is also known as East Turkestan. Could some, both inside and outside Turkey, connect the outbreak of violence with the Turkish president's visit to the region? Though there has not been any implicit or explicit reference to his visit in relation to the conflict in the major Western media, the Doğan Media Group's *Hürriyet* daily ran news reports in Turkey with headlines such as "After President Gül's visit, violence has broken out in the Xinjiang region." President Gül was wisely quick to stress that Turkey has always viewed the Uighurs as a means to improve friendship between China and Turkey.

Prime Minister Erdoğan was in a relatively different and rather awkward position regarding the ongoing violence among the Uighurs, the Han Chinese and the Chinese security forces. He initially deplored the violence against the Uighurs and then described it as genocide-like. Though the target of that accusation was somewhat vague, the Chinese Foreign Ministry's rapid response, when it described the conflict as an internal matter, suggested that the Chinese government took note of the prime minister's accusations. Moreover, apparently giving in to the populist demands and provocation that he should say "one minute!" to the Chinese government as he did to the Israeli president in Davos, Prime Minister Erdoğan has not softened his rhetoric against the Chinese government. Consequently, he stated that Turkey would bring the issue to the UN Security Council, where China is a permanent member. He also announced that so-called Mother Uighur Kadeer, a millionaire businesswoman and American citizen living in Fairfax County, Virginia, would be granted a visa to visit Turkey. Kadeer and Uighurs in general welcomed the prime minister's harsh criticism of the Chinese government and especially his description of the violence as "genocide-like."

Unless necessary measures are taken by Ankara, Turkish-Chinese relations are likely to be strained in the coming weeks. The Chinese government holds Kadeer primarily responsible for instigating the Uighurs in Xinjiang to rebel against the Chinese authorities. In this context, coupled with the prime minister's hitherto criticism of the Chinese government, Kadeer's announced visit to Turkey will most likely cause further tension in Turkish-Chinese relations. There is no need to mention that right-wing parties such as the Nationalist Movement Party (MHP) and the Felicity Party (SP) would take extreme advantage of Kadeer's presence in the country to bring themselves into the spotlight with various public activities.

Whether or not Kadeer is responsible for instigating the protests as the Chinese government argues, and regardless of whether what happened was really "genocide-like," as the prime minister argued, the prime minister was wrong to say that for diplomatic reasons. Ankara should be prepared for tough direct and indirect measures by the Chinese government, which may not necessarily materialize immediately. One of these measures could be China's opposition to every proposal brought to the UN Security Council by Turkey. Another one, and a much more painful one, could be the Chinese-American diaspora's alliance with and financial support for Turkey's traditional sources of headaches in Washington. Is it difficult to grasp that there are countless organizations in Washington and in the other capitals which would readily exploit the prime minister's description of the recent Uighur massacres as "genocide-like" and Beijing's frustration with such a remark?

Obviously concerned with the possible ramifications of Ankara's critical stance, Foreign Minister Davutoğlu sought to soften Turkey's position and compensate for any damage already done. During his telephone conversation with his Chinese counterpart, Yang Jiechi, Davutoğlu stressed that Turkey does not have any intention of meddling in China's internal affairs and respects China's territorial integrity while hoping that those responsible for the violence will be brought to justice immediately.

Mediation between the Uighurs and the Chinese government

The Turkish foreign minister's apparently impartial and yet non-neutral approach to the conflict was a move in the right direction. Ankara should maintain its impartiality between the Uighurs and the Chinese government by constantly stressing its belief in the conflict being an internal Chinese matter and yet manifest its non-neutrality regarding the conflict by advocating the betterment of the socioeconomic and political conditions of the Uighurs in the China's Xinjiang autonomous region. Maintaining a neutral distance from all parties to the conflict, Ankara can position itself as an able and desirable mediator between the Chinese government and its Uighur minority. For the former, Turkey's mediation would be preferable, for it would give the Chinese government an opportunity to settle one of its potentially explosive internal problems via the cooperation of a rather insignificant partner (compared to the US or the EU) that is unlikely to use the mediation process as leverage against China. For the latter, Turkey's mediation is preferable because the Uighurs have confidence in Turks' genuine sympathy for their long suffering.

As a potential mediator, Ankara should impartially analyze the conflict and point out that the satisfaction of the mutual interests of the Uighurs and the Chinese government does not necessitate independence for the Uighurs. It rather necessitates the cessation of discrimination against the Uighurs in access to the labor market and of the coordinated influx of the Han Chinese into the region to change its demographics. Moreover, it necessitates the Chinese government's revocation of legislation which restricts the Uighurs' practice of religious and cultural traditions. Finally, it necessitates that the Chinese government give an appropriate share of its economic development to the Xinjiang region by bringing in major industries and thereby providing the Uighurs with employment opportunities. In response to the gestures from the Chinese government, and utilizing the resources of the Uighur diaspora, Turkey should urge the Uighurs in the Xinjiang region to further integrate into Chinese society and benefit from the expanding socioeconomic and political opportunities, not only in their autonomous region, but more importantly in Beijing.

Following such a constructive course, both the Uighurs and the Chinese government would be better off. Certainly, Turkey would benefit tremendously from it, not only by bolstering its image as an international peacemaker, but also by avoiding the backlash that the otherwise sentimentally driven and critical stance against the Chinese government may cause.

BREAKING THE VICIOUS CYCLE

Time to Change the Course on Cyprus[28]

The second-round talks between the Turkish and Greek Cypriots on the unification of the two sides of the island were supposed to start on Sept. 3. However, what was hoped to be a final step toward the resolution of one of the most troublesome conflicts of the last century has stalled yet again.

According to news reports, the Greek Cypriot leadership "postponed" the second-round negotiations on the pretext that some dozen Greek-Cypriots were denied entry into the north, and that, according to Greek Cypriot leader Dimitris Christofias, it apparently demonstrated the Turkish Cypriot's ill will to block the progress of the negotiations.

On the other hand, Turkish Cypriot Prime Minister Derviş Eroğlu remarked that the Greek-Cypriots had deliberately set up the row over the entry by sending individuals without the proper documentation, so that they could withdraw from, or at least stall, the negotiations. Similarly, frustrated by his Greek Cypriot counterpart's last-minute step back, the Turkish Cypriot president, Mehmet Ali Talat, stated that the negotiations would not last forever and that the Turkish Cypriots would resort to alternative solutions if the Greek Cypriots rejected the solution to be proposed in the second-round negotiations. Talat implied that these alternative solutions might lead to a permanent partition of the island.

Under the shadow of such tense remarks, the second-round negotiations began on Sept. 10. Given the historical characteristics of the relationship between the two communities, and more so the leaderships, the negotiations are not likely to yield any substantial solutions,

---

28 First appeared in *Today's Zaman* daily on September 24, 2009.

or if any, one that will soon be shattered by yet another row between the two sides of the island on a trivial issue.

The recent disruption in the negotiations is just more of the same in the general course of the Turkish-Greek Cypriot relationship. However, it raises a question critical to the possibility of achieving a long-term solution to the Cyprus problem: Under the current circumstance of disparity in political power between the two sides of the island, is a long-term solution even possible? If not, what is the step to take to break the vicious cycle of endless negotiations?

Is a long-term solution even possible on the island?

During a seminar on peacemaking and preventive diplomacy in Oslo, I was asked by a prominent Greek-American expert/professor of diplomatic negotiations whether a long-term solution in Cyprus is possible now, given that the political leaderships on both sides of the island and in the guarantor states (Greece and Turkey) have changed and that they all seem resolved to move on. My answer was "no, it's not possible" under the current circumstances, because the partition of the island itself was illegitimate and unjustified in the first place, the Turkish Cypriots had had legitimate territorial claims over the south, from where they had been ethnically cleansed and forcefully evicted to the north and because neither the Greek nor the Turkish Cypriots seem to be interested in a conclusive solution to the Cyprus problem.

The professor's explanation of why the Greek Cypriot leadership had rejected the Annan plan in 2004 has only reinforced that under the current circumstances of the unjustified partition of the island, the prospect for a sustainable solution is quite low. She argued that the Greek Cypriots were economically much better off compared to the Turkish Cypriots, the Greek Cypriot government was internationally recognized as the sole representative of the whole of Cyprus and the Greek Cypriot side would have been accepted into the European Union anyway, with or without their acceptance of the Annan plan. So, she contended, there was no incentive for the Greek Cypriot leadership to accept a plan that would substantially transform the political structure and the balance of power on the island.

Moreover, the current position of the Turkish Cypriot leadership suggests that there is no sustainable solution to the problem in sight in the foreseeable future, at least with the current leaders. During his interview with the Turkish daily *Milliyet*, Turkish-Cypriot leader Talat noted that the prospects of a permanent partition of the island were becoming ever greater, the discussions with the Greek Cypriots would not last forever and the international recognition of the Turkish Republic of Northern Cyprus (KKTC) was just a pipedream. With his apparently diminishing faith in the possibility of international recognition of the nation he presides, Talat is increasingly reminiscent of his predecessor, Rauf Denktaş, who infamously commented that "the non-solution is the solution on the island," and as such raises questions, once again, about the Turkish Cypriot leadership's resolve and ability to achieve an amenable long-term solution to the Cyprus problem.

The futility of the mere talks between the Turkish and Greek Cypriot leaderships is nothing new. In his *The Road to Bellapais: the Turkish Cypriot Exodus to Northern Cyprus*, Pierre Oberling reminds us that starting in 1968 at the initiative of then-President Archbishop Makarios, and representing, respectively, the Greek Cypriot and the Turkish Cypriot communities, Glafkos Klerides and Denktaş met on a weekly basis for six years to discuss a settlement. However, argues Oberling, there were many on both sides who wanted the talks to fail. For the Greek Cypriots, the establishment of a bi-communal government for the entire island would lead to the dismissal of hundreds of Greek Cypriots from the government and bureaucratic posts and would bring back what they called Turkish Cypriot "obstructionism." It was a kind of obstructionism which they accused the Turkish Cypriots of for using their veto power within the framework of the 1960 Constitution to prevent legislation that would marginalize the Turkish Cypriot presence in the national and local governments. Similarly, argues Oberling, the Turkish Cypriots were content to have achieved a de-facto separation, thanks to Turkey, which spared their lives from the ensuing Greek Cypriot terrorism. In addition, Ankara's aid for food and protection against a would-be aggressor was sufficient for the Turkish Cypriots not venture into another round of duels with the Greek Cypriots.

So, after some 40 years, there is not much change in the dynamics of the talks between the Greek and Turkish Cypriots of the island. According to the apparent mindset of the Greek Cypriots, now as a member of the European Union, they have much more to lose with a solution that requires them to share the government with the Turkish Cypriots. However, the reluctance of the Greek Cypriot leadership and the inability of its Turkish Cypriot counterpart to solve the problem once and for all are only one part of the reason for the absence of a solution on the island. It appears that the bitter memories of the 1960s and 1970s entrenched in the psyche of the Turkish Cypriots may well engender a major impediment to a solution that does not address the issue of reparation for their losses.

The necessity of addressing the losses of the past has recently become clear once again as the Turks and Armenians have sought ways to settle their relations. It would probably take some time for both sides to figure out the extent of the tragedies they inflicted on each other. Nevertheless, the acknowledgement is a first and crucial step to take for a long-term solution. Similarly, any long-term solution on the island requires both Greek and Turkish Cypriots to acknowledge what they have inflicted on the other side.

The historians on both sides should shed light on their pasts no matter how bitter the realities it may reveal. Oberling contends that the Turkish Cypriots' exodus to the north had intensified by the end of 1963 and the beginning of 1964. He writes:

> Giorgio Bocca, the correspondent of *Il Giorno*, an Italian daily of the time, reported: "Right now we are witnessing the exodus of the Turks from their villages. Thousands of people abandoning homes, lands, herds; Greek terrorism is relentless. This time, the rhetoric of Hellenes and the busts of Plato do not suffice to cover up barbaric and ferocious behavior… Threats, shootings and attempts at arson start as soon as it becomes dark. After the massacre of Christmas that spared neither women nor children, it is difficult to put up any resistance."[29]

---

[29] Oberling, *The Road to Bellapais: the Turkish Cypriot Exodus to Northern Cyprus*, NY: Columbia University Press, 1982.

Moreover, as quoted in Oberling's work, the *UN News Bulletin* in May 1964 describes the situation as follows:

> The Greek Cypriots continued to build up their arms and war equipment by purchasing heavy weapons, ammunition, aircraft and vehicles from abroad… The Turkish communities remained surrounded by the overwhelming Greek forces and were constantly subjected to all kinds of abuse, vexations and pressure. Freedom of movement on the island was totally denied to the Turks; their economic situation continued to deteriorate rapidly, as they were not allowed to sell their produce in the markets, to cultivate their fields, to graze their flocks and to go to their jobs in areas dominated by Greeks.
>
> In the villages which the Turks had abandoned in the face of Greek attacks, the houses were put on fire, the properties looted and the harvest confiscated. From March to June the Turkish Cypriots continued to be murdered and the Greeks did not give up their abhorrent method of taking hostage among the innocent people.

The grim reality of the island's past is probably caught best by Archbishop Makarios' confession of his genocidal intentions toward the Turks of the island in 1974. Oberling notes, "While the [Turkish] air raid was in progress, Makarios, in a paroxysm of grief and frustration, threatened that unless the Turkish Air Force left the scene within half an hour he would order the massacre of the entire Turkish Cypriot population."

The Turkish Cypriots have long been terrorized by such organizations as the EOKA (Ethniki Organosis Kypriakon Agoniston—National Organization of Cypriot Fighters) and other smaller paramilitary groups and been victimized by such ideologies as Hellenizing the entire island and uniting with Greece. Interestingly, however, the hitherto Turkish Cypriot leaderships and Ankara in part have continued to stand pathetically apologetic. What is even more problematic is that none of the Turkish Cypriot leaders has ever voiced the Turkish Cypriots' rightful claims over the territories in the south, from where their forefathers were forced out. It is difficult, or maybe not, to understand why former Turkish Cypriot leader Denktaş had never made the demand for reparations by the Greek Cypriots a part of his political discourse;

his very hometown was Paphos, a small town on the western coast of southern Cyprus, where his forefathers had been persecuted.

In the end, it is more obvious today than ever that in a conflict involving different ethno-religious groups no long-term solution is even possible without mutual acknowledgement of the tragedies the parties inflicted on one another. In this regard, both Greek and Turkish Cypriots should be bold enough to investigate their common past and be ready to accommodate the demands of the other side for their losses. After all, what do they have to fear if they have not done anything wrong?

UNCONVENTIONAL WARFARE AND INTERNATIONAL RELATIONS

Political Assassinations and Biological Attacks as a Means to Destabilize Turkey[30]

Turkey's relations with its neighbors have been rapidly evolving over the last few years. Some are improving unexpectedly well, and some are deteriorating unexpectedly fast. One can argue that Turkey's relations overall as such are evolving for the better. However, the historical characteristics of some of the neighbors which Turkey has been severing ties with requires Ankara to be extremely vigilant and to prepare accordingly against the damage that those particular neighbors may inflict upon it.

In line with the Justice and Development (AK Party) government's "zero problems with neighbors" principle, Ankara has improved in a very short span of time its relations with Damascus, from the brink of waging war to the level of removing visa requirements between the two countries and holding joint ministerial meetings. Similarly, it secured Baghdad's substantial cooperation in dealing with the outlawed Kurdistan Workers' Party (PKK), the terrorist group that has long used Iraqi territory to launch attacks on Turkey. Moreover, Ankara gained Baku's critical support in fulfilling the Nabucco pipeline project, which many critics used to view as a pipedream named after an opera. In addition, Ankara has become a champion for an immediate and sustainable solution in Nagorno-Karabakh, where Armenia's continuing occupation has turned one million Azerbaijanis into homeless refugees. Finally, Ankara has managed to accomplish the unthinkable and

---

[30] First appeared in *Today's Zaman* daily on November 01, 2009.

recently signed the protocols that officially started the process for the normalization of its relations with Yerevan.

However, at the same time, Ankara's relations with Israel have been dramatically worsened over a series of issues, which included, as the American journalist Seymour Hersh revealed, Israel's clandestine military assistance to the Kurds in northern Iraq; Israel's apparently intentional delay in delivering the "Heron" unmanned aerial vehicles (UAV) Ankara agreed to buy from it in 2005; Israel's recent military operation against Gaza where some 1,400 Palestinians, mostly women and children, died; the Davos incident in which Prime Minister Recep Tayyip Erdoğan walked out of a panel discussion after he had fiery quarrel with the Israeli president, Shimon Peres; and finally the Turkish TV series called "Ayrılık" which depicts the Israeli occupation of Gaza and which Israel is not so comfortable with.

In light of these developments, Turkey's increasingly active posture in regional affairs brings to the fore an urgent need for Ankara to improve its ability to counter possible threats that such prominence may engender, especially when it challenges the regional status quo. Turkey's military might and strategic importance for global energy security minimizes the prospects of it facing any threat of conventional warfare waged by its neighbors. However, unconventional warfare by those states which are not so fond of Ankara's regional policies is always likely to be waged against Turkey. As a matter of fact, Turkey may have already been exposed to such warfare, especially by those states that are so used to manipulating Ankara through their influence over a small number of the ultra-secularist elite, be they businessmen, judges or generals.

Unconventional warfare: Bringing a nation to its knees

The US Department of Defense defines "unconventional warfare" as follows:

> Unconventional warfare is a broad spectrum of military and paramilitary operations, normally of long duration, predominantly conducted through, with, or by indigenous or surrogate forces who are organized, trained, equipped, supported, and directed in varying

degrees by an external source. It includes, but is not limited to, gue-
rilla warfare, subversion, sabotage, intelligence activities, and unconventional assisted recovery.

More practically, unlike the conventional warfare where the parties involved aim to maximize the damage inflicted on each other's
military capabilities, unconventional warfare targets the civilian population and political bodies, thereby making the military might of the
enemy irrelevant in due process.

The state waging the unconventional warfare tries to propagate
the belief within the targeted country that the deteriorating socio-economic, political and security conditions are merely caused by the sitting government and that everything will be better once the government is replaced by another, or agrees to make concessions in certain
policy areas. In a way, the perpetrator of the unconventional warfare
(UW) manipulates the fears and sensitivities of the society to affect
the political dynamics in the targeted country. In order to do that, the
UW perpetrator may utilize both military and non-military means. By
definition, it may provide military assistance, training and funds to
groups within the targeted country, which would, in turn, create military and security problems. Similarly, the UW perpetrator may seek to
destabilize the targeted country by playing one or more groups against
each other by exploiting the fears and sensitivities of those groups. The
most efficient means of doing this is certainly through the exploitation of the mass media, and the best example of this is to mobilize the
so-called secular military against the so-called Islamist civilian groups
or civilian government.

Turkey at war

From this point of view, a quick look into Turkey's republican history may suggest that the country has always been a target and victim
of a never-ending unconventional warfare waged against it. The country has long suffered from the ultra-secular center versus traditional
periphery divide, the military's dominance over politics, the paradigm
of being surrounded by sea on three sides and by enemies on four,

the idea that the Turks are not capable of accomplishing anything and that the only way to prosperity is through an unconditional mimicking of the West and finally the fear that Kurdishness or the manifestation of any other ethno-religious identity poses an existential threat to Turkishness. Improvements in areas from the legal system to domestic/foreign policy and to the economy throughout the past seven years indicate that Turkey has learned quite a bit about how to counter these types of unconventional warfare tactics.

However, with the advancement of technology comes new ways and means of unconventional warfare, and therefore it becomes ever more urgent for Turkey to improve itself in order to cope with the evolving threats. Two of the most effective tactics of contemporary unconventional warfare are political assassinations and biological attacks, which can be disguised as accidents and as natural disasters or pandemics, respectively.

In the recent past, Turkey has experienced the seemingly "natural deaths" of a number of its political leaders. For instance, former Prime Minister Adnan Menderes, whose coming to office marked Turkey's transition to multiparty democracy, was sentenced to death and duly executed after a seemingly normal judicial process. Former Prime Minister and President Turgut Özal, whose dream was the unification of the Turkic world, is believed to have passed away because of a heart attack, although there has been speculation that he had gradually been poisoned over a long period of time, which led to the heart attack. Former Governor Recep Yazıcıoğlu, who stood against the foreign corporations that sought to explore for uranium in Denizli province, was seemingly killed in a tragic car accident while on his way to Ankara to investigate the deaths of engineers who had been killed in mysterious car accidents as well. In addition to these political figures, many journalists and academics such as Uğur Mumcu, Ahmet Taner Kışlalı and Hrant Dink have also been killed in such mysterious ways that these deaths eventually fanned the animosities between different segments of society.

Similarly, the deliberate spread of certain infectious diseases and viruses constitutes another dimension of unconventional warfare. One historic example of that is the mass death of the American Indians in the 17th century caused by the Europeans who migrated to the New World and considered the spread of smallpox among the American Indians as an effective way to vacate the land where they intended to settle. Today, although they are not nearly as deadly, the outbreak of such contagious diseases as bird flu, swine flu and many others yet to come poses a grave danger to the countries that are not capable of producing their own vaccines against these diseases, but instead are dependent on the mercy of the other states that are able to produce these vaccines. This exemplifies the current situation that Turkey finds itself in. Although Turkey recently secured the purchase of 500,000 doses of the swine flu vaccine, it does not eliminate the country's vulnerability to the threat posed by swine flu or other such pandemics that are likely to emerge in the near future. Accordingly, the fate of a government that may seem unable to protect the population against epidemic diseases would also be at stake.

As Prime Minister Erdoğan becomes openly critical of a particular state in the neighborhood, and as such, Ankara defies an almost century-long status quo that its relations are built upon with this unconventional neighbor, the AK Party government is likely to be challenged time and time again in the near future by the ever evolving tactics of unconventional warfare. It is not something to be afraid of in itself, but a critical challenge to be prepared for as Turkey gradually rises to become a regional leader.

WHAT IS PLAN B, IF THERE IS ONE?

The Nuclear Menace Looming Over
Turkey's Neighborhood[31]

From the very beginning, Turkey has seemed to have a firm and clear stand on Iran's nuclear activities by simply stating that it is against the presence of all kinds of nuclear weapons in the region. Yet, in line with the UN-chartered Nuclear Non-Proliferation Treaty, Ankara tacitly acknowledged Tehran's legitimate right to develop and acquire nuclear technology for civilian and non-military purposes, while at the same time becoming increasingly vocal about Israel's getting away unchecked with its nuclear arsenal.

In the meantime, the opposition to the Iranian nuclear program, namely the loud criticism by the US, UN, EU-3 (UK, France, and Germany) and Israel, and somewhat silent worries of the other regional Arab states, mainly Egypt, Syria and Saudi Arabia, have been largely characterized as much talk and little, if any, action. The current Iranian nuclear debate began in August 2002, when the National Council of Resistance of Iran, an Iranian dissident group, publicly revealed that two nuclear sites were under construction in the country. The only real progress since then seems to be the progress in the construction of these nuclear facilities and the overall progress in Iran's nuclear program. As of today, the debate is at a point where the US refuses to hold talks with Iranian officials any time before January 2010, Iranian leaders clearly assert that the nuclear debate is over and Iran continues its nuclear program.

From a realpolitik perspective, whether Iran's nuclear program is legitimate or not and whether Iran will use its nuclear technology to

[31] First appeared in *Today's Zaman* daily on December 30, 2009.

produce weapons or not are, and should be viewed by Ankara as, a secondary concern for Turkey. Instead, Ankara should be primarily concerned about the fact that Tehran has already made substantial progress in acquiring nuclear technology. If it does reach the point where transforming that technology is no longer a matter of ability but of choice, then it will certainly strike the regional balance of power in favor of Tehran and thereby create a region with new nuclear realities. Then, Ankara would hardly be in a position to deter a possible nuclear conflict (i.e., between Iran and Israel) or counter any deterrence imposed on Turkey. Such a scenario is not far from possibility. After all, as many would argue, both Iran and Israel are somewhat equally crazy enough to use nuclear weapons against each other, and both have somewhat similar views that their long-sought end days mentioned in their respective religious doctrines will come only after apocalyptic clashes. Similarly, Ankara may fall short of matching Tehran's growing influence across the region.

Then, the questions are whether Turkey is prepared for the new nuclear realities in the region, whether it can afford not to have nuclear weapons and finally what Ankara can do in order to benefit from the changing dynamics in its neighborhood.

Iran's word not very convincing

The Iranian leaders, most notably President Mahmoud Ahmedinejad, have time and again repeated that Iran is not interested in developing nuclear weapons, but in acquiring nuclear fuel-cycle ability for civilian purposes. Apparently, the Iranian leadership's word is not very convincing for its Western counterparts in the debate, and certainly not for Israel. Even if Tehran has some convincing way to guarantee that it will not produce nuclear weapons, the very fact that it has been actively pursuing a nuclear program, which is conducive to giving Iran an ability to produce nuclear weapons, will sooner or later induce the neighboring nuclear and non-nuclear states into a nuclear arms race. Such a vivid possibility will eventually and understandably lead Iran as well to develop nuclear weapons even if it has not yet contemplated doing so. Moreover, it will give the neighboring Arab states a raison d'être to acquire nuclear weapons against a possible threat, which the US and the EU-3 can empathize with and which they have hitherto lacked vis-à-vis the West in their opposition to Israel's nuclear arsenal.

A Taoist anecdote in *Journey to the West*, one of the four great novels of the Ming dynasty (1368–1644), presents a unique analogy as to what to expect regarding Iran's course of action on the nuclear matter and that of the neighboring and the Western capitals in response:

> A magical monkey founds a monkey civilization and becomes its leader by establishing a territory for the monkeys. Subsequently the monkey king overcomes a "devil confusing the world" and steals the devil's sword. Returning to his own land with the devil's sword, the monkey king takes up the practice of swordsmanship. He even teaches his monkey subjects to make toy weapons and regalia to play at war. Unfortunately, though ruler of a nation, the monkey king is not yet ruler of himself. In eminently logical backward reasoning, the monkey reflects that if neighboring nations note the monkeys' play, they might assume the monkeys were preparing for war. In that case, they might therefore take pre-emptive action against the monkeys, who would then be faced with real warfare armed only with toy weapons. Thus, the monkey king thoughtfully initiates the arms race, ordering pre-pre-emptive stockpiling of real weapons.

As far as Turkey's interests are concerned, not only its national security in the face of a possible nuclear threat (not necessarily posed by Iran), but also the diminishing of its diplomatic clout in the face of Iran's growing regional influence is at stake.

Nuclear Iran vs. non-nuclear Turkey: What is the game plan?

Iran is hardly likely to pose a direct nuclear security threat to Turkey, for several reasons. First, both Iran and Turkey pride themselves on having the most stable border in the region since the 17th century. Second, the two have increasingly lucrative commercial ties, mostly based on oil and gas, and in many ways Turkey is a gateway for Iran to the world, from which it has long been forcibly isolated. Third, Iran's security doctrine is mainly based on defense, and as such, Tehran is very unlikely to use the military card in its relations with Turkey unless in

an ultra-hypothetical scenario it decides to lead an all-out Shiite uprising against the Sunnis. Fourth, Iran would not want to alienate the rest
of the Muslim world by militarily threatening another Muslim country such as Turkey, which is increasingly popular and influential. At this
point, it is worth remembering that it was not Iran which started the
eight-year war with Saddam Hussein's Iraq in 1980, but the other way
around. Finally, Iran already has a legitimate adversary with a heavy
nuclear arsenal in the region, toward which Tehran may want to make
use of its prospective nuclear weapons for most likely defensive and
less likely offensive purposes. There is no need to mention that engaging in such a military confrontation with Israel would rapidly boost
Iran's popularity throughout the Muslim world as well. So, Turkey is
hardly in a position to be worried about Iran's prospective nuclear weapons as a national security threat. In this line, recently asked about Iran's
nuclear program, Turkish Foreign Minister Ahmet Davutoğlu stated
that Turkey does not perceive any of its neighbors, including Iran, as
a security threat.

Nevertheless, Turkey should be concerned about the potential
growth of Iran's diplomatic influence throughout the region once the
latter acquires nuclear weapons capabilities on top of its already increased
economic and political influence. The last eight years has witnessed
an unprecedented increase in Iran's regional influence thanks to the
US invasion of Afghanistan and Iraq as well as Israel's never-ending
aggression against Lebanon and Gaza.

Former Iranian President Mohammad Khatami notes, "Regardless of where the United States changes regimes, it is our [Iran's] friends
who will come to power."[32] It looks like it has just been so. The US
invasions have ousted Iran's enduring adversaries, respectively, the Taliban in Afghanistan and Saddam Hussein's Baath Party in Iraq. Similarly, Israel's aggressions toward Lebanon and Gaza have again enabled
Iran to increase its influence and popularity in these parts of the region
through its support of Hezbollah in Lebanon and Islamic Jihad and
Hamas in Palestine. It is obvious that Iran will follow bolder policies

---

[32] Khatami, quoted in Vali Nasr, *Forces of Fortune*, 2009.

in its support of such groups once it gains the protective shield of nuclear weapons against any possible threat either from Israel or from its Western allies. In addition, Iran will be admired by the masses throughout the region for its not bowing to the demands and pressures of the West, in general, and of the US, in particular.

In the final analysis, Iran's nuclear program presents dangers for some and opportunities for others. Turkey is in a unique position to be presented with both. As Davutoğlu reiterated recently, Iran's nuclear program does not pose a military threat to Turkish national security. However, it does threaten Turkey's diplomatic influence across the Middle East. As such, it is the problem of not only Turkey, but also the West. At the end of the day, Turkey may have to consider acquiring its own nuclear weapons capability as a Plan B in order to counterbalance the new nuclear realities in its neighborhood.

ONE MILLION TURKS TO JERUSALEM

What should be the next step in the Turkish-Israeli relations?[33]

There seems to be no end in sight for the bumpy ride in Turkish-Israeli relations. A crisis between the two countries recently caused by Israeli Deputy Foreign Minister Danny Ayalon's attempt to humiliate Turkey's ambassador to his country not only strained already bitter relations between Israel and Turkey but also signaled a major characteristic change in bilateral relations.

The two neighbors should turn these crises into opportunities in order to strengthen their socio-economic and political relationship in a way that would at the same time help solve other ensuing problems, such as the plight of the Palestinians within Israel, Gaza and the West Bank.

The latest crisis in bilateral relations was sparked on Jan. 11 when Israel's deputy foreign minister summoned the Turkish ambassador to Israel in order to protest against a Turkish TV series ("Valley of the Wolves"), which recently depicted Israeli diplomats involved in a sort of child abduction. During the meeting, Mr. Ayalon, speaking in Hebrew, told reporters they should notice that he did not shake hands with the Turkish ambassador, that he was not smiling, that the Turkish ambassador was seated on a lower sofa and that there was no Turkish flag on the table. Once the humiliating intention became apparent, Ankara sent a diplomatic note to Tel Aviv requiring an explanation and an apology for the unfortunate incident.

---

[33] First appeared in *Today's Zaman* daily on January 28, 2010.

Turkish President Abdullah Gül and Prime Minister Recep Tayyip Erdoğan weighed in, demanding immediate action from their Israeli counterparts to prevent any further escalation of the crisis. Mr. Gül stressed that unless Israeli authorities apologized in writing to Ankara by that evening, the Turkish ambassador to Israel would fly back to Ankara to start consultations on a structural Turkish response to Israel's perceived insult to Turkey. In response, differing reactions came from Tel Aviv. Initially, Prime Minister Benjamin Netanyahu dismissed Ankara's demand for an official apology by suggesting that the explanation made by Mr. Ayalon was sufficient. However, Ankara continued to exert pressure on Tel Aviv, demanding a written statement clearly expressing the latter's apology. Tel Aviv's official apology letter, sent to Ankara on Jan. 13, prevented any further escalation of the crisis.

From a militarized to a civilized Turkish-Israeli relationship

So, what is happening to the Turkish-Israeli relationship? What do these recent crises mean in the long run? The recent series of crises in Turkish-Israeli relations started in 2006, when a Turkish movie titled "Valley of the Wolves: Iraq" pictured an Israeli surgeon involved in trading the organs of dead Iraqis. Although three years later, in 2009, FBI officials arrested five rabbis who led a network of some 40 people, including politicians, and charged them with involvement in human organ trafficking between Brooklyn, New York, Deal, New Jersey, and Israel, what the Turkish movie showed then was quite a daring allegation about Israeli involvement in the US-led invasion of Iraq. Consequently, Ankara was pressured not only by Israel, but also by Jewish-American lobbies in New York and Washington.

Since then, Turkish-Israeli relations improved to the extent that Turkey mediated indirect peace talks between Syria and Israel, only to be outraged by Israel's military operation in Gaza in January 2009, which left some 1,400 Palestinians dead and dashed hopes for sustainable peace in the region. The already soured relations between the countries were further challenged during the World Economic Forum's (WEF) January 2009 summit, when Israeli President Shimon Peres crossed the due boundaries of diplomatic courtesy by trying to brush off Turkish Prime Minister Erdoğan following his criticism of Israel over its military operation in Gaza. Prime Minister Erdoğan had some two weeks earlier called Israel's use of phosphorus and cluster bombs against civilians, mainly women and children, a war crime and a crime against humanity.

Only 10 months later, in October 2009, the not-yet-healed Turkish-Israeli relations were once again strained over another TV film series, "Ayrılık" (The Separation), which allegedly depicted the Israeli military forces' brutality against the Palestinians during Israel's invasion of Gaza in January. While Israeli Foreign Minister Avigdor Lieberman accused the Turkish government of being the force behind the TV series and his Turkish counterpart, Ahmet Davutoğlu, dismissed the allegation, another crisis between Ankara and Tel Aviv had been looming. It was about Israel not delivering Heron unmanned aircraft that Ankara ordered and paid for in 2001.

After all these, from a conceptual perspective, what is happening in the Turkish-Israeli relationship is that the two countries' long-militarized state-to-state relationship is becoming civilized. The two countries' relationship dates back to the early 1950s, when it was first initiated under the auspices of Turkish Prime Minister Adnan Menderes and Israeli Prime Minister David Ben Gurion as part of the latter's peripheral alliance strategy. The relationship has deepened over time, albeit under heavy military control and far from civilian scrutiny, eventually turning into a strategic partnership in 1997, again with heavy Turkish General Staff oversight. Since 2002, however, on both sides, civilians including media outlets, civil society organizations and business networks are becoming more aware and vocal about the relations between the two countries. It is certainly so for Turkey, and the proliferation of criticism of Israel in the Turkish media is the most immediate effect of that change.

Critics of the Justice and Development Party (AK Party) government inside and outside Turkey apparently blame Prime Minister Erdoğan and his party for the increased Turkish criticism of Israeli policies in the occupied Palestinian territories. However, it is not the AK

Party but the growing Turkish civil society that brought the AK Party into office and that is responsible for Turkey's increasingly critical attitude toward Israel, and this is a sort of democratic change in Turkey that Israel has to live with from now on.

Eliminate visa requirements between Turkey and Israel

Nevertheless, repercussions for Israel from this change can be minimized with a series of reforms. These reforms should aim to deepen the civilian dimension of the Turkish-Israeli relationship by creating conditions that would boost the exchanges between the two countries. In line with Ankara's emphasis on lifting visa requirements between Turkey and as many countries as possible, it would be an important step in the right direction to eliminate the visa requirement between Turkey and Israel. Accordingly, Ankara should encourage more and more Turks to visit Israel for touristic, business, humanitarian and educational purposes. Turkish businesses should develop long-term economic relations with their Israeli counterparts, and mainly with Arab Israelis. Similarly, Turkish media and civil society organizations should increase their presence, especially in Jerusalem, in order to ensure the continued stream of objective and accurate news to the Turkish audience.

The present visa policy between Turkey and Israel restricts only the Turks' travel to Israel, but not the Israelis' travel to Turkey. Practically speaking, almost no Israeli visitor is denied entry into Turkey. Both the ease of getting a Turkish visa and its proximity to Israel make Turkey a preferred destination for many Israelis. According to a *Jerusalem Post* report, Turkey was the second most popular tourism destination for Israelis after the United States, and every year about 300,000 Israelis came to visit Turkey. They visit not only major cities and touristic spots such as Istanbul, İzmir, Antalya and Cappadocia, but also the most unusual ones such as Hopa, Artvin, Rize and Trabzon. Part of the reason for Turkey's high popularity among Israelis should be the hospitality and welcoming environment they find throughout Turkey. Israeli Defense Minister Ehud Barak's recent dismissal of allegations that anti-Semitism was on the rise in Turkey speaks to that fact.

However, the mutual visa policy of the two countries is not at all as favorable to Turks as it is to the Israelis. While any Israeli can easily obtain a Turkish visa in Israel, or in 10 minutes at the Istanbul Atatürk Airport, Turks intending to travel to Israel have to wait for days, if not weeks, for an Israeli visa before enduring hours of random questioning while entering and exiting Tel Aviv's David Ben Gurion Airport.

Should Israel be convinced to reciprocate Turkey's goodwill on visa policy, better yet, to mutually lift the visa requirement, Turks could and should make Israel, especially Jerusalem, one of their most preferred destinations for business, education and touristic activities. Doing so would enable Turks to better understand contemporary Israel and its aspirations in the region. It would also enable Turks to contribute to strengthening the Palestinians' socio-economic conditions, thereby creating better prospects for a sustainable two-state solution. For a start, Ankara may aim to raise the number of Turks visiting Israel and the West Bank to one million per year. Given that Jerusalem is the third holiest city for Muslims after Mecca and Medina, and a former Ottoman territory, it would not be difficult to increase that number thereafter.

In the final analysis, the recent series of crises in the Turkish-Israeli relationship is not a sign of deterioration. On the contrary, they symbolize normalization and a change in the over-militarized nature of that relationship into a civilized one. Both Ankara and Tel Aviv should take advantage of these crises and turn them into opportunities to foster multiple channels of communication between the Turkish and Israeli societies. Following such a course would not only pave the way for Israel to normalize its relationship with its neighbors in the region, but also enable Turkey to better contribute to the resolution of the so-called Israeli-Palestinian conflict.

SONER CAGAPTAY FINALLY GETS IT!

Fethullah Gülen Is Indeed behind
Turkey's Democratization[34]

In a recent commentary, "What's Really Behind Turkey's Coup Arrests," published in *Foreign Policy* magazine on Feb. 25, 2010, and another one, "Turkey's Turning Point," published in *Newsweek* the following day on Feb. 26, 2010, Soner Çağaptay of the Washington Institute for Near East Policy (WINEP) accuses Fethullah Gülen, 72, a retired preacher, prolific writer, and an advocate of interfaith-intercultural dialogue who lives in a self-imposed exile in a small town of Pennsylvania, of being the one responsible for the recent arrests of the former Turkish army generals who apparently plotted several times to overthrow Turkey's democratically elected Justice and Development Party (AK Party) government.

Although he intentionally interprets and portrays it falsely and misleadingly, Çağaptay finally got at least one thing right. Gülen can indeed be plausibly argued to be a force, albeit indirect, behind the Turkish authorities' recent crackdown on the unlawful, dictatorial and anti-democratic formations nested within the Turkish army, police, bureaucracy, academia, business and wherever they hinder democratization of the Turkish society.

Gülen has so far been denied the credit he much deserves for his efforts to make Turkey a more open, more democratic and more liberal country, integrated into the rest of the international community. It is mostly because of Gülen's humble nature, which instructs him not to claim any credit for the accomplishments of the faith-based civil society movement, which he inspired worldwide and which academics and

---

[34] First appeared in *Today's Zaman* daily on February 28, 2010.

researchers have practically called the Gülen movement. It is also because of the above-mentioned antidemocratic establishment's constant persecution of Gülen and of whoever sympathizes with his ideas. As he alarmingly charges Gülen with leading a shadowy Islamist movement and extending its influence into the Turkish political life, Çağaptay simply illustrates the antidemocratic establishment's infamous attitude toward Turkey's citizens whenever they challenged, through democratic means, the establishment's grip on the state and its resources. That is, Çağaptay and similar voices of the antidemocratic and secularist establishment have always suppressed its challengers by discrediting them in the eyes of the public with false allegations.

Such allegations by Çağaptay should be a wake-up call to any concerned person inside and outside Turkey to really investigate what is really behind the antidemocratic secularist establishment's witch-hunt not only against Gülen, but also against whoever sympathizes with him.

In an article like this or many others, which apparently would hardly, if ever, find a place in the *Foreign Policy* and *Newsweek* magazines either because of the magazines' possible bias or because no such article would ever be sponsored by a formidable Washington think tank like WINEP, one can go into detail convincingly disputing each and every allegation made by Çağaptay. But it is neither the right nor ethical thing to do. It is not right because Çağaptay himself apparently knows that what he says simply is not true given the logical problems in his factually baseless allegations. It is not ethical because Çağaptay simply distorts the facts in an attempt to manipulate public opinion; and, as such, dignifying him with a response would simply make his unethical act look legitimate. What one should instead do is delve into the issues, which Çağaptay seems to be portraying purposefully falsely and misleadingly.

Why were the army generals arrested?

In his *Foreign Policy* commentary, Çağaptay rightly states as follows:

> For the last several decades, the Turkish military was untouchable;
> no one dared to criticize the military or its top generals, lest they

risk getting burned. The Turkish Armed Forces were the ultimate protectors of founding father Kemal Atatürk's secular legacy, and no other force in the country could seriously threaten its supremacy. Not anymore.

Çağaptay is perfectly right that just as it would be in any military dictatorship or in an authoritarian society where the elected governments are subservient to the whims and wishes of the army generals, the Turkish military was untouchable, no matter how badly its generals violated the laws, hindered democracy and banned individual human rights and freedoms.

Most probably for this very reason, better to say for this self-entitled military supremacy over civilian subjects, months after the AK Party government took office through free and fair elections, a junta of army generals dared to plot overthrowing the AK Party government through a military coup d'état. On Jan. 20, 2010, the liberal Turkish daily newspaper *Taraf* exposed a coup plan titled the *Balyoz* (Sledgehammer) Security Operation Plan, drafted in 2003, shortly after the AK Party government came to power. According to the *Taraf* report, the masterminds of the plan were the then commander of the First Army, retired Gen. Çetin Doğan, then Air Forces Commander retired Gen. İbrahim Fırtına and retired Gen. Ergin Saygun. Soon after the report, a series of voice recordings from the alleged meeting of the generals leaked to the media (also to YouTube) and substantiated the *Taraf* report.

According to the report, and obviously understood in the voice recordings, the Sledgehammer coup plot was agreed upon at a military meeting attended by 162 active Turkish Armed Forces (TSK) members, including 29 generals. According to the plan, the military was to systematically foment chaos in society through violent acts, among which were bomb attacks on two major mosques in Istanbul during the Friday prayer. Consequently, provocateurs were to incite widespread rallies to protest the AK Party government's inability to ensure public security. Similarly, a series of bombs were to be detonated at museums crowded with children in order to heighten the already emerged sense of insecurity.

In addition to increasing violence in Turkey, the junta aimed to create tensions with Greece in an attempt to demonstrate the government's inability to handle international security threats. In this regard, a Turkish military aircraft was to provoke Greek pilots by entering Greek airspace, and the ensuing dogfight between the Turkish and Greek jets would lead to the crash of a Turkish jet. The plans noted that in case the dogfight attempt failed, then the junta's air force branch would intentionally down the Turkish jet and blame it on the Greeks. In the meantime, media organs close to the junta would accuse the AK Party government of failing to ensure the security of the country. Then, the circumstances would not only justify, but also necessitate the army's intervention.

The coup arrests which Çağaptay so alarmingly mentions in his commentaries are actually the detentions of some 49 retired and active duty military officers as part of the investigation into the alleged Sledgehammer coup plot. Consequently, two of the alleged masterminds of Sledgehammer, former Air Force Commander Gen. Fırtına and retired Gen. Saygun, respectively, were released after testifying to prosecutors. The ringleader, retired Gen. Doğan, was arrested as he was revealed to have already booked his flight to Mexico and was about to flee the country only a day after the police suddenly detained him. At this point, both Doğan and the other generals who have been released are waiting to stand trial in civilian courts. If they are innocent, they will be freed anyway.

What does this have to do with Gülen?

So, what does all this have to do with a retired preacher living in self-imposed exile in a small town of Pennsylvania for the last decade? The answer offered by Çağaptay is the following: "The only quality that ties together all of those arrested is their opposition to the AKP [AK Party] government and the Gülen movement." What else could one expect? Actually, it would be quite odd if those who plotted to bomb their own people and crash Turkey's own jet did not oppose the AK Party government and the Gülen movement. After all, the latter two are everything that the coup plotters would not like.

A more plausible explanation as to what it all has to do with Gülen could be the following: Gülen certainly is not just a small mosque preacher. Throughout the last four decades, with his writings, public speeches and most importantly with worldwide civil society initiatives, Gülen has revolutionized the Turkish society's imagination. With his help, the Turkish society, which had so far been intimidated and humiliated by the antidemocratic, dictatorial and secularist establishment, has recognized its potential.

Gülen convinced the Turkish people that it was their judiciary, their army, their academia, their industry and their own art and sciences; and as such, they had the legitimate right to claim their place in all these areas of life while preserving their piously Muslim identity. This success of Gülen seems to have scared the establishment to death as it now terribly risks losing its absolute grip on every aspect of life in Turkey.

This point is actually well addressed in Çağaptay's own writing in his *Newsweek* commentary: "This campaign could become the final battle for control of Turkey." Çağaptay is right; this is the battle between Turkish society and the dictatorial establishment for the control of Turkey. This explanation is of course an attempt to understand the root causes of the ongoing witch-hunt against Gülen and his sympathizers. Any concerned individual should not suffice with this explanation, but make his or her own judgment by delving into who Gülen is and what the Gülen movement is about.

In the final analysis, suggesting that Gülen is the cause of the recent arrests of the coup plotting army generals is tantamount to merely distorting the facts, and attempting to manipulate public opinion against both Gülen and whoever sympathizes with his ideas. This is exactly what Çağaptay seems to be doing, and it does not look credible even if his allegations appear in credible publications like the *Foreign Policy* and *Newsweek* magazines. It is also hard to argue that Gülen and the individuals associated with him are the only force behind Turkey's consistent march toward democracy. However, it is certainly plausible to argue that among Turkey's other democracy and freedom supporters,

Gülen and whoever is associated with him are a formidable force behind Turkey's recently accelerated march toward democracy.

Çağaptay not only keeps distorting the facts about the ongoing judicial process, but also violates fundamental human rights of a prominent Turkish intellectual by constantly accusing him with baseless allegations. What Çağaptay does is not an objective intellectual engagement, but a mere witch-hunt and a campaign to discredit. Neither Gülen nor anyone who feels threatened by Çağaptay's baseless accusations should try to respond to him. Yet, they should immediately take Çağaptay's case to the courts of justice and make Çağaptay himself substantiate his allegations.

HUMILIATION AS AMERICAN EXPERIENCE

US Public Diplomacy Shattered at the JFK Airport[35]

In the first days of President Barack H. Obama, who campaigned on the promise of change in Washington's policies and vowed to revitalize the long-stagnated so-called Middle East peace process, Israelis used to tease Americans and whoever was hopeful about the new administration by suggesting the following:

"Do you have a problem somewhere in the world? Have President Obama deliver a nice speech about it, and then the problem is solved."

The United States' image abroad, especially in the Muslim world, is a problem much more critical than one that can be solved only with the nice words in President Obama's famous inauguration and Cairo speeches or by the mere appointment of a so-called special representative to Muslim communities around the world and a special envoy to the Organization of the Islamic Conference (OIC). Before anything else, US authorities, and especially the State Department, should recognize the damage inflicted upon the US image in the minds of the non-Americans by its very own consular and immigration officers, who successfully manage to do away with the remaining last bit of sympathy toward the United States.

America unloved

The United States has long been criticized and eventually hated, rightfully or wrongfully, for various reasons. Among many of them are its

---

[35] First appeared in *Today's Zaman* daily on February 28, 2010.

military presence in more than 40 countries, two military invasions in Afghanistan and Iraq, which led to the deaths of more than four million civilians and created less secure and less stable environments both in these countries and in their surrounding regions, American soldiers' treatment of Afghan and Iraqi civilians, its disrespect for multilateralism and heedlessness to the concerns of the international community, its unwavering support to Israel that has time and again been condemned by almost the entire world community, its transgressions of international norms and laws under the pretext of the so-called American exceptionalism, and finally what has become common knowledge worldwide—American arrogance.

In addition to Washington's overall policies, the attitude of various civil society organizations, which claim to act in defense of American interests, toward Islam and its adherents has only further led to the deterioration of the United States' image across the globe. The unique cases in point are the so-called Virginia Anti-Shariah Taskforce (VAST), the Traditional Values Coalition (TVC), and Act! for America. These three organizations have recently urged hundreds of Americans to boycott the Virginia House of Delegates for inviting Johari Abdul-Malik, a local imam, to offer the opening prayer at the daily session on the House floor. Earlier during an interview with the Australian Jewish News the head of Act! for America, Brigitte Gabriel, who *The New York Times Magazine* described as a radical Islamophobe, suggested that every practicing Muslim was a radical Muslim. When asked whether Americans should oppose Muslims who want to seek political office in the United States, Gabriel said:

> Absolutely. If a Muslim is a practicing Muslim who believes the word of the Koran to be the word of Allah, who abides by Islam, who goes to mosque and prays every Friday, who prays five times a day and who believes in the teachings of the Koran, [he or she] cannot be a loyal citizen to the United States of America.

Along a similar line, in a Capitol Hill press conference on Oct. 14, 2009, Representatives Sue Myrick (R-NC), John Shadegg (R-AZ) and Trent Franks (R-AZ) publicly endorsed David Gaubatz's book titled *The Muslim Mafia*, where he accuses Muslim congressional interns of being part of espionage and subversive jihad against the United States. To what extent these radical Islamophobes represent mainstream American people is, of course, questionable. Yet, the extent of their impact at the political and social level both inside and outside the United States is unquestionable.

Therefore, the list of reasons as to why non-Americans criticize or hate the United States goes on and on. For these very obvious reasons, the new administration in Washington with a star-like president and secretary of state made it a top priority on its agenda to reach out to the Muslim world in particular and the world communities in general in an attempt to revitalize America's positive image, which has been shattered throughout the infamous eight years of the Bush administration. Immediately after taking the office of secretary of state, Hillary R. Clinton appointed American of Kashmiri origin Farah Pandith as a special representative to Muslim communities around the world. Although her job description is somewhat bleak and what she has accomplished so far in that capacity is unknown, the appointment itself was perceived as a show of the new administration's willingness to reconnect with the Muslim world. Similarly, on Feb. 13, 2010 President Obama appointed Rashad Hussain, an American of Indian origin raised in Dallas, Texas, as a special envoy to the OIC. This appointment as well raised hopes and expectations for the Obama administration's promise for change to materialize in both US-Muslim world relations and in the protection of the civil rights and dignity of Muslims both living in and visiting the United States.

However, there is one particular area that seems to remain outside the radar of the new administration as a source of international resentment against the United States. It is the contemptuous and humiliating treatment that non-Americans are exposed to at US consulates abroad while seeking a US visa and at the airport immigration offices in the United States while seeking entry into the country. These rather unusual and mostly unnoticed sources of resentment are actually causing more enduring damage to the American image abroad than Washington's political preferences or some so-called patriotic American Islamophobes do because they directly and negatively affect individuals who would normally be instrumental in revitalizing America's positive image abroad.

The JFK effect on America's deteriorating image

Technically there are two groups of people seeking entry into the United States: one that intends to inflict harm onto the United States through terrorist activities and which is microscopic in size at best, and all the rest, who intend to travel to the United States for purposes ranging from business to education to tourism, and as such constitute some fifty million people visiting the US every year.

During the eight years of the Bush administration, the US authorities' caution against the first group turned into a hysteria that consequently haunted the second group entirely, thereby precisely serving the purposes of the first group.

Understandably, the US authorities raised the level of security and hence the level of scrutiny at the airports after the Sept. 11 terrorist attacks. However, their sense of insecurity at the same time paved the way for airport security and immigration officers to become extremely hostile and insensitive towards the passengers going in and out of the United States. If there has been one change introduced with the new Obama administration after the eight years of the Bush administration, it is certainly not a change in US immigration officers' treatment of visitors seeking entry into the United States. Obviously, it requires concrete policy changes and not just nice words about reaching out to the Muslim world.

These visitors may be esteemed scholars, journalists, artists, musicians, religious leaders, politicians, students, businessmen or businesswomen. No matter who they are in their own countries, once they arrive at New York's John F. Kennedy Airport after hours of tiring flight, they are immediately reduced to mere beggars in front of the immigration officer, hoping to clear their entry into the United States with a minimum amount of humiliation. The very fact that a passenger's entry into the country is contingent on the decision of the immigration officer he or she is talking to at the kiosk and that it does not really matter whether or not the US consulate back home issued a valid visa is humiliating enough. Having invested so much time, money and hope in the process of obtaining a US visa, the passenger is forced to compromise the last bit of dignity in order not to be denied entry into the United States at the last moment.

Such compromises include being scorned and yelled at by someone who is barely a high school graduate and hardly speaks proper English, having to wait for long hours without knowing the reason for waiting, having to remain silent while that officer is sniffing through your private belongings such as photographs in your digital camera and personal items in your purse, being questioned in a small room like a terrorism suspect, and finally not being able to object to the mistreatment because you do not want to get yourself into any further trouble. After all, no matter who you are and no matter whether you have a valid visa, the immigration officers apparently have the right to deny you entry into the United States and oblige you to return to your home country at your own expense, if you do not behave.

The travesty in US immigration practices is not limited to civilian passengers only. There are even major international organizations that suffer from the implications of the immigration policies deliberately devised to restrict their movement. The case in point is the diplomatic status of the Organization of the Islamic Conference (OIC) in the United States. As a matter of fact, it is the absence of the diplomatic status of the organization, which is second in size only to the United Nations. The OIC represents 57 Muslim countries and countries with substantial Muslim populations. It is a major partner of the United Nations in areas ranging from poverty reduction to protection of human rights and to maintenance of international peace and security. The US president has had a special envoy to the OIC for the last nine years. Yet, the same organization is not as privileged as the International Coffee Association, International Fertilizer Development Center, Pacific Salmon Commission, International Cotton Institute and Israel-U.S. Binational Industrial Research and Development Foundation to have diplomatic status in the United States. The representatives of the OIC, including its ambassador to the United Nations, are denied the diplomatic immunities and privileges that the representatives of other regional and international organizations naturally enjoy while functioning within the territories of the United States. It does not really make sense for the US president to appoint a special envoy to an organization he does not even see as on par with the International Fertilizer Development Center. Or perhaps it does make sense in explaining how much substance President Obama puts into such an appointment.

At the end of the day, nice speeches and bombastic promises do not solve America's image problem abroad, especially in the Muslim world. Before embarking on a so-called campaign to earn the hearts and minds of those who already dislike, if not hate, the United States, the White House and the State Department should start checking the US consular and immigration practices that encourage tens of thousands of non-Americans every day to resent the United States due to the humiliation that they are exposed to at the US consulates abroad and at the immigration offices at US airports.

ARMENIAN IRREDENTISM

The Real Obstacle to Turkish-Armenian Rapprochement[36]

Yerevan's unilateral decision, as Turkish Foreign Minister Ahmet Davutoğlu describes it, to put the Turkish-Armenian rapprochement on hold should have had a cold shower effect on those who had long been fed up with the overcooked so-called Armenian genocide debate.

On April 22, Armenian President Serzh Sarksyan signed a decree suspending the ratification of the "Protocol on Establishing Diplomatic Relations between the Republic of Armenia and the Republic of Turkey" and "Protocol on Opening the Border between the Republic of Armenia and the Republic of Turkey." In his televised address to his fellow Armenians, Sarksyan stated as follows:

> Our political objective for normalizing relations between Armenia and Turkey remains valid, and we shall consider moving forward when we are convinced that there is the proper environment in Turkey and the leadership in Ankara is ready to reengage in the normalization process.

Referring to Ankara's demand for Armenia to end its occupation of the Nagorno-Karabakh region of Azerbaijan before Parliament ratifies the protocols, the Armenian president charged Ankara with causing the breakup in the normalization process by making the end of Armenian occupation a precondition to the ratification.

While Ankara repeatedly reiterated its wish to continue the normalization of relations with Yerevan, on April 24 Armenian demon-

---

36 First appeared in *Today's Zaman* daily on April 26–27, 2010.

strators burned Turkish flags as well as posters of Turkish President Abdullah Gül, Prime Minister Recep Tayyip Erdoğan and Davutoğlu during the so-called Armenian genocide commemoration ceremonies attended by President Sarksyan and other Armenian officials. Like the Armenian officials, some inside and outside Turkey have criticized Ankara for pushing the end of Armenian occupation in Nagorno-Kara-bakh as a precondition to the ratification of the protocols. Some even argued that there was no relationship between the occupation and the normalization of Turkish-Armenian relations and that Azerbaijan stood as an obstacle to normalization.

As a matter of fact, the real obstacle to Turkish-Armenian rap-prochement is Armenia's irredentist attitude toward its neighbors. As such, Armenia's irredentism not only constitutes a national security threat to Turkey, but also is the major obstacle to any step toward sus-tainable security and stability in the South Caucasus. So long as Yere-van does not irreversibly change this attitude, it is unlikely to achieve any sustainable relationship between Turkey and Armenia.

Armenia is an irredentist country. That is, it is a country with aspi-rations on a part of another country's land, over which it claims to have the political right to control. Article 11 of the Armenian Declaration of Independence reads, "The Republic of Armenia stands in support of the task of achieving international recognition of the 1915 Genocide in Ottoman Turkey and Western Armenia," referring to contemporary eastern Turkey as Western Armenia. Article 12 reads as follows:

> This declaration serves as the basis for the development of the con-stitution of the Republic of Armenia and, until such time as the new constitution is approved, as the basis for the introduction of amend-ments to the current constitution; and for the operation of state authorities and the development of new legislation for the republic.

So obviously, the crux of the Armenian Constitution and of the guideline for the state authorities is Yerevan's unrelenting aspirations to seize eastern Turkey as well as other possible monetary and politi-cal reparations.

Yerevan has proven its characteristic as such by invading and occu-pying 20 percent of a neighboring country—Azerbaijan. Consequently, another neighboring country, Turkey, which has long been the main target of Yerevan's irredentist aspirations, closed its common border with Armenia. Although Turkey and Azerbaijan do have deep cultural, ethnic, social, economic and political ties and as such Turkey's closure of the border may seem and has long been portrayed as an emotional response to Armenia's invasion of Azerbaijan's territories, Turkey's response to the invasion is purely a rational one.

It is only normal for a country to seal its common border with an irredentist neighbor to maintain its national security and territorial integrity.

It is more so given that Armenia has never officially recognized and acknowledged its common border with Turkey, constitutionally considers part of Turkey's lands as its own, and worse, has for almost two decades been occupying 20 percent of another neighboring country. So, the reason Turkey shut its border with Armenia and why Turkey should keep it as such is not simply Turkey's affinity with Azerbaijan, but Armenia's irredentist nature and the security threat that it clearly poses to its neighbors. The fact that Armenia cannot dare to confront Turkey militarily neither ceases its aspirations on Turkish territories nor changes its malignant nature that has long obstructed progress toward security and stability in the South Caucasus.

Moreover, the impunity Armenia has long enjoyed despite its continuous violations of international law, humanitarian law, Geneva conventions and United Nations Security Council resolutions during and after its invasion of Azerbaijani territory makes Yerevan even more reckless about paralyzing its peace talks with Turkey and Azerbaijan. According to the UN Security Council Resolution S/RES/822 which was adopted on April 30, 1993, the Council,

> Noting with alarm the escalation in armed hostilities and, in particular, the latest invasion of the Kelbadjar district of the Republic of Azerbaijan by local Armenian forces…, Expressing grave concern at the displacement of a large number of civilians and the humanitarian emergency in the region…, Reaffirming also the inviolability of international borders and the inadmissibility of the use of force for the acquisition of territory, [the UN Security Council] demands the immediate cessation of all hostilities and hostile acts with a

> view to establishing a durable cease-fire, as well as immediate with-
> drawal of all occupying forces from the Kelbadjar district and other
> recently occupied areas of Azerbaijan.

This resolution came after Yerevan-backed local Armenian forces
killed 613 Azerbaijani civilians, including 106 women and 83 children, in the town of Khojali on Feb. 25-26, 1992. Instead of ceasing
their attacks, the Armenian forces expanded their killing campaign to
beyond the Nagorno-Karabakh region into surrounding districts such
as Lachin, Kubatly, Jebrail, Zangelan, Aghdam and Fizuli. As Armenian forces continued to invade these districts, the UN Security Council adopted resolutions 853, 874 and 884 in the same year demanding a cease-fire and the withdrawal of Armenian forces from the occupied Azerbaijani territories.

To this day, however, these districts, totaling 8.9 percent of Azerbaijani territory, as well as the Nagorno-Karabakh region remain under
the control of Armenia. The way Sarksyan recalls the Khojali massacres
is quite telling:

> We don't speak loudly about these things. But I think the main point
> is something different…Before Khojali, the Azerbaijanis thought
> that they were joking with us, they thought that the Armenians were
> people who could not raise their hand against the civilian popula-
> tion. We were able to break that [stereotype]. And that is what
> happened.[37]

By that, President Sarksyan also implies what they aspire to do so
long as the circumstances permit.

The way forward

In the final analysis, the current leadership in Yerevan does not seem to
be ready to acknowledge its past transgressions, let alone make due reparations to their victims. Yet it can start by revisiting Armenia's irredentist characteristic and finding ways to get rid of it instead of asking
Ankara to give up its precondition to the ratification of the protocols.

---

[37] Thomas de Waal, *Black Garden: Armenia and Azerbaijan through Peace and War*,
NY: NYU Press, 2004, p.172.

In the meantime, Ankara should recognize that the normalization of Turkish-Armenian relations is directly contingent to not one but two preconditions: First, Armenia must end its occupation of the Azerbaijani territories in the Nagorno-Karabakh region as well as the surrounding districts, and second, it must remove from its constitution the articles that describe eastern Turkey as "Western Armenia." In the absence of the other, satisfying one of these conditions is not enough, because while one literally certifies Yerevan's irredentist aspirations toward Turkey, the other practically illustrates that Yerevan would seek to fulfill those aspirations once the circumstances permit. Until then, Turkey's common border with Armenia should remain sealed.

CHOOSING THE LESSER EVIL

Nuclear Balance of Power Vs. Perpetual Conflict in the Middle East[38]

T urkish Prime Minister Recep Tayyip Erdoğan and Brazilian President Lula da Silva have finally managed to convince their Iranian counterpart, Mahmoud Ahmadinejad, to agree on the UN-brokered nuclear swap deal.

Thanks to the unwavering efforts of their respective foreign ministers, Ahmet Davutoğlu and Celso Amorim, and days of negotiations, Tehran agreed to abide by the agreement, according to which Iran will ship its low-enriched uranium to a third country (Turkey) in exchange for enriched uranium. This deal would prevent Iran from enriching its uranium to a high level, but at the same time, Iran would be able to use the enriched nuclear fuel it receives to produce medical isotopes for civilian purposes. The agreement with Iran was apparently the easiest part of the task in defusing the escalation over Iran's controversial nuclear program.

What seems to be more difficult, perhaps even unlikely, is convincing the US-led Western troika (US-UK-France) within the UN Security Council to heed that agreement. Although the agreement is exactly what was proposed by the United Nations to Iran some seven months ago, the Obama administration was quick to view, and hence dismiss, it as Iran's opportunism to avoid a fourth round of UN sanctions without making any real concessions on its nuclear program. The US secretary of state had already suggested earlier that Brazil and Turkey's efforts to find a diplomatic solution would fail anyway.

---

[38] First appeared in *Today's Zaman* daily on May 24–25, 2010.

On the other hand, Russia has not yet commented on the deal. Russian diplomats say it is too early to do so before knowing the details of the agreement. However, another UN Security Council member, China, which is capable of vetoing any sanction resolution, has welcomed the agreement as a positive development paving the way to further interaction between the international community and Iran for a sustainable solution. Going even further, Turkish Foreign Minister Davutoğlu voiced the opinion that there was no longer a need for the UN sanctions against Iran, given that Tehran has already accepted the UN-proposed nuclear swap agreement.

Yet, the latest announcement by US Secretary of State Hillary R. Clinton only two days after the Brazil-Turkey-Iran agreement indicates that the dispute over Iran's nuclear program is far, if not farther than before, from being resolved. Testifying to the Senate Foreign Relations Committee, Secretary Clinton said:

> We have reached agreement on a strong draft [on the fourth round of UN sanctions against Iran] with the cooperation of both Russia and China...I think this announcement is as convincing an answer to the efforts undertaken in Tehran over the last few days as we could provide.

The announcement is certainly a blow to Ankara and Brasilia's efforts. Or more figuratively, it is a big fat slap in the faces of both the Turkish and Brazilian leaders for daring to oppose the P5+1 engineered sanctions against Iran.

As the case now stands, it is unclear whether the Brazil-Turkey-Iran agreement will even be implemented. What is crystal clear though is that the way the US handles the issue will certainly polarize the international community over the sanctions against Iran and tilt the global public opinion in favor of Iran. In addition, Washington's apparent obsession with the sanctions will further strengthen the widely held belief that the US administration is simply pursuing Israel's agenda against Iran, as it did almost a decade ago against Iraq. Ironically, it seems, the US is pressuring Iran, a Nuclear Non-Proliferation Treaty (NPT) signatory, on its alleged attempts to acquire nuclear weapons, while it is providing nuclear assistance to Israel, a nuclear weapons possessor and a non-NPT signatory. The irony is not the US' pressure on Iran, but its silence on Israel's apparent nuclear arsenal, and even worse, its continuing nuclear assistance to Israel while the latter continues its absolute defiance of the NPT.

The looming feud over Iran's controversial nuclear program between the P5+1 and basically the rest of the international community may actually be the starkest indication of the necessity of revising the global security doctrine, which has been embodied within the nuclear non-proliferation principle. Where nuclear non-proliferation and disarmament is not verifiably possible and when the nuclear weapons states are not keen on giving up their entire nuclear arsenal, the very possession of nuclear weapons may actually be more useful to ensure their non-use by any of the nuclear weapons states. After all, the idea of the world free of nuclear weapons is nothing but a dream, a dream that may possibly engender nightmares.

The Obama administration recently announced its Nuclear Posture Review (NPR), which underlines that even if the US substantially reduces its nuclear arsenal over time, it would never give up its nuclear weapons entirely unless the world is cleared of all nuclear weapons.

The US' caution over total nuclear disarmament may be understandable given its superpower and balancing role within the international system. Similarly, French President Nicolas Sarkozy recently declared that France would "never" give up its nuclear weapons and make France vulnerable to external security threats. The nuclear arsenals of Russia, China and the UK are not likely to be eliminated either.

While even France and the UK are not willing to give up their military nuclear capabilities despite the fact that they are not only in the middle of the so-called prosperous and peaceful European Union zone, but also somewhat at the helm of the EU's security structure, would Iran ever be willing to give up its nuclear military capabilities if it acquires or has already them? Would Israel ever want to lose its military superiority and hence dominance over its perceived arch enemies in the Middle East? Would Israelis ever risk total annihilation in the face of their perceived nuclear threat? How about Iran? Would Iran's guardians of the so-called Islamic Revolution ever want to risk a military invasion or a substantial military attack? Iran's president, Ahmadinejad, argues that what America has given to Iranians is two wars and instability on both sides of Iran, in both Afghanistan and Iraq. Would Iran risk suffering the same military offensives, while those who got the US to attack Iraq look even more obsessed about getting the US, as well as the entire international community, to attack Iran? Neither Israel nor Iran would be interested in giving up their military nuclear capabilities or arsenals.

There are really only two options left to the international community—and these two differ only by the level of evil in their natures. One is a perpetual conflict in the Middle East, which would sooner or later be triggered by Israel, and which would certainly drag the United States in with its nuclear arsenal. The other is the deliberate establishment of a balance of nuclear power in the region. Pursing the second option would inevitably strain the nerves, but eventually ensure non-aggression to a great extent among the regional powers, because the mutually assured destruction capability that nuclear weapons give each state would at the same time inhibit them from using those weapons against other regional states.

Nuclear Middle East may actually be the solution

It would be desirable if nuclear weapons had never existed, if Iran were not suspected of pursuing nuclear weapons possession and if it were possible to eliminate all the nuclear weapons on earth with verifiable certainty. However much it is desired, implementing it is practically impossible. So long as nuclear weapons technology exists in one way or another, in the hands of one country or another, so will the possibility of state or non-state actors acquiring or developing nuclear weapons. This is actually why the US' NPR underlines that the US would retain its nuclear weapons arsenal until all the nuclear weapons on earth are definitely eliminated. It means that the US would never give up its nuclear arms entirely, neither would the others. Nor would the non-nuclear weapons states stop aspiring to acquire nuclear weapons or the capability to build them. Unfortunately, this is the cold reality that one has to reconcile. One has to perceive the nuclear threat as it is, not as it should be.

Then, more specifically, what is the sustainable and reliable mechanism to prevent possible nuclear aggression in the Middle East? What could be more reassuring than the mere wish for nuclear disarmament, nonproliferation and peaceful use only? Crippling economic and political sanctions against Iran, as the P5+1 seek? Pre-emptive military strikes on Iran's nuclear facilities, as Israel has long been lobbying for? A diplomatic solution, which Turkey and Brazil hope to achieve? None is likely to provide as reliable a solution as a nuclear balance of power would.

The most vivid illustration of a security guarantee ensured by the balance of nuclear power is the fact that never in history has a nuclear weapons state attacked with or without nuclear weapons another nuclear weapons state, but a nuclear weapons state has attacked a non-nuclear weapons state with nuclear weapons. There is no need to mention that nuclear weapons states keep attacking non-nuclear weapons states as they wish, though not with nuclear weapons. Of course, under such an arrangement in the Middle East, tiny but mighty Israel will no longer be the only nuclear weapons state in the region and hence will be forced to restrict its recklessness under international and regional agreements. However, the heightened prospects for peaceful survival and prosperity should be a good enough reward for Israel in exchange for its nuclear monopoly in the region.

RETHINKING ISRAELI POLITICS

Does Israel Need a Foreign Minister?[39]

T he never-ending row between Turkey and Israel's Likud government under Prime Minister Benjamin Netanyahu has escalated to a whole new level since Israeli commandos raided the Mavi Marmara, a Turkish humanitarian aid ship headed to Gaza, in international waters, killing nine Turkish citizens and injuring 38 others.

Immediately after the unfortunate incident Turkish Foreign Minister Ahmet Davutoğlu convened the United Nations Security Council for an emergency meeting to discuss the matter. Similarly, at the Turkish foreign minister's initiative, the NATO council gathered and, along with its condemnation, urged Israel to release all the participants in the Freedom Flotilla captured during the raid. Moreover, the Organization of the Islamic Conference's (OIC) executive council convened to formulate the 57 member states' common response to Israel's aggression. Concurrently, the Arab League member states also convened to condemn the Israeli attack on the humanitarian aid ships headed to the Gaza Strip, which has long suffered under the Israeli blockade. All major international and regional organizations unequivocally condemned Israel, demanded the immediate release of the captured and insisting on a thorough investigation into the raid.

The Israeli foreign minister, on the other hand, remained rather silent on the day of the raid. The next day, in a phone call to the UN secretary-general, Avigdor Lieberman complained about the international community's reaction. "The hypocrisy and double standards taking root in the international community regarding Israel is to be regretted," he lamented. "In the past month alone 500 people were killed in

---

[39] First appeared in *Today's Zaman* daily on June 05, 2010.

various incidents in Thailand, Afghanistan, Pakistan, Iraq and India, while the international community remained silent and passive and generally ignored the occurrences, while Israel is condemned for unmistakably defensive actions," he continued. "The subject of yesterday's incident was the basic right of Israeli soldiers to defend themselves against an attack by a gang of thugs and terror supporters who had prepared clubs, metal crowbars and knives in advance of the confrontation."

This time, even the US administration was unable to defend the Israeli government's actions. The State Department announced that contrary to what was argued by the Israeli officials, there was no tie between the Humanitarian Aid Foundation (İHH) and al-Qaeda. Similarly, the Obama administration said the Israeli blockade on Gaza was no longer sustainable and that the Israeli government had to develop another approach regarding Gaza.

All in all, the way the Israeli government managed—or, more accurately, mismanaged—this international crisis has raised questions not only about the viability and legitimacy of the Israeli blockade on Gaza, but also about the utility of the Israeli foreign minister. After all, whatever Israel does directly impacts the non-Israeli Jews around the world as well as the Israeli Jews, and the Israeli foreign minister is the primary person who is supposed to be capable of determining the nature of that impact.

Non-Israeli Jews between a rock and a hard place

Aside from the Palestinians themselves, the group most affected by Israel's unrelenting aggression is Jews who do not condone Israel's hawkish policies. On the one hand, both liberal and Orthodox Jews around the world and especially in the United States have raised their opposition to the brutal policies of consecutive Israeli governments toward the Palestinians living either in the West Bank or in Gaza. When Israeli troops invaded Gaza in the first days of 2009 and killed some 1,400 civilians, mostly women and children, among those crying out against Israel's invasion were prominent Jewish scholars and opinion leaders. Similarly, they joined the masses in condemning Israel's destructive blockade of Gaza, which has long nurtured instability in the region and paralyzed the so-called peace process between Israelis and Palestinians. Again, most recently, when the Israeli commandos attacked the humanitarian aid flotilla headed to Gaza, Jews—in Turkey, the US, Europe and elsewhere—were among the first to condemn Israel. They too joined the masses in front of Israel's embassies to protest Israeli piracy and banditry in international waters.

On the other hand, the very same Jews around the world and in the United States have long been victimized by the common antipathy rapidly growing against Jews due to successive Israeli governments' constant breach of international laws and norms, complete heedlessness of international public opinion and continued violence unleashed upon Palestinian civilians. This phenomenon in a way resembles the pitiful case of Muslims around the world who are reduced to potential suspects allegedly sympathizing with such terrorist groups such as al-Qaeda and the Taliban. However, just as the terrorist nature and activities of al-Qaeda and the Taliban should not define Muslims in general, those of the Israeli government should not determine the common public perception of Jews, wherever they may be.

It is questionable, though, to what extent it is possible under the current circumstances for an ordinary man on the street to distinguish between hawkish and dovish Jews. Either hawkish or dovish, and regardless of their nationality/citizenry, all Jews seem to be staunch supporters of the state of Israel (though not necessarily its every policy), although Israel is simply another state/country other than their own. Imagine a Country X whose senators, congressmen, ministers and ordinary parliamentarians do not shy away from publicly prioritizing the interests of Israel over those of Country X. Imagine a Country X where those in charge make substantial cutbacks in funding to educational, scientific and social programs that benefit their very Country Xians while they either cannot or do not even think about slightly holding back Country X's monetary, military and all other forms of assistance to Israel. And imagine a Country X where politicians categorically reject any policy proposal, even if it greatly serves the interests of Country X, unless they serve those of Israel, let alone considering con-

4446666

flict against them. Or imagine a Country X where the non-Jewish Country Xians are scared to death to say anything negative about Israel due to their fear of losing their public, private or academic positions on the grounds of allegedly being anti-Semitic. It is quite difficult to distinguish between those extremists that condone every act of aggression and terrorism for the sake of the so-called Jewish state from those extremists like the al-Qaeda and Taliban bandits who perpetrate every kind of aggression and terrorism in the name of the so-called Islamic state. What is the difference? One blows up a hotel with hundreds of innocent civilians in it just to punish those officials who oppose the establishment of the so-called Jewish state and the other blows up a bus full of innocent civilians in order to spread the sense of fear among those who oppose the establishment of a so-called Islamic state.

It is equally difficult to discern where the real loyalty of Country X's Jews lie, when some of them rush to suffocate Country X's relationship with its allies every time the latter encounters a problem with Israel, even if doing so would be detrimental to the interests of Country X. In such cases, a propaganda machine starts to run at full force. The latest crisis between Turkey and Israel is just one example of this. All of a sudden, so-called op-ed pieces by so-called Turkey experts from so-called prominent think tanks started to appear in the so-called foreign policy journals, reminding Country Xians of the "Islamist" roots of the Turkish government and seeking to sow seeds of discord among Turkish leaders by seemingly praising one while smearing the other. Similarly, so-called prominent columnists of so-called newspapers of record started to propagate the false argument that Turkey is a more dangerous enemy to Country X and Israel than Hamas is.

So, the situation has always been quite complicated for non-Israeli Jews. As such, it becomes an ever more critical question as to whether Israel should have a foreign minister and what kind of foreign minister Israel should have, because he or she is in a position to determine what kind of impact that complicated situation would have on public opinion not only about Israel, but also about the non-Israeli Jews around the world.

The kind of foreign minister Israel needs

Given the unchecked and abundant political, military and financial support it is receiving from states such as Country X, one may be tempted to conclude that Israel does not really need a foreign minister that has to explain Israel's actions to and foster friendships within the international community. Moreover, recalling the example of the former US Secretary of State Henry Kissinger, who reportedly once told his Syrian counterpart seeking US intervention to stop the so-called Six-Day war between Israel and Egypt-Jordan-Syria that "we do not have any problem with the war going on, so long as Israel is the one winning it," some may actually suggest that Israel already has more than one foreign minister.

However, given the magnitude of the troubles the consecutive Israeli governments have been creating not only for the Palestinians, but also for Jews around the world and for the international community in general, Israel needs not a foreign minister, but perhaps a group of foreign ministers. A group of foreign ministers whose sole responsibility would be to foster constructive relations with Israel's immediate neighbors in particular and with the international community in general. A group of foreign ministers who would formulate long-term constructive foreign policies that would help Israel be accepted as an ordinary and legitimate member of the international community. Again, a group of foreign ministers who would earn Israel's right to exist through gaining the consent of other countries, not through squandering the political and economic resources of a few countries such as Country X.

It is only obvious toward that end that Lieberman is completely useless as foreign minister of Israel. As a matter of fact, Lieberman as a foreign minister is quite detrimental to the interests of Israel as well as of the non-Israeli Jews who feel somehow connected to the state of Israel. Perhaps Prime Minister Netanyahu too subscribes to the idea that Israel does not really need a foreign minister and that is why he left an otherwise very important post in his cabinet to Mr. Lieberman.

RETHINKING TURKISH POLITICS

Has Turkey gone too far over Gaza?[40]

In diplomacy, there is a fine line between credibility and incredibility, between the serious and the ridiculous. Recently, over the tragic fate of Gaza, Turkey was made to walk that fine line, when the genuine but unwise and untimely humanitarian mission triggered an inhumane action by Israeli forces. The ensuing popular reactions to the killing of nine Turkish citizens by Israeli commandos, and the tendency of some groups, both inside and outside Turkey, to exploit these reactions to bolster an Islamist rhetoric, anti-Semitism and a false image of Turkish guardianship over the Middle East have marred Turkey's genuine diplomatic efforts in the aftermath of those killings.

The question is: Why did Turkey do what it did? And, has Turkish foreign policy already lost its credibility?

What was Ankara outraged about?

Ankara was naturally outraged by Israel's brutal reaction to the humanitarian aid mission to Gaza. The Israeli commandos' killing of Turkish citizens demanded Ankara's immediate attention to the matter. In his address to the UN Security Council, which convened that day in emergency session, Turkish Foreign Minister Ahmet Davutoğlu did not defend the aid activists' right to break Israel's unlawful blockade on Gaza, nor did he advocate the legitimacy of the Humanitarian Aid Foundation (İHH)-organized flotilla, but condemned Israel's killing and injuring of civilians in international waters with total and shameless disregard for international law. Davutoğlu underlined the following fact:

---

[40] First appeared in *Today's Zaman* daily on June 13, 2010.

> The Israeli Defense Forces [IDF] stormed a multinational, civilian endeavor carrying humanitarian aid to Gaza in international waters— 72 nautical miles off the coast to be exact—killing and wounding many civilians. This action was uncalled for. [The] Israeli actions constitute a grave breach of international law.

He further condemned the Israeli government's banditry and piracy:

> It is murder conducted by a state. It has no excuses, no justification whatsoever. A nation-state that follows this path has lost its legitimacy as a respectful member of the international community.

He also deplored Israel's inappropriate and disproportionate use of force against civilians. Israel's action is also a violation of international law as well as of international humanitarian law, which ensures the protection of civilians even during wartime.

So, in response to Israel's criminal act, Ankara did not seek military action to punish Israel but urged the international community and the United Nations to take appropriate action immediately. In this regard, Turkey was not the sole country, but one of many states within the international community, doing just that. Davutoğlu stressed that: (1) An urgent inquiry must be undertaken; (2) Appropriate international legal action must immediately be taken against the perpetrators of and authorities responsible for this aggression; (3) A strong sense of disappointment and warning must be issued by the United Nations. Israel must be urged to abide by international law and basic human rights; (4) The countries concerned must be allowed to retrieve their deceased and wounded immediately; (5) The ships must be expressly released and allowed to deliver the humanitarian assistance to its destination; (6) The families of the deceased, wounded, NGOs and shipping companies concerned must be compensated to the full extent; (7) The blockade of Gaza must be ended immediately and all humanitarian assistance must be allowed in; and, finally, (8) Gaza must be made an example by swiftly developing it, to make it a region of peace. So, Ankara only sought to exercise its legitimate rights under international law to protect its citizens as well as the citizens of other nationalities harmed by Israel's criminal act.

Ankara should also have been outraged by the fact that out of all six aid ships only the one carrying Turks was raided by Israeli commandos and that the soldiers reportedly killed the Turkish activists while uttering derisive "One minute! One minute!" slogans in mockery of Turkish Prime Minister Erdoğan's outburst at Israeli President Shimon Peres at the infamous Davos forum.

So Ankara had already had enough reason to be outraged and to do what it did. However, just as the anti-Semites sought to exploit this crisis to incite hatred against Jews and Israel, some inside and outside Israel rushed to exploit Ankara's reaction in order to demonize the current Justice and Development Party (AK Party) government in Turkey. In his article titled, "Erdoğan and the Decline of the Turks," Robert Pollock of *The Wall Street Journal* alleges that the flotilla could not have been organized without the approval of Turkish Prime Minister Erdoğan, who, Pollock says, cannot "bring himself to condemn a fictional blood libel [that the organs of the dead Iraqis were being shipped to Israel]." At the expense of embarrassing himself, Pollock argues in the same article that Turkish Foreign Minister Davutoğlu calls on Turkey to loosen ties with the West, including with the US, NATO and the European Union. In his article titled, "Flotilla raid offers Israel a learning opportunity," David Ignatius of *The Washington Post* suggests that Turkey is "a more dangerous foe than Hamas" for Israel, and that Prime Minister Erdoğan is "a Muslim populist with a charismatic message" and "a genuinely tough if erratic rival" whereas Iran's president, Mahmoud Ahmadinejad, is "often a buffoon." In his interview with Pat Robertson on CBN News, Daniel Pipes of the Middle East Forum said, "Turkey is no longer 'our' [the United States'] ally, but an opponent of the United States."

Nevertheless, the very fact that many Jews both inside and outside Turkey as well as in the United States joined others to protest the Israeli attack on the humanitarian aid flotilla justifies Ankara's reaction in the aftermath of Israel's terrorist attack in international waters. Yet, understanding the true reasons behind Ankara's reaction is only one part of the assessment as to whether Turkey has gone too far over Gaza, and the answer to this part of the question is that Ankara has not gone too far but only carried out its natural duty to pursue justice and hold Israel accountable for its crime.

What has the flotilla accomplished?

The second part of the assessment is about the original idea of organizing a humanitarian aid flotilla to break the unlawful Israeli blockade of Gaza. The question is whether it was the right thing to do in the first place in order to bring aid to Gaza, or to lift the blockade altogether, for that matter. How reasonable was it for an NGO or for a group of NGOs to defy the authority of a sovereign state, whether or not this is a legitimate authority? What would it accomplish in favor of the Palestinians in Gaza? Would it better highlight the plight of the Palestinians suffering under the Israeli blockade to the world? Or, would it demonstrate how brutal and unlawful Israeli practices were?

There is nothing justifiable about the heinous Israeli attack on the peace activists. The Israeli commandos raiding the Mavi Marmara and did not hesitate to shoot a 19-year-old US citizen of Turkish origin in the head five times. The Israeli commandos did not hesitate to shoot an Indonesian doctor treating one of those commandos injured during the raid four times in the stomach. Nor did they refrain from taking hostage a 1-year-old baby and using him as a means to psychologically torture his parents. Nor did Israel's so-called defense forces refrain from using cluster bombs of phosphorus to burn and kill Palestinian children during Israel's December 2008-January 2009 invasion of Gaza.

No matter how brutal Israel is to the Palestinians, the best way to help the Palestinians in either the West Bank or in Gaza is to work through legitimate means, even if one has to engage with an illegitimate authority to do that. The İHH president stressed that they could not trust the Israeli authorities to distribute the aid in Gaza. They did not have to. They could have delivered the aid to the United Nations Relief and Works Agency (UNRWA) for distribution or worked it out with the Red Crescent. Similarly, they could have worked with the Egyptian authorities, if not the Israelis, to find ways to deliver the aid to Gaza. It was not necessary to try to break the unlawful Israeli block-

ade to deliver the aid. If, however, the only goal was to break the blockade, the flotilla would not do that, either.

The way forward

According to the Lebanese newspaper al-Mustaqbal, the Turkish prime
minister has been "weighing the possibility of travelling to the Gaza
Strip in order to break the Israeli blockade on Gaza, and even informed
the US of his intention to ask the Turkish Navy to accompany another aid flotilla to Gaza." Though such a plan has not been confirmed
by the prime minister, and this could be just another piece of disin-
formation spread about his government, realizing such a plan would
not only be disastrous for stability in the region and for prospects of
proximity talks between the Israelis and the Palestinian Authority but
also political suicide for Prime Minister Erdoğan and his AK Party
government. It would eliminate Turkey's prospects for EU membership—at least with the AK Party government in office. Turkey has not
gone too far over Gaza, but if it attempts to fulfill such a wild plan, it
will really have gone too far. There is no need to even mention its possible impact on US-Turkish relations because there would be none in
existence.

FREEDOM TO MAKE MISTAKES

Is Turkey's Ahmet Davutoğlu Infallible?[41]

Turkey's foreign policy achievements in the last eight years have mesmerized most Turks and some outside admirers so successfully and raised their expectations so high that it has consequently and unfortunately diminished Ankara's and, most notably, Foreign Minister Ahmet Davutoğlu's, freedom to fail, or freedom to make mistakes in either formulation or implementation of the country's foreign policy.

Now it is harder for the government to step back from certain foreign policy moves, even if it becomes apparent that they are not helpful. This development is an unhealthy and destructive one for the fate of Turkey's foreign relations, and for both its regional and global image. It misleadingly portrays the country not only as a regional hegemonic aspirant seeking to revive its imperial heritage, but also as a whimsical and irrational actor that is willing to readily risk its long established diplomatic relations with its partners. In addition, such excessive admiration, without due criticism, of the AK Party government's foreign policy not only pushes its leadership to have a relatively higher opinion of itself, but also makes it vulnerable to both internal and external manipulation.

Turkish foreign policy in recent years has been marked by souring Turkish-Israeli relations, which followed Israel's invasion of Gaza in January 2009, continued with the infamous Davos incident and reached its apex when Israeli soldiers killed eight Turkish citizens and one Turkish-American in international waters on May 31, 2010. The changing nature of Turkish-Israeli relations and the way Ankara han-

---

[41] First appeared in *Today's Zaman* daily on July 20, 2010.

dles this change provide a unique case to assess the AK Party government's performance in managing Turkey's foreign relations, and to predict its future.

Who's Ahmet Davutoğlu? What's extraordinary about him, if anything?

Any attempt to make such an assessment, however, should follow a clear understanding of who the Turkish foreign minister, Ahmet Davutoğlu, is, because of his central role in both the formulation and implementation of Turkey's response to Israel.

Turkey's foreign minister is most widely known both inside and outside the country as the man who has been trying to restructure Turkish foreign policy according to the so-called "zero problem with neighbors" principle. Theoretically, this is not a groundbreaking idea that would suffice to distinguish him, because that principle had already been enshrined the famous quote of Atatürk, the first president of the Turkish Republic, "Peace at home, peace abroad." Oddly enough, however, the republican elite that hastily isolated Atatürk in his last years and took absolute control over state affairs immediately after his death used the very same quote in order to rein in Turkish diplomacy. This elite created a paranoid foreign relations approach that perceived every state (except Israel after 1948) as an existential threat to Turkey. With his multidimensional foreign policy approach viewing every state as a potential ally, unless proven otherwise, Davutoğlu seems to be undoing this paranoid perception by reaching out not only to the West, but also to the East, not only to the Bosnian Muslims, but also to the Serbian Orthodox Christians. In that regard, he may be considered as the one who is for the first time endeavoring to fulfill Atatürk's vision for Turkish foreign policy.

Simply speaking, Davutoğlu is just an ordinary academic and a relatively observant Muslim, turned into a politician. There are and will be many people like this as Turkey progresses into this century. One has to admit, though, that this is quite a strange practice for Turkey, while it has been a long-established tradition in democratic countries.

Throughout the history of the republic, one had to be a high-ranking army general, or at least a civilian of the secular-fundamentalist breed, in order to somehow influence the country's foreign policy. Although Davutoğlu is first of his kind, he is still ordinary in the sense of what he has been doing.

However, what is extraordinary about Davutoğlu, compared to either his Turkish predecessors or foreign counterparts, is his apparent passion for actively involving himself in all dimensions of international politics, and to restructure it by redefining the fundamental theories of international relations. He seems to be attempting a mental transformation of states from a purely "selfish national interest" conception to one of "altruistic national interest" as the fundamental driving force of foreign policy decision-making. In his rhetoric and practice, the notions of the collective interests of states and justice outweigh the notion of selfish national interest.

That is, if there are two options for a state to pursue—one, a higher gain which may harm the wellbeing of another nation, and the other, a relatively lower gain which may benefit another nation, or at least not harm it—then that state actor should pursue the second option. This way of thinking may be the reason why Davutoğlu is trying to integrate Armenia into the economic structure of the Caucasus, instead of further weakening Armenia's already impoverished economy by exclusively cooperating with Georgia and Azerbaijan. Again, this may be why he encourages cooperation between Bosnia and Serbia, instead of boosting relations exclusively with Muslim Bosnians and isolating the Serbs, who a little more than a decade ago perpetrated the Bosnian genocide under the watch of EU heavy weights like France, Germany, Italy, and the United Kingdom. So, given the pattern of his preferences, Davutoğlu seems to be a rational man who thinks that Turkey's national interests are truly secured only if its neighbors' interests are also secured, and who seeks to build partnerships instead of pursing old animosities.

Then, what is the problem with Israel? Why did Davutoğlu suggest that Turkey would cut off its diplomatic relations with Israel unless the latter officially apologizes for the deliberate killing of eight Turk-

ish citizens and one Turkish-American by Israeli soldiers? Was it a
mistake to do so?

Ankara's reaction to Israel's aggression:
What else would it be?

In his address to the United Nations Security Council, Turkish Foreign Minister Davutoğlu appealed to the UN secretary-general to set
up an international committee to investigate the attack. In addition,
Davutoğlu urged Israel to immediately release all the civilians who survived the Israeli attack, return the Mavi Marmara to Turkey, pay com-
pensation for those killed and officially apologize to Turkey. For the
time being, the Netanyahu government has met none of these demands,
except for releasing the survivors upon Washington's unofficial ultimatum. As time passes without any concrete progress with regard to
the international investigation, Davutoğlu may have wanted to imply
that the Israeli leaders would not be able to get away easily with Turkish blood on their hands.

However, it was a major mistake to announce that Turkey would
ever cut off its diplomatic relations with Israel. While any democratically elected government in Ankara holds a legitimate right to cut off
those relations, whether it can freely exercise that right depends on a
number of domestic and international factors. Aside from that, Israel
is actually way too important of a regional neighbor for Turkey to cut
off relations with, because it currently controls areas even more important than itself.

Therefore, instead of cutting off its relations with Tel Aviv, Ankara may want to consider promoting a "balanced" and "mutually beneficial" Turkish-Israeli relationship. There are a number of areas where
Turkey can do so. Traditionally, Turkey has been the second most preferred tourism destination for Israelis after the United States, averaging about 300,000 Israeli tourists per year. Davutoğlu should insist
that Tel Aviv eliminate visa requirements for Turks visiting Israel, and
accordingly encourage Turks to visit Israel, especially Jerusalem, every
year to balance the Israeli tourist inflow to Turkey. Just like the Israe-

lis visiting Turkey, the Turks visiting Israel, too, should be able to obtain a visa at the airport without any obstacles or questions. Similarly, he should insist on regulations that would ease the establishment of Turkish NGOs and businesses in both East and West Jerusalem or elsewhere in Israel.

In addition, Ankara should minimize its military relationship with Israel as much as possible, be it arms purchases, military equipment overhaul contracts or joint military maneuvers. Under the current circumstances, Turkey lacks the technological expertise to balance its military purchases with similar military sales to Israel. Nor would it be appropriate to do so even if it could, given continuous Israeli offensives against Turkey's Arab allies in the region. Hence, such an imbalanced military relationship negatively affects Turkey's neutrality towards Israel and its Arab neighbors, thereby eliminating its ability to be an impartial mediator between the two.

While promoting a "balanced" and "mutually beneficial" Turkish-Israeli relationship, Ankara should engage with the Israeli President Shimon Peres instead of Prime Minister Benjamin Netanyahu, and the Minister of Industry, Trade and Labour Binyamin Ben-Eliezer instead of Minister of Foreign Affairs Avigdor Lieberman, since both Netanyahu and Lieberman are apparently either indifferent or incapable of developing friendly relations with Turkey. In the meantime, the Turks should give their foreign minister the freedom to make mistakes and a chance to correct them with a completely different, and at times opposite, course of action if necessary. Otherwise, not only his reputation as the architect of Turkey's multidimensional foreign policy vision, but also his and his successors' ability to pursue such a vision will be dramatically diminished by domestic and international factors.

FINDING A MIDDLE WAY

Is an Islamic Center Necessary at Ground Zero?[42]

The controversy over the proposed construction of an Islamic center at Ground Zero, where once stood the World Trade Center in Lower Manhattan, is growing with full speed.

It all started when the Cordoba Initiative, headed by American Imam Feisal Abdul Rauf, applied to the New York City Council for a license to build an Islamic center and mosque only 180 meters from where, according to most of its opponents, the "Islamists" struck the hardest blow to America. The planned Islamic center is intended to function more like a community center which includes, in addition to a Muslim prayer room, a 500-seat auditorium, a theater, a performing arts center, a fitness center, a swimming pool and a food court serving halal dishes. The construction of this center, reportedly, is also aimed at eradicating the feelings of ill will generated by the memory of the 9/11 attacks, and promoting interfaith understanding.

Although the project has lofty intentions behind it, the way it has been perceived and portrayed not only signals more harm than good for interfaith understanding, but also raises suspicions as to whether it is yet another stage in the whole setup to increase interfaith discord, to the contrary of the naïve intentions of its proponents.

The reactions to the Ground Zero mosque vary greatly. The opponents have primarily argued that building a mosque where some 3,000 people died due to an act of "Islamist" terrorism would and does offend the loved ones of the dead. This feeling was obvious in some of the protest posters that read "A mosque at ground zero spits on the graves of 9/11 victims!" Giving political meaning to the project, some took it even

---

[42] First appeared in *Today's Zaman* daily on August 11, 2010.

further: "Building a mosque at Ground Zero is like building a memorial to Hitler at Auschwitz," "You can build a mosque at Ground Zero when we can build a synagogue in Mecca," "Mosques in NYC=200+, Synagogues, Churches in Mecca=0" and "Build Churches in Saudi Arabia!" Apparently, hoping to benefit from an already electrified atmosphere, some sought to serve a rather more nuanced agenda as well, carrying "Boycott Turkish goods and products."

The source of funding for the project has also caused controversy. Opponents point to the fact that according to NBC and the *New York Post* Imam Feisal told a London-based Arabic language newspaper that he would seek funding from Muslim nations, whereas he earlier told American authorities that he would raise money from the local Muslim community. Recently, a Jewish organization, the Anti-Defamation League (ADL), has joined the debate with a public announcement in which it argued that the proposed construction was neither an issue of rights, nor the right thing to do because it would cause more pain to the loved ones of those who perished in the Sept. 11 terrorist attacks. Although the ADL president later on declared that they would not fight against the proposed mosque, he urged authorities to scrutinize the foreign sources of the funding.

On the other hand, the proponents of the mosque and those who condone its construction argue for the legitimacy of the project on the basis that just like Christians and Jews, Muslims living in New York are entitled to the right to build their places of worship so long as they do not violate the law. Among them, New York City Mayor Michael Bloomberg welcomed the mosque as an expression of freedom of religion exercised in the United States. Many others, including Massachusetts Governor Deval Patrick, supported the construction, arguing that it would help dissociate Islam and peaceful Muslims from those terrorists who act in the name of Islam. Similarly, Rabbi Arthur Waskow of the Shalom Center said the mosque would stand as a living example that Islam is not a tradition of violence, but peace.

Nevertheless, the controversy is gradually turning into a national debate across the United States, attracting the reaction of opponents rather faster than that of supporters. In Florida, a priest and his followers protested outside a Florida mosque and started a Facebook page titled "International Burn a Koran Day." The group is planning and inviting all to "burn the Koran on the property of Dove World Outreach Center in Gainesville, Florida, in remembrance of the fallen victims of 9/11 and to stand against the evil of Islam."

So, what should one make of the brewing controversy over this proposed Islamic Center at Ground Zero in lower Manhattan? Is all what it seems to be? Or, could it yet be another move in a bigger design in the making to further damage relations between the West and the Muslim world?

It looks like the more of the same

Throughout the last decade the relationship between the West and the Muslim world has been tested and strained so many times over so many issues, both critical and trivial, that one cannot help but suspect the existence of a group of masterminds manipulating the masses on both sides, playing with them like mice in a lab and feeling overwhelming ecstasy every time those masses tear each other apart. First, came the terrorist attacks on the World Trade Center on Sept. 11, allegedly by "Islamic" terrorists who cannot stand the "Western way of life," and cannot tolerate "liberal democracy and freedom." Then, came the "normal reaction" of the two military invasions: one of Afghanistan, which reportedly aimed to pre-empt another terrorist attack on American soil, and the other of Saddam Hussein's Iraq, which aimed to eliminate an existential threat to the "free world" posed by weapons of mass destruction that had in fact never existed. Once the general framework is set up, the rest has only to follow.

On the one hand, the increased sense of insecurity in the West, particularly in the United States, has occasionally turned into paranoia and fed racist and xenophobic sentiments against Muslims. On the other hand, the skyrocketing number of Afghan and Iraqi casualties, which was never even seriously counted, fanned the growing hatred across the "Muslim world" against the United States and its accomplice, the United Kingdom. The Abu-Ghraib and Guantanamo tortures were followed by the London and Madrid bombings. In the meantime, the

Israeli-Palestinian conflict continued like business as usual. Ariel Sharon's Israel fought with Hezbullah of Lebanon in 2006 when the latter fired rockets into Israeli border towns and snatched two Israeli soldiers. Ehud Olmert's Israel invaded Gaza in the last days of 2008 in response to the rockets fired into Israeli border towns from Gaza and in order to rescue the Israeli soldier Gilad Shalit. The invasion left some 1,400 Palestinians dead under the watch of the US, thereby further inflaming the hatred against the latter.

On the intellectual front of the "West-Muslim world" battle, the situation has not been much different. In the Netherlands of the "free world," the director Theo van Gogh was assassinated in 2004 by an "Islamist" because he produced the film "Submission," which was critical of the treatment of women in Islam. In Denmark of the "free world," the cartoonist Kurt Westergaard barely survived an axe attack in 2005 by another "Islamist" because he had earlier drawn 12 insulting cartoons of the Prophet Muhammad. In 2008, Dutch parliamentarian Geert Wilders sparked another wave of reaction from the "Islamists" that do not belong to the "free world" when he released "Fitna," a short film arguing that Islam encourages acts of terrorism and violence against women. Lately, France of the "free world" is likely to take the lead in sparking violent extremism among the "Islamists" as it bans Islamic headscarves in public spaces and continues to set an undemocratic example for other European states of the "free world" that are likely to follow suit.

So, given this sequence of unfortunate events that has strained relations between the West and the Muslim world in the last decade, how should one interpret the latest controversy over the proposed mosque at Ground Zero? One thing is certain: When such a mosque is eventually built as planned, it should not be a surprise to anyone if Christian and Jewish groups living in majority Muslim countries claim their rights to build places of worship and similar religious centers for their communities. While they have every right to do so, it is also obvious that almost none of those Muslim majority countries are prepared and open enough to reciprocate the gesture, unless they undertake dramatic reforms in the realm of freedom of expression and freedom of religion. For that matter, it should not be surprise, either, if "an extremist Christian American who could no longer bear the haunting burden of his loss on 9/11" bombs the Islamic center only to incite further violence from the so-called Muslim world. At the end of the day, the eventual construction of the mosque at Ground Zero is likely to spark further tension between the so-called West and the Muslim world under the current circumstances.

How about an interfaith center instead of an Islamic one?

Yet, the question persists: Is it necessary to build an Islamic center or a mosque at Ground Zero? Not really. In fact, it may be even counterproductive to do so given the bitter controversy it has already sparked.

However, what is urgently necessary is to build proper venues for Muslims to perform their daily prayers as well as the weekly Friday prayer. According to a *New York Daily News* report, today more than half a million Muslims live in New York City, including 10 percent of all public school children and more than 1,000 Muslim officers in the New York Police Department. One should also add to this the number of Muslim immigrant workers and visitors. As their number grow, it becomes harder and harder for the Muslims of New York City to perform their daily or Friday prayers in warehouses, building basements, or outside on the sidewalks. Muslims have been part and parcel of New York City ever since 1840 when the first Muslim immigration to the US started with the Yemenites and Arabs of the Ottoman Empire. As they continue to be part of and contribute to the prosperity of American society, Muslim-Americans in cooperation with the authorities should establish proper worship places all around New York City instead of symbolic mosques in symbolic locations. As for the proposed Islamic center at Ground Zero, it would be much better if it was turned into an "interfaith center" with the exact same amenities plus Christian, Jewish, Hindu and Buddhist worship places.

DETERRENCE

The Missing Dimension of Turkey's Multidimensional Foreign Policy[43]

The General Debate of the 65th session of the United Nations General Assembly next week is likely to be a milestone for Turkish diplomacy. In its capacity as the Chair, Turkey will be convening the Security Council at the heads of states and governments level to assess the UN's role in maintaining international peace and security on September 23, and at the ministerial level to discuss global counterterrorism measures on September 27. Certainly, these are all the results of Turkey's increased prominence, which is both cause and effect of Turkey's burgeoning soft power. Ankara has never seemed as active and influential as it is today within the international community. But what does it really mean for Turkey? How independent is Ankara in terms of charting its own path within the realm of international diplomacy? Is its freedom in that regard at the mercy of the usual global and emerging regional powers?

"No country can warn Turkey or Turkish prime minister," remarked recently Turkish foreign minister Ahmet Davutoğlu in order to stress that Turkey is as independent as it can be in terms of formulating and implementing its own foreign policies. Three days earlier, the British daily *Financial Times* had reported, "President Barack Obama personally warned Turkey's prime minister that unless Ankara shifts its position on Israel and Iran, it stands little chance of obtaining the US weapons it wants to buy," referring to Turkey's interest in purchasing American drone aircraft to fight the terrorist PKK (Kurdish Workers Party).

---

[43] First appeared in *The Washington Review* in September 2010.

The incident has already been forgotten, without creating any tension, once the White House spokesperson denied the *Financial Times* report, and stated that no ultimatum was given to Turkey. Yet, it raises a number of questions regarding Turkey's capabilities. Can Turkey sustain the growth of its soft power without attaining formidable hard power? Does it have sufficient deterrence capability to eliminate threats to such growth? Is soft power only sufficient vis-à-vis a potential foe with formidable hard power? Is Turkey really a country, as it currently stands, that no other country can warn, or impose its will onto, on the negotiation table? For instance, would the course of developments be the same in the aftermath of the infamous Israeli attack on the "Freedom Flotilla"?

Sources of strength in diplomacy

Technically, there are two sources of strength for a country on the negotiation table: one, its ability to benefit; and the other, its ability to harm the other party. Accordingly, both kinds of abilities derive from that country's hard and soft power. Given its destructive potential in the short and long term, a county should be primarily concerned with its counterpart's ability to harm coming from its hard power meaning military/warfare capabilities. Similarly, given the high cost and risks associated with state-to-state military confrontation through the means of conventional warfare, a country like Turkey should be concerned by a potential foe's unconventional (nuclear, chemical, biological, and cyber) warfare capabilities. Not less important is a potential foe's psychological warfare capability deployed through the means of the media, lobbies, think tanks, and academia. Having these capabilities does not automatically make a country threat to Turkey. However, whether or not Turkey is equipped to counter any threat posed to it through such capabilities determines whether or not Turkey is a country that "can be warned."

Nuclear weapons capability is not something that a nuclear power would openly threaten to use against a non-behaving counterpart. However, the non-behaving state with no nuclear weapons capability would always know its due boundaries vis-à-vis a nuclear power. The historical experience has demonstrated that nuclear powers have never attacked, and tend not to attack another nuclear power; but they have attacked, and are apparently prone to attacking non-nuclear powers even if they are signatories to all kinds of international treaties banning the use and possession of nuclear weapons. Currently, there are only a handful of nuclear powers and a nuclear "almost-there", which include the United States, Russian Federation, China, United Kingdom, France, India, North Korea, Pakistan, Israel and Iran. Apparently, Turkey is not one of them.

Chemical and biological weapons are not unfortunately as symbolic as nuclear weapons. They do get to be used by either states or non-state actors such as terrorist networks, which might well be acting as proxies of those very states within the enemy states. Although these type of weapons are not frequently used by military units, even possibility of using them against civilian populations suffice to spread fear and sense of constant insecurity in the enemy state, especially in its metropolitan cities. Chemical and biological attacks can be used in order to terrorize a nation, and thereby disorient and destabilize its political process by diminishing public trust in the incumbent government's ability to provide security and to govern.

Chemical and biological attacks do not have to be carried out against the civilian population in order to be fearsome. In most cases, they are carried out against the targeted nation's agriculture and livestock in order to demoralize and impoverish people by rendering its vast lands uninhabitable and non-arable. One infamous example of this tactic was the use of herbicides and defoliants by the US military with the tacit approval of the then Secretary of State Henry Kissinger in Vietnam and Cambodia in 1960s. The purpose was to defoliate rural and forested lands, and hence deprive the guerillas of both food and cover. The impact, however, has gone far beyond the intent. Even today, half a century later, babies in these affected regions are born physically disoriented, missing their body parts, or with body parts misplaced. Today, in addition to the nuclear weapons states, even countries like Albania, Bulgaria, Israel, Poland, Netherlands, and Ukraine possess chemical and biological weapons, but Turkey does not.

Finally, for certain countries that have it, cyberwarfare capability has increasingly become the most formidable source of strength in their practice of diplomacy. Cyberwarfare is basically the act of a state or non-state actor to penetrate another state's digital networks for multiple reasons, which include, but are not limited to, control, disruption, sabotage, manipulation, and espionage. In this regard, the primary points of attack in the targeted country would be telecommunication networks, electric grids, banking infrastructure, automated supply chains, government and military intelligence, Internet service providers, energy distribution lines, databases of major public and private companies, and so on. At the individual level, the cyberwarfare also include gathering intelligence about the private lives of the target country's political and military leaders, which in turn becomes quite instrumental in manipulating those leaders and waging a systematic psychological warfare across the country.

Is Turkey strong enough yet to sustain its influence?

So, where does Turkey stand with respect to its ability to counter evolving security threats posed by unconventional warfare capabilities of other states? It is actually hard to know, but not so hard to predict whether Turkey is equipped to ably counter such threats. The website of the Turkish Armed Forces (TAF), where apparently two of the TAF priorities are respectively to count the number of both Turkish and foreign nationals visiting the Anitkabir (Ataturk's mausoleum) and to teach proper use of Turkish language grammar, does not provide useful information to assess whether Turkey has sufficient defense capabilities in that regard. However, the scandals after scandals revealed in the recent months about the high-ranking army generals as well as the illegal networks nested within the army suggest that the Turkish Armed Forces is far from standing against any credible threat of nuclear, chemical-biological, cyber or psychological warfare.

These scandals include, but are not limited to, respectively the Daglica, Aktutun, and Hantepe incidents, during which the PKK terrorists raided the Turkish military outposts, slain in total 35 soldiers, kidnapped 12, and the Armed Forces failed to aid its ambushed soldiers. It has been later on revealed that the army failed to do so, despite the fact that not only the army had been provided with the relevant intelligence about the coming raids days before, but also during the Hantepe raid, 30 different military bases were streamlined real time video from the UAVs of the terrorist attacks which lasted for hours. Asked about the army's failure to respond, while its fighter jets and helicopters could have reached the attacked post in only 7 minutes, and simply blow up the entire terrorist unit, the Chief of Army General Staff sufficed to state in a press release that the jets and helicopters did not took off to aid, "because the weather was cloudy and there was dust in the air." The statement also noted that had they arrived at the point of attack, the helicopters would be under the risk of being shot down by the PKK's heavy weapons.

Such a mind-boggling excuse actually makes it futile and embarrassing even to ask if Ankara is capable of countering possible nuclear, chemical-biological, or cyber attacks posed against Turkey. Yet, one keeps wondering what Ankara's options are, if any, under such circumstances. What would Ankara do, for instance, if a hostile capital threatened to use its nuclear arsenal in a final showdown with Turkey; if a biochemical agent such as anthrax or sarin gas was released to a crowded shopping mall in one of the metropolitan cities, and caused the death of hundreds; if such an attack was deliberately blamed on the PKK in an attempt to portray every Kurd as a potential terrorist and a security threat; and finally if the country's telecommunication networks, electric grids, online banking infrastructure, automated supply chains, government and military intelligence, Internet service providers, energy distribution lines, databases of major public and private companies were all compromised. Under the current circumstances, Ankara does not seem to have many options.

Therefore, it is not really quite reasonable to assume that no other country can impose its will on Turkey, or admonish its leaders. Instead, a wiser course of action for a state with certain vulnerabilities such as Turkey would be to remain discrete about whatever it is not capable of doing, try doing whatever it is capable of, and seek ways to attain a deterrence capability commensurate with its aspirations. For that, reforming the Turkish armed forces with its all aspects would be a good point to start.

TURKEY'S ABDULLAH GÜL SHOULD RUN FOR THE UN SECRETARY GENERAL[44]

T he last month has clearly demonstrated how far Turkish diplomacy has come. *The New York Times* recently reported that no country was as outspoken as Turkey in terms of projecting a new image during the opening of the 65th UN General Assembly. But the *Times* was not applauding. Contrasting Turkish President Abdullah Gül's meeting with Iranian President Mahmoud Ahmadinejad and his unavailability to meet with Israeli President Shimon Peres, the paper portrayed Turkey as indifferent to U.S. efforts to reach peace in the Middle East and tackle the growing nuclear threat posed by Iran. On the other hand, Foreign Minister Ahmet Davutoğlu, with his head-spinning bilateral and multilateral meeting traffic, contributed to Turkey's assertive image as the new power broker in town.

Davutoğlu has clearly been identified as the author of the new Turkish foreign policy orientation and subsequently his popularity has increased exponentially inside and outside Turkey. But if Turkey's new diplomatic clout is to be institutionalized, it will have to develop beyond the person of Davutoğlu. Mobilizing the entire country for a commonly-appealing specific goal, such as the election of President Gül as UN secretary-general in 2016, will simultaneously institutionalize Turkish foreign policy while also moderating it.

Gül would make an excellent UN secretary-general, as he served as foreign minister, prime minister and president of a country which shares almost the entire UN agenda from promoting development in Africa to countering terrorism and incitement to hatred on the basis of religion and race. For the candidacy in 2016, Ankara would be

---

[44] First appeared in *Foreign Policy Magazine* on October 20, 2010.

required to pursue an intensive lobbying campaign not only at the UN, but also in every capital represented at the UN. This effort would temper Ankara's foreign policy as it should feel obliged not to disagree with the permanent members of the Security Council on issues that are sensitive to them. For instance, had such a campaign already been underway, Ankara would probably have avoided calling Beijing's handling of the riots in the East Turkistan genocide even if it had been the case. Ankara might have reacted in a less strident manner to the Israeli assault on the Mavi Marmara and the killing of Turkish civilians.

Such a role for a Turkish diplomat could also help Turkey cement its multifaceted policy in the foreign ministry bureaucracy as well. The current multidimensional foreign policy orientation or at least its current pace is unlikely to survive without the AK Party at the helm. In his article on the *Radikal* daily ("Davutoğlu's 'Self' Conception," 15 June 2010), Akif Beki, former adviser to PM Erdoğan, argued that Davutoğlu's policies were driven not by Turkey's national interests, but by an obsession with self-promotion. In fact, Turks should be thankful to Davutoğlu, as the idea of a multidimensional Turkish foreign policy is certainly unprecedented. Yet, it is peculiar for this to have been exclusively associated with the current AK Party government and the foreign minister. Its sustainability and applicability have not yet been tested by a possible replacement of the current government. Besides, all three of the Republican Peoples Party (CHP), the Nationalist Action Party (MHP), and the Peace and Democracy Party (BDP), which are represented in the Turkish parliament, have their own ideological limitations that would bar them from embracing such a foreign policy orientation.

Gül's campaign for UN secretary-general would promote Turkey's ability to be a power broker while simultaneously forcing Ankara to rationalize its policies and avoid sentimentalism when dealing with sensitive issues. This would strengthen its legitimacy, increase its viability and help spare the popular Davutoğlu from unfair allegations of self-promotion. In any event, even if Gül were not elected as the UN secretary-general, Turkey would benefit from the process in multiple ways.

ORGANIZATION OF THE ISLAMIC CONFERENCE

A Quest for Reform across the Muslim World[45]

T he despicable assassination in Pakistan of Punjab's provincial governor, allegedly due to his disparaging views on Islam, has once again prompted many to question what century they are living in.

The heinous attack on the Coptic Christian Church in Egypt's Alexandria by terrorists who either claim or are claimed to have done it in the name of Islam shows that multi-religious communities are not immune to incitements of violence. Similarly, in Tunisia the recent popular uprising because of socio-economic and political deprivation has led to the deaths of many civilians. These and many other unfortunate incidents taking place across what is dubbed the Muslim world make it ever more necessary for Muslims to proactively revisit their problems and come up with their own sustainable solutions. In this process, the onus is on reformist leaders, institutions and intergovernmental organizations, the most overarching one of which is the Organization of the Islamic Conference (OIC).

Ekmeleddin İhsanoğlu, secretary-general of the OIC, has recently authored a book titled *The Islamic World in the New Century: the Organisation of the Islamic Conference*. It has been published respectively by Hurst & Company of London in Europe, and by the Columbia University Press in the United States. The book explains the historical formation of the organization, which prides itself on being the sole intergovernmental representative of the world's Muslim population, and

---

[45] First appeared in *Today's Zaman* daily on January 24, 2011.

the process of transformation that this organization has gone through in terms of both its structure and vision. Since taking office in 2005, the OIC's first elected secretary-general, İhsanoğlu, has led this organization through major changes such as the revision of its charter and the adoption of a Ten-Year Programme of Action. Yet the single most daunting challenge for him remains to be convincing its some 57 member states to transform their lofty pledges into actual and sustainable action when it comes to countering extremism, injecting higher doses of moderation into the fabric of societies, ensuring respect for freedom of expression, human rights, rights of religious minorities and gender equality and attaining democratic governance, rule of law and accountability. Beside the unprecedented reforms he has introduced, the extent of the pressure that he puts on OIC member states to deliver on those pledges will define İhsanoğlu's legacy as the ninth secretary-general of the OIC.

Criticisms aimed at the OIC

Headquartered in Jeddah, Saudi Arabia, the OIC has long been criticized for being insignificant, if not incapable, in defending the interests of Muslims around the world, which it claims to be representing, as well as in resolving regional conflicts and in influencing the international decision-making process on regional or global matters. Naturally the harshest critics of the organization originate from societies who have high expectations of it. As İhsanoğlu acknowledges in the book, the OIC used to be heavy on rhetoric but less so on implementation. For the most of its history, it hardly remained relevant to the international system that it was supposed to be an active part of, and ideally influence. This failure resulted from a number of reasons, which included but were not limited to divergence among the member states politically, socio-economically, culturally and ideologically; cronyism in filling key administrative positions; lack of organizational vision commensurate with the changing international environment and globalization; and an underlying sense of reactive existence.

Ironically though, in recent years, the OIC has gained publicity and visibility in the Western media, especially in the United States, albeit increasingly negatively. It stems largely from the common tendency of normally distinct groups to demonize the OIC over their own concerns about the OIC-sponsored resolution titled "Combating Defamation of Religions." Civil rights groups accuse the OIC of trying to restrict freedom of expression by criminalizing any derogatory comment on religions and their revered figures and personalities. Freedom House suggests that the OIC initiative is an attempt to reshape international human rights instruments by linking "insult on religion" with "incitement to hatred" against the adherents of that religion, and as such to criminalize opinion. It is also concerned that the revision of law in that direction at the international level would legitimize blasphemy laws at the national level, thereby leaving freedom of expression at the mercy of the national authorities in any given country.

Beside civil rights groups, anti-Islamist groups and individual Islamophobes have spared no effort to spread their phobia by the way of demonizing the OIC, its secretary-general and its member states on the basis of that resolution. Critics of the resolution, going beyond the scope of the resolution, referred to honor killings, wife beating and female genital mutilation, among other inhumane practices stemming from local tribal cultures, as Islamic practices. The OIC has become an easy target to demonize Islam through, and the most convenient scapegoat for every "misbehavior" committed around the world by Muslims, whether in the name of Islam or not. The fact that the OIC has been at the forefront during contentions, from the cartoon crisis in Denmark to the minaret ban in Switzerland, makes it an even easier target to attack.

Transformation at the hands of Ihsanoglu

Amid these tensions, Secretary-General İhsanoğlu's structural and substantial overhaul of the OIC has gone mostly unnoticed both in the member and non-member states, if not deliberately ignored. Probably, his most important contribution was the shift of a paradigm that defines the very existence of the OIC. He has transformed the OIC's institutional purpose of existence from the one that is defined by the past grievances of its member states and that aims to reactively guard against the repetitions as such, to the one that is future oriented and that aims to proactively make the Muslim world a constructive and integral part of the international community. Accordingly, under İhsanoğlu, the OIC has prioritized the improvement of the socio-economic, legal and political environment in OIC member states. He argues that the future of the Muslim world depends on the development of principles of good governance, together with the establishment of a tradition of pluralistic democratic practices, respect for human rights, empowerment of women, rule of law, transparency and accountability of the administrative authority. With the adoption of a new OIC Charter in 2008, these values and concepts have officially entered into the lexicon of OIC member states.

Observers and OIC officials acknowledge that Secretary-General İhsanoğlu was influential in the preparation of the new charter by providing guidance. The OIC General Secretariat sources cite the inclusion of an independent and permanent human rights commission as an OIC organ in the new charter as an example of the many innovations that would not have been possible without his leadership and persistence.

Under the current circumstances, Secretary-General İhsanoğlu cannot be expected to pick on any OIC member state for its misconduct that paves the way for violations of human rights or an increase of religious extremism, just like the UN secretary-general is expected not to interfere in the domestic or foreign policies of UN member states. Understandably, he has to be aware of various sensitivities. However, at the same time he has to be vocally critical of such misconduct, even if doing so may make him less popular in the eyes of conservative elements of some OIC member states. There are a plethora of contentious issues from blasphemy laws to the treatment of homosexuals in which misconduct has so far not only tainted the image of OIC member states, but more importantly resulted in wider defamation of Islam. It is inconceivable that Islam does not provide solutions for these kinds of contentious issues, while it is the religion that enabled former slaves to lead nations some 1,400 years ago, whereas so-called beacons of democracy of our time have not received that level of inclusiveness and democracy even today. The OIC can greatly contribute to elucidating the true Islamic approach to any contemporary issue by revitalizing its subsidiary organ, the International Islamic Fiqh (Jurisprudence) Academy as an independent and scholarly institution, whose rulings are to be heeded by the entire Muslim world. It is quite promising that, as he indicates in the book, Secretary-General İhsanoğlu prioritizes the revitalization of the Fiqh Academy as an essential part of OIC reform.

The need for an Islamic jurisprudence authority

Current challenges faced by Muslim-majority countries, radicalization among Muslim youth in the West and the concurrent trend of Islamophobia, existence of radical elements to incite Muslim-Christian strife from the Philippines and Pakistan to Iraq, Egypt and all the way to West Africa necessitate the existence of a resourceful, proactive and moderate Islamic jurisprudence authority. In order to prove itself as a credible international organization, the OIC should assume wider and proactive roles in dealing with challenges and crises affecting the Muslim world. Secretary-General İhsanoğlu is said to have a strong conviction about the OIC's responsibilities in this regard. He has been pushing the limits of existing mechanisms to encourage the OIC membership to devise comprehensive approaches, particularly for Somalia and Afghanistan, by taking into account the OIC's comparative advantages.

In conclusion, the OIC symbolizes a colossal intergovernmental organization that has existed for more than 40 years, but only recently started to figure in international relations thanks to its reformist leadership. It has the potential to lead democratic change across the Muslim world and contribute to international peace and security. However, for that to happen, Secretary-General İhsanoğlu needs to be more of a general when it comes to convincing member states to deliver on their respective pledges to support the new reformist vision of the organization. Otherwise, not only does the OIC run the risk of regressing back to oblivion once this reformist and visionary man completes his tenure, but the world community will also lose a formidable partner.

IN THE AFTERMATH OF THE THIRD ARAB REVOLT

What can Turkey do for the Middle East's freedom-seeking peoples?[46]

About a century ago, Arabs revolted against the Ottoman Empire in a campaign masterminded and guided by the Europeans in order to allegedly liberate themselves from the Turks. About half a century ago, Arabs revolted against the Europeans in a campaign led by nationalist Arab leaders in order to liberate themselves from their European colonizers.

Today, Arabs are revolting against their leaders in a campaign led by ordinary citizens in order to liberate themselves from leaders that have long been backed by the Europeans and the US—and they have just deposed one in Egypt who had long seemed to be the most invincible. What is odd, if the foregoing is not, is that today Europeans are suggesting that Arabs should take Turkey as a model for development and democratization. A recent *Financial Times* editorial has suggested that the European governments help the Arab countries to evolve into free societies following the example of Turkey. Perhaps, it is better just to leave the Arabs alone, and let them figure out the best way forward for their countries.

However, the frequent references to the so-called Turkish model in the aftermath of the third Arab revolt have brought to the fore once again Turkey's potential role in the democratic transformation of that region by presenting a model of success, which has combined Islam and

---

46 First appeared in *Today's Zaman* daily on February 14, 2011.

democracy. Can Turkey really serve as a model for the Arab countries in the Middle East?

Various commentators have readily suggested that the Egyptian generals follow the example of their Turkish counterparts without questioning whether it should be the army generals leading Egypt's transition in the post-revolution period. Without implicitly condoning the meddling of the Turkish army, or of the Egyptian army for that matter, with politics, the United Kingdom's former Secretary of State for Foreign and Commonwealth Affairs David Miliband and *Newsweek*'s Fareed Zakaria suggested that the Egyptian generals emulate their Turkish counterparts in terms of stepping back into their barracks after their intervention in country's political process. Similarly, Soner Çağaptay of the Washington Institute for Near East Policy praised the Turkish military for serving as an effective restraint on the civilian governments.

As Steven Cook of the Council on Foreign Relations rightly put it, however, modernization and democratization in Turkey have developed not by the grace and leadership of the army, but despite the rogue elements within the army, which has traditionally dominated politics. Three-and-a-half different military coups, one of which led to the execution of a democratically elected prime minister and two ministers of his government on the charges of treason, speak well to that fact. So obviously, it is certain that with its historical attitude toward civilian governments, the Turkish military cannot set a commendable example for the armies in any of the Arab nations seeking democracy and freedom. Yet, it may certainly do so if it acknowledges its rightful place subordinate to the democratically elected civilian government, and acts accordingly. Thankfully, it seems to gradually be becoming the case in Turkey.

A model of success?

And how about the civilian governments of Turkey, and specifically the Justice and Development Party (AK Party) government? Do they provide a model of success for the Arab governments? Is the AK Party government in a position to advise its Arab counterparts on the way forward toward creating democratic and free societies? It goes without saying that the civilian governments that ruled before the AK Party came to power and under the heavy control of the rogue elements within the Turkish military can present only bad examples for their counterparts in the region. After all, it was the complacency of these civilian governments that enabled those rogue elements to roll time back for Turkish democracy. Yet, the case seems somewhat different with regard to the AK Party government's ability to present a model of success.

According to Robert Fisk of *The Independent*, Turkey, with the AK Party government at the helm, presents the ultimate success model where Islam and democracy coexist. Similarly, Joshua Walker of Brandeis University thinks that its unprecedented economic success and hyperactive diplomatic dynamism has brought Turkey back to the region, from which it has long remained detached, as "kingmaker."

Probably, such optimistic views of the Turkish model have led Prime Minister Recep Tayyip Erdoğan to join President Barack Obama in calling upon Egyptian President Hosni Mubarak to listen to the demands of the Egyptian people, do the right thing and step down. Perceiving it as interference in Egypt's internal affairs, Cairo was quick to react to the prime minister's advisory comment.

Whether such a call amounts to interference in another country's internal affairs is open to interpretation. After all, as foreseen by the UN agreements, the protection and promotion of human rights transcend the national boundaries as the lack or violation of fundamental human rights constitute the core cause of extremism and violence, which consequently pose threats to regional and global security. However, such a reaction to the prime minister's remarks clarifies one thing, and it is that the contemporary political structures of the Middle Eastern states do not tolerate any sort of political engagement with them that defies the regional and national status quos, which were established during the Cold War and are of either a patrimonial, nationalist or so-called Islamist nature. Nor will it be any different so long as the same political elites rule, even if the leader is no longer in control.

Under the current circumstances, the best Turkey can do for the freedom-seeking peoples of the Middle East is not to advise them on the way forward, but to re-energize its own political and economic reform process, which would ensure individual freedoms and respect for human rights, as well as respect for multiculturalism and minority rights to an extent that would dwarf even those available in the European countries. Doing so, Turkey will not only get the Arabs to question how Turkey has transformed itself in a period as short as a decade, but also inspire them to build their own types of democracy in a similar fashion. Today it is more obvious than ever that the Arabs who revolutionized their countries need, not advice, but inspiration, and they realize that they may suffer from the same problem a century from now unless they seize control of their countries today.

WHAT IS IN IT FOR THE AMERICANS?

A UN Resolution as a US Public
Diplomacy Nullifier[47]

Rumor has it that when Canadians travel abroad, especially in the Middle East and increasingly in Western Europe after the Bush administration's decision to invade Iraq, they tend to wear something authentic to the distant corners of their country to recognize each other as true Canadians in foreign lands. The reason is that American tourists also wear outfits or accessories featuring the traditional Canadian maple leaf when traveling abroad to pose as Canadians and spare themselves from harsh reactions from locals or at least from unfriendly stares in countries where they travel.

On Feb. 18, when US Ambassador to the UN Susan Rice raised her hand with a grin on her face to block the adoption of the Security Council resolution that condemned the illegal Israeli settlements in the occupied Palestinian territories, she created yet another reason for American tourists abroad to prefer outfits with the Canadian maple leaf. The resolution, which 127 countries co-sponsored and 14 members of the Security Council supported, was rejected only because the United States opposed it.

This result affects the United States in a much more negative way than it does Israel. From Casablanca to Jakarta, every single Muslim detests the United States for unconditionally, unfairly and shamelessly supporting Israel to the detriment of the Palestinians under any circumstances. At the same time, some of those very same people might even be admiring Israel for its ability to manipulate the US, a gigantic super power, to fulfill Israel's each and every wish. In the end, it is

---

[47] First appeared in *Today's Zaman* daily on March 6, 2011.

not Israel but the US that gets the blame for the failure of every attempt to resolve the Israeli-Palestinian conflict.

The US government's unconditional support for Israel

So, what is in it for the Americans? What benefit do they get from their government's unconditional support for Israel? These questions have long occupied the minds of many Americans, including Jewish Americans. There is no point, however, in asking these questions, as it is a futile exercise given the emotional, religious and racial attachment of many US legislators and policy makers to the State of Israel. Whether such an attachment is good or not is one thing, but it is a reality that anyone has to take into account before expecting a favor from a sitting US government on any issue pertaining to Israel, or the Palestinian territories, for that matter. A Jewish American, Ami Kaufman of *The Jerusalem Post*, charges President Obama with keeping the "good old" paradigm of "Israel + US = everlasting occupation," despite his promise of change. As is the case with the +972 Israeli online magazine, some go even further describing the situation rather harshly, as the Israeli occupation of the US Congress. By this token, so long as this occupation continues, so will the Israeli occupation of the Palestinian territories. Similarly, some argue that even the Israeli Knesset is more critical of the Israeli government's practices than the US Congress is, while others argue that certain legislators in the US Congress are more Israeli than American. Under these circumstances, it would be a pipe dream to expect President Obama to overhaul the traditional US position on the Israeli-Palestinian issue.

Nevertheless, the decision to abstain on, if not support, the resolution in the Security Council was more of a strategic one. What did the American people earn when the US blocked the adoption of the Security Council resolution condemning illegal Israeli settlement activities? In fact, the US could have simply abstained and let the resolution pass, thereby adding only one more to many UN resolutions that have so far condemned illegal Israeli activities, and which Israel has apparently not cared a bit about. By so doing, the US could keep alive not only the hope that the Israel-Palestinian negotiations may eventually result in a sustainable peace, but also the hope for change, which President Obama promised to bring about.

One legitimate question may be whether the content of the resolution was something that the US was diametrically opposed to. The resolution reaffirmed that the "Israeli settlements established in the Palestinian Territory occupied since 1967, including East Jerusalem, are illegal and constitute a major obstacle to the achievement of a just, lasting and comprehensive peace"; reiterated the "demand that Israel, the occupying power, immediately and completely ceases all settlement activities in the Occupied Palestinian Territory, including East Jerusalem, and that it fully respect all of its legal obligations in this regard"; and urged the "intensification of international and regional diplomatic efforts to support and invigorate the peace process towards the achievement of a comprehensive, just and lasting peace in the Middle East." As such, the resolution, which was supported by the United Kingdom, France and Germany as well, did not seem to contradict the previously adopted UN resolutions.

Nor did Ambassador Rice criticize the content of the resolution when she explained the US opposition to it after the vote. Instead, she said that the US thought this resolution risked hardening the positions of the Israelis and the Palestinians, thereby encouraging them to stay away from direct negotiations. In this regard, it is important to note that while 129 states, the EU, the US and the International Court of Justice along with many Jewish Americans and Israelis call the Israeli settlements illegal, the official US statements call these settlements "illegitimate—not authorized by law" as opposed to "illegal—contrary to law, or forbidden by law." Although she meticulously used the words and spoke delicately, what the entire world and all Arabs and Palestinians so bluntly saw was that the resolution failed only because the US vetoed it.

So, there remains only one possible explanation as to why the US is going to such an extent to humiliate itself before the international community when it comes to Israeli settlement activities, completely diminishing the hope for a new beginning between the US and Muslim communities around the world, which President Obama himself promised in his historic Cairo speech. In addition, when he stated during his address to the UN General Assembly in September 2010 that he wished to welcome Palestine as a sovereign state to the next opening of the General Assembly one year later, President Obama, the so-called "leader of the free world," thrilled the Arabs. Yet, the recent US veto sent one clear message: No matter who the US president is and no matter what he or she says, it is Israel whom the US will side with. It is so, even if it is the Israel of the racist governments such as that of Benjamin Netanyahu and Avigdor Lieberman. That message multiplies any US public diplomacy effort by zero.

Finally, one should realize that what is sweeping the entire Arab world today is not a Facebook or Twitter revolution, but the Arab youth's revolution, which they carry out through the use of Facebook, Twitter and all other sorts of technologies. It appears there is absolutely no reason to believe that this youth cannot and would not use the same frustration, anger, dynamism and skills to undermine US interests regionally and internationally, if they happen to believe that Washington will never, ever care about their concerns vis-à-vis Israel's actions. So, what is in it for the Americans, when their government is made to look like it supports Israel blindly and unconditionally? A lot is there in quite a negative way.

THE REAL AND OPPORTUNITY COSTS OF THE LATE TURKISH FOREIGN POLICY[48]

There are less than 90 days left before Turkey's upcoming parliamentary elections on June 12, and it is almost certain that Prime Minister Recep Tayyip Erdoğan's Justice and Development Party (AK Party) government will easily proceed to its third term in office, provided that the elections take place freely, fairly and in a secure environment.

So, an important matter of curiosity for voters is not whether the incumbent AK Party government will make it to another term, but whether it will be able to increase its electoral support from the 47 percent of all votes it received during the last general elections. Similarly of interest is whether the Nationalist Movement Party (MHP) will be able to secure any seat at all in Parliament given its rapidly shrinking support base, and whether the accidental leader of the main opposition party, Kemal Kılıçdaroğlu of the Republican People's Party (CHP), will be able to remain at the helm of his party after another electoral defeat. Nevertheless, all three of these issues are becoming more or less predictable as election day draws closer.

However, what is and has always been the real matter of curiosity in Turkish politics is how the prime minister forms his or her new Cabinet. In this case, which ministers will Prime Minister Erdoğan retain? Which new figures will he bring on board to replace those who are to willingly or unwillingly give up their respective posts? Even though it may be argued that this practice has resulted in cronyism in Turkish politics, as it would in any other democracy, it gives the prime minister a chance to recalculate the real costs and opportunity costs

---

[48] First appeared in *Today's Zaman* daily on March 30, 2011.

incurred by his earlier Cabinet appointments. Therefore, with a view to improving Turkey's overall foreign policy performance in his third term, maximizing the fulfillment of certain ministers' potential and minimizing the avoidable irritation caused by Ankara's heightened diplomatic dynamism, Prime Minister Erdoğan may want to reconsider certain appointment decisions.

The AK Party government's second term in office has been starkly different from its first term in terms of European Union accession and in terms of the intensity of negotiations in that direction. According to a recent poll by the Turkish-German Foundation for Education and Scientific Research (TAVAK), 60 percent of Turks are opposed to Turkey's EU membership. While the credibility of such a poll can always be questioned, it is obvious today that many Turks seem to lack any enthusiasm for EU membership. It is partly because of the EU's erratic attitude toward Turkey; the consistent opposition by the current governments in France and Germany; the AK Party government's domestic preoccupations, ranging from questionable closure cases against it to coup attempts by rogue elements within the army; and burning regional and international problems such as the question of nuclear Iran, a matter in which Ankara adopted a position that was contrary to that of its European counterparts. Under these circumstances, it would be unfair to expect the AK Party government to have been as dynamic in its second term in its pursuit of EU accession as it was in its first term.

The role of the chief EU negotiator

However, there has never been a real discussion about the performance of Turkey's chief EU negotiator in discharging his responsibilities and duties and keeping public enthusiasm on the subject high. Oddly enough, according to a report in the *Hürriyet* daily, the chief negotiator has recently reacted to the military operations led by the EU countries such as France, United Kingdom and Italy against the Gaddafi regime in Libya by suggesting, "We would not leave our Libyan brethren to the European Gaddafis." It is yet to be seen whether Turks will debate this specific element of Turkey's EU accession efforts in the coming weeks and months. Also yet to be seen is how Prime Minister Erdoğan will act in his third term in order to boost Turkey's negotiations with the EU.

Even more critical is the opportunity cost borne by Turkish foreign policy due to the appointment of Professor Ahmet Davutoğlu as foreign minister, and consequently by Ankara's preference to actively pursue a visible political engagement with its immediate neighbors. As economist John Stuart Mill, who developed the concept, put it: the opportunity cost is the next-best choice that one foregoes while picking among several mutually exclusive choices. In this case, the next best choice that Prime Minister Erdoğan has foregone was to keep Professor Davutoğlu as his and the president's chief foreign policy adviser with extended oversight and mandate. Consequently, the next best choice that Ankara has foregone was to focus exclusively on its socio-economic and cultural engagement with its immediate neighbors while pursuing a "behind-the-scenes" political engagement with them.

Davutoğlu's role

These two next best choices, if taken, could have provided Turkey with a number of advantages. First of all, Professor Davutoğlu would not have been exposed to widespread and unfair criticism as the man behind Turkey's alleged shift of axis from the West to the (Middle) East. Secondly, he would be able to deepen Turkey's political engagement with its neighbors through silent (behind the scenes) diplomacy, which he had already proven effective when he spearheaded the secret talks between Syria and Israel. Thirdly, as an independent thinker, he would have enjoyed a wider freedom to make mistakes, since his every action and statement would not be under public scrutiny, while the opposite is the case as long as he is the foreign minister. In addition, free from the day-to-day and bureaucratic duties of a foreign minister, Davutoğlu would be in a better position to oversee not just the foreign ministry, but all elements of the state apparatus, improving Turkey's foreign policy, both regionally and further afield. Moreover, mainly through civil society initiatives and people-to-people interactions, Ankara would have continued to pursue more socio-economic, cultural and humanitarian engagement with its immediate neighbors

as well as its distant counterparts, while continuing its political engagement with them behind the scenes.

However, since Professor Davutoğlu became a foreign minister
in 2009, not only has he brought the regional political engagements
he was involved in to the fore, but also he has been exposed as a clear
target for those looking for a scapegoat for every foreign policy move
by Ankara that they find irritating. Furthermore, as a foreign minister, he came into a position where he has become both the master-
mind and the chief executive of Turkey's foreign policies; as a result,
Turkey has started to rather more readily venture into certain political
issues from which it would or could otherwise stay away. Similarly,
Foreign Minister Davutoğlu's sudden emergence on the international
scene as an unusually passionate leader and his growing popularity in
the Middle East as such may have led Prime Minister Erdoğan to feel
obliged to weigh in on foreign policy issues more than he used to and
more than he would do otherwise, thereby paving the way for a confrontational and emotional foreign policy approach. Plus, some leaders' tendency for a selective reading of their history and nationalist
myths that surround it may have led contemporary Ankara to aspire
beyond what it can realistically achieve under the current circumstances and in the foreseeable future.

In the final analysis, as Prime Minister Erdoğan proceeds towards
his third term in the office, there are a number of challenges that his
government will be facing, probably the most formidable of which
will be maintaining its popularity and credibility as a progressive democratic government as well as a reliable international and regional partner. Politically unrivaled and seasoned thanks to the past two terms,
the AK Party government may naturally be tempted to be more assertive and unyielding. Moreover, in the face of consistent resistance from
such EU capitals as Berlin and Paris to Turkey's EU membership, the
AK Party government may further disengage from Turkey's quest for
full membership. Similarly, Ankara's interest in taking a publicly active
role in the resolution of political turmoil in its neighborhood, such as
a mediatory role between the Gaddafi regime and its opponents, may
get Turkey unnecessarily bogged down in prolonged conflicts in

which the real parties whose interests need to be reconciled are not actually the ones that are fighting. In light of these challenges, the upcoming parliamentary elections and his almost certain electoral victory provides Prime Minister Erdoğan with a unique opportunity compensate for the real and opportunity costs incurred by recent Turkish foreign policy during his second term in office.

WHY DO THEY LIE ABOUT FETHULLAH GÜLEN?[49]

For many of those who have admired the ideas of the scholar Fethullah Gülen and at varying levels took part in fulfilling those ideas for the service of humanity, it has been a lamentable fact that the international community does not know as much as it should about either Gülen or the worldwide Hizmet (Service) Movement he has inspired.

From a causality perspective, it was he who masterminded the idea of teaching the children of all nationalities, races, creeds and religions a common language of peace, love and harmony, so that as responsible adults of tomorrow they could build a better and more peaceful world. It was this idea and his selfless efforts that have led to the mobilization of millions of volunteers across the world to found modern and secular schools and intercultural dialogue centers as well as humanitarian aid organizations in more than 140 countries, including in impoverished and conflict-stricken places such as Haiti, Darfur and Afghanistan. Gülen was the first Muslim scholar to publicly denounce the Sept. 11 attacks as an act of terrorism, and going even further challenged its perpetrators on Islamic grounds by saying, "A terrorist cannot be a Muslim, nor can a true Muslim be a terrorist." All in all, given the magnitude of his service to humanity, many believed that Gülen should have long ago been awarded the Nobel Peace Prize. Yet, his strict principle of not promoting himself, accepting any credit for the good works attributed to him, and actually giving the credit to the volunteers of those works, has so far kept him away from the attention of the international community. In fact, many have been decorated with such

---

[49] First appeared in *Today's Zaman* daily on April 19, 2011.

awards for merely dreaming and speaking about global peace, while over the past several decades Gülen has been patiently laying the foundations for such peace to actually come about.

Apparently, this will no longer be the case thanks to his opponents, who have been systematically flooding the Internet and print media with wild allegations about him and the movement. After all, who in his or her sane mind would hear such a wild allegation as Gülen being the "most dangerous Islamist on Earth," and not bother to do a Google search for "Fethullah Gülen"? Then, what he or she will find, in addition to some more of those allegations, is rather scholarly research on Gülen's thoughts and practice, some of which include Jill Carroll's *A Dialogue of Civilizations: Gülen's Islamic Ideals and Humanistic Discourse*, Helen Rose Ebaugh's *The Gülen Movement: A Sociological Analysis of a Civic Movement Rooted in Moderate Islam*, Muhammed Çetin's *The Gülen Movement: Civic Service Without Borders*, and John Esposito and Ihsan Yilmaz's *Islam and Peacebuilding: Gülen Movement Initiatives*. More importantly one would find Gülen's very own writings and statements as well as the actual works produced by volunteers inspired by his ideals. So, bringing him to the attention of those who would otherwise not know anything about Gülen and the global civic movement he has inspired, Gülen's adversaries are inadvertently making him ever more popular and well-known worldwide through their systematic defamation campaign. In this regard, one should expect Gülen soon to be recognized by the international community for his contributions to world peace. Then, one should also expect his adversaries to allege in self-denial that Gülen himself had designed this defamation campaign in order to attract global public attention.

But the question is, why do they make such wild allegations about Gülen and the Hizmet Movement, which, based on all available and credible evidence, seem to be unsubstantiated and untrue beyond any reasonable doubt? Subsequently, in what ways do they carry out their defamation of Gülen as an individual and the millions of people from different nationalities, races, creeds and religions, whose voluntary service makes up what is called the Hizmet Movement? At this point, one should note that as Kerim Balcı of *Today's Zaman* rightly puts it, those allegations take different, and often self-contradicting, forms depending on the perceived fears of the target audience. For instance, if the target audience is Russian, then Gülen and his initiatives are accused of being the US's and more specifically the CIA's designs. If the audience is Americans and Christians, then he is accused of being an Islamist terrorist aspiring to establish a global Islamic empire. If it is the audience is Jewish, then he is portrayed as being anti-Semitic. If it is anti-democratic Arab leaders, then he is argued to be not only a Turkish nationalist bent on reviving the Ottoman Empire, but also an agent of the Greater Middle East Project by the US, that foresees the overthrow of those leaders. In terms of methodology, just like John Mearsheimer describes the different forms of public lies, these allegations too vary from outright false statements to the true facts spun in a way that would lead the target audience to make erroneous conclusions about Gülen and the Hizmet Movement.

In the American context, they lie about Gülen and his work, because the latter stands as living examples that repudiate the deliberately produced stereotypes of Islam being inherently violent and hostile, and of Muslims being a potential threat to the so-called "Judeo-Christian" nature of American society. This in turn threatens the socio-economic and political interests of those who have not only consistently injected such stereotypes into the American conscience, but also cashed in heavily on the fears fed by these stereotypes by manipulating America's domestic and foreign policies accordingly.

Defamation of Islam and demonization of Muslims in the American conscience

As Edward Said puts it in his *Covering Islam*, for Americans, Islam and Muslims have been no more than mere elements within and of political and security concerns by the US; not because they are indifferent to learning about Islam and Muslims, but because the news coverage and the so-called expert analyses of the incidents taking place within Muslim communities had often engendered too simplistic and rather negative views of Islam and Muslims in the minds of Americans. According to the prevailing discourse, Islam was, and according to a considerable number of Americans still is, a heretical religion/cult predominant across regions where the US has massive political and economic interests. It was the system that oppressed women, restricted freedom of thought and religion and encouraged its adherents to fight Jews and Christians. Academics like Samuel Huntington and Bernard Lewis, as well as commentators such as Daniel Pipes, built up such a skewed image of Islam inch by inch over the last several decades.

When Lewis argued in *Islam and the West* that history was simply a struggle between Christians and Muslims for world domination and in *What Went Wrong?: The Clash Between Islam and Modernity in the Middle East* that Muslims are enraged by the West in general and the US in particular because Islam lacks the cluster of "Western" values such as democracy, human rights and freedoms, he was basically producing pseudo-academic arguments for the disposal of the like-minded academics, policy makers, journalists and opinion leaders. Along similar lines, in his book, *The Clash of Civilizations: Remaking of World Order*, Huntington coined the concept of "the bloody borders of Islam," suggesting that at any given time most of the conflicts across the globe either involved, or took place within "Muslim" communities, because Islam was inherently violent and not open to pluralism. Following this line, Pipes and many other like-minded pundits/columnists in prominent American newspapers and analysts at influential think tanks have frequently written rather short "opinion" pieces as well as "policy" papers propagating the same argument. Consequently, the American public has to a great extent digested this false image of Islam and Muslims. In his recent opinion piece titled "Ambitious Turkey," Pipes' use of heavily loaded and defamatory descriptions such as "the tyrannical, Islamist, and conspiracist mentality generally dominating Muslim peoples," well illustrates the case in point.

So, for Americans, who have so long been bombarded with the violent images and perceptions of Muslims, Gülen and the work he inspires is an unexpected but most welcome surprise. However, for those who have for decades portrayed Islam as anything and everything that the so-called "Judeo-Christian" nature of American society is not, Gülen, his ideas, the people who are inspired by his ideas and the humanitarian-educational work that they have produced are understandably posing a threat. Such a threat exists not because of the very nature of the work that they produce, but because it defies the deliberately constructed and established image of the "Muslim" as a savage from the Middle Ages who is inherently against the Western way of life and eager to wage a "jihad" against Americans.

Consider the following cases: (1) Following protests and Quran burning in the United States hundreds of "Muslims" in Afghanistan resort to violence, killing seven UN workers; and (2) "Muslim" civil society and humanitarian aid organizations, including both men and women, were among the first to reach "non-Muslim" Haitians immediately after the devastating earthquake, serving 40,000 Haitians hot meals and constructing a hospital in Port-au-Prince to meet the medical needs of impoverished Haitians. Or, (1) An "Islamic" leader vows to wipe Israel off the map (possibly by nuking it), as well as destroying its main sponsor, which he calls the Great Satan; and (2) An "Islamic" scholar publicly suggesting that any humanitarian assistance to Palestinians should be delivered through coordination with Israeli authorities and without breaching international law. Or, (1) "Muslim" children in Hezbollah camps in southern Lebanon are indoctrinated with fundamentalist "Islamic" ideology and receiving armed training with AK-47s in their hands; and (2) "Muslim" students in cooperation with their non-Muslim counterparts from around the world compete in the international science competitions and undertake research in such vital fields as curing cancer, eradicating poverty, preventing environmental pollution and overcoming global energy shortages. The latter example in each pairing is what Gülen and the movement engenders. Quite understandably, in a country like the United States, where the news is more of an instrument manufactured to manipulate public opinion to accept certain socio-economic and political practices, any development that challenges the established "negative" image of Islam and Muslims would be unwelcome by those who have a vested interest in the perpetuation of such a negative image.

How they try to defame Gülen

In this regard, there are two major allegations that are currently employed in the United States by Gülen opponents in order to discredit and cause fear mongering about him: One is that the charter schools opened in various states by Turkish-Americans are connected to Gülen, and that they are spreading "Islamic fundamentalism;" and the other is that Gülen is behind the ongoing Ergenekon investigation in Turkey, which has led to the detainment of many active duty and retired army officers as well as journalists. The first allegation begs the following question: Would the US authorities that have authorized and overseen these schools, not be aware of any such wrongdoing, if any? The second allegation is a mere distortion of the facts on the ground. Currently there are 26 journalists being detained in relation to the Ergenekon investigation, and none of them are being held because they exercised their freedom of expression, but rather because of their suspected involvement in verified coup plans that aimed to overthrow Turkey's democratically elected government. In fact, it is similar to the case of *The New York Times'* Judith Miller, who was sentenced to 18 months in jail in 2005 due to her involvement in the leaking of an active CIA officer's identity. One wonders if anybody then opposed the court decision by arguing that she was exercising her freedom of expression as a journalist. Similarly, was a Hutu radio host exercising his freedom of expression when he incited his fellow Hutus to massacre Tutsis ahead of what eventually amounted to the Rwanda genocide? Furthermore, even if a prosecutor or a police officer who happens to admire Gülen and is involved in the Ergenekon investigation went rogue and broke the law, what does it have to do with Gülen himself or the millions of others who admire his ideals?

In the final analysis, the real threat perceived by accomplices of Gülen opponents, in major capitals including Washington, D.C., actually seems to be the possibility of Turkey's Ergenekon investigation inspiring and encouraging peoples of other countries, as well as investigating deep state arrangements that have long been running in the veins of their own societies. For them, the threat is clear and imminent: Apparently, Turkey is no longer the old Turkey, where it was easy to deal with the "real" owners of the regime, meaning corrupt military generals, bureaucrats and politicians; but with its growing civil society and strengthening economy, it is no longer easy or possible to manipulate Turkey. What if the same happens in other countries that have long been in the orbit of special interest groups within these major capitals? More importantly, what if their own masses mobilize to break the glass ceilings and claim their rightful share of political and economic resources that have traditionally remained under the monopoly of these special interest groups? Speaking of a so-called "Islamist" threat in the United States, the real questions that disturb the adversaries of Gülen are the following: What if Muslim Americans want to serve as judges on the US Supreme Court, and as senators and representatives in Congress? What if they want to command the US armies as generals? What if they want to manage giant American corporations? And, what if, one day, one of them were to become the president of the United States? What is at stake with the democratization of Turkey is quite high and critical for those whose interests have depended on it remaining an anti-democratic satellite state. It is only normal then that in all their despair, hopelessness and panic, adversaries of Gülen both inside and outside Turkey are trying to demonize him, for he and the millions inspired by him are in fact behind the democratization of their country.

MISREPRESENTATION OF FETHULLAH GÜLEN IN ENGLISH-LANGUAGE MEDIA[50]

For an average American and European reader, the name Fethullah Gülen may not necessarily be a familiar one. That Gülen is a scholar who has inspired millions of volunteers across the world to engage in educational and intercultural initiatives, that he publically denounced Osama bin Laden for the shame that the latter brought upon Islam, and that he advocated Turkey's full membership in the European Union at a time when his counterparts opposed it by simply viewing the EU as a Christian club with Zionist touches, are not something that the average reader would know, either. Recently, it seems that the English-language media, and particularly American and European media, are increasingly covering Gülen and the worldwide civil society initiatives he has inspired.

However, the language in general and the way certain politically significant words are used in some of this media coverage are somewhat problematic in the sense that they fail to present the full picture about Gülen, if not deliberately create doubts and prejudices about him. A recent *Financial Times* report titled "Turkey: Inspiring or insidious" by Delphine Strauss as well as reports by two Turkey-based correspondents, Amberin Zaman of *The Economist* and Claire Berlinski of the Manhattan Institute for Policy Research, are quite indicative of such a tendency. In so doing, they appear to appeal to a basic human instinct of fearing what one cannot comprehend, contain or control, and as a result, developing a hostile attitude toward it. These reports also consistently belittle Turkey's efforts to reckon with its antidemocratic past through the Ergenekon investigation on the alleged involve-

---

[50] First appeared in *Today's Zaman* daily on May 15, 2011.

ments of active duty and retired army and police officers, journalists, bureaucrats and others in coup plots, thereby raising doubts about their journalistic objectivity and neutrality on either subject.

Financial Times' insidious coverage

"But in Turkey, opinion is sharply divided between those who see Mr. Gülen as a force for social mobility and tolerance, and those who suspect he is insidiously undermining the country's secular foundations," writes Strauss. First of all, it is hard to say that opinion in Turkey is sharply divided with regard to Gülen. As of today, there has been no poll carried out by Turkish researchers or authorities to determine public opinion about him. However, according to a poll conducted by Professor Akbar Ahmed of American University, for his book, *Journey into Islam: the Crisis of Globalization*, 84 percent of Turks have a favorable opinion of Gülen and the initiatives he has inspired. In addition, a poll carried out by the magazines *Foreign Policy* of the United States and *Prospect* of the United Kingdom demonstrated that Gülen is the world's top public intellectual. In the aftermath of this poll, some apparently unpleased with the result claimed that the "followers" of Gülen had rigged the poll. One wonders what the difference is between simply voting for someone and rigging a poll. Would one of the candidates not eventually come first in the poll? If another candidate was voted the world's top public intellectual, then would his or her supporters not have "rigged" but "voted" for that candidate? At the end of the day, any poll can be misleading depending on how one designs it. Perhaps, it is about time to carry out multiple polls in Turkey by various pollsters in order to assess whether opinion about Gülen is "sharply divided" or if it is just a small marginal group that opposes him and the initiatives he has inspired.

Strauss further suggests, "His followers have been described as 'Islamic Jesuits'—and as Turkey's equivalent of Opus Dei." Again, this is another simplistic method increasingly utilized in order to reduce Gülen to just another charismatic religious leader, and his admirers as blind followers of that leader. It is also a somewhat derogatory description of them, which aims to inject into the reader's mind doubt about their true intentions. The word "follower" has quite a loaded meaning and can be easily exploited. What does it mean to follow? Follow to achieve what, or get to where? Who is more of a "follower"—the young college graduate who foregoes job offers with lucrative salaries and volunteers to go to a country which he or she cannot even point out on the map, in order to help that country's children receive a modern education; the woman who donates everything, including her beautiful keepsakes and jewelry, to support the start-up of a school, which she is most unlikely to visit in her lifetime; the Assyrian Christian priest who is thankful for and supports Gülen's interfaith dialogue efforts; the Jewish businessman who vouches for the apolitical nature of a Gülen-inspired Turkish school in a foreign country; an atheist writer who participates in the activities of the Journalists and Writers Foundation (GYV), which is associated with Gülen; the Turkish diplomat who is proud to see a Gülen-inspired school in a country where even the Turkish state does not have official representation; or, one who follows Gülen's twitter account? So, who is a "follower" of Gülen? What does it take to become a so-called "Gülen follower"?

How many unsubstantiated allegations make one credible premise?

Moreover, what does it mean "… have been described as Islamic Jesuits?" Who is it that makes such a description? It may well be one of those currently detained because of alleged involvement in alleged coup plots, or someone who is unhappy with the ongoing Ergenekon investigation on the alleged outlawed network nested in the army, police, bureaucracy and other parts of the state apparatus. Why would the *Financial Times* use such an unsubstantiated allegation? Does such a statement have any credibility without a reference to its source? As it stands, it is hardly different from mere defamation of Gülen and his admirers under the disguise of "neutral" reporting. This defamation is further deepened by likening what is called the Gülen movement to Opus Dei, which is known to Westerners as a secretive, powerful and controversial formation within the Catholic Church.

After all, how credible would it be if a newspaper report read, "It is widely believed that the *Financial Times* and the other media outlets owned by Jewish media moguls like Rupert Murdock are intentionally misrepresenting Fethullah Gülen and his admirers, whom they think are the driving force behind Prime Minister Recep Tayyip Erdoğan's Justice and Development Party [AK Party] government, which they adamantly want to get rid of due to Israel's growing uneasiness with Turkey under that government." Just like the *Financial Times*' quote of unsubstantiated allegations about Gülen by unreferenced sources, this quotation would not have any credibility, either.

Perhaps the answer as to why the *Financial Times* is using such language is in the report itself: "Yet there is little doubt that the movement [Gülen] inspires is now an important force shaping Turkish society, part of a broader evolution in which leaders emerging from a religious, business-minded middle class are gradually eclipsing older, fiercely secular, elites." Objective observers of Turkey would rather say, "Older, fiercely secular, elites, who have traditionally dominated the economic and political spaces as well as the state apparatus, who did not refrain from resorting to anti-democratic and criminal practices from targeted killings and massacres of civilians to military coups ousting democratically elected governments, and some of whom, as a result of recent democratic reforms and transformations in state institutions, are being investigated for their alleged involvement in these criminal acts."

Moreover, Strauss argues, with regard to the Gülen-inspired schools, "Though officials from the traditionally secularist foreign ministry have tended to keep their distance from Gülen-inspired projects, ministers appear to view them as a useful extension of Turkey's soft power." Here too, the report seems like it is aiming to instill two misleading perceptions about these schools: One is that the Turkish diplomatic corps is generally not sympathetic to the contributions these schools are making to the emergence of a positive image of Turkey abroad; and the other is that they are instruments of a new Turkish foreign policy orientation that is associated with the AK Party government. First of all, it is increasingly evident that in most of the countries where these schools operate, Turkish diplomats, regardless of them being conservative (if there are any) or secular, seem to publicly appreciate these schools or other Gülen-inspired initiatives. Unless Strauss knows of something more than meets the eye, then the *Financial Times* reporter's allegation is wrong at best, if not intentionally misleading. Secondly, when the first Gülen-inspired school was established outside Turkey, those with whom the new Turkish foreign policy orientation is associated today were still either students at college or junior professionals in bureaucracy and academia. So, unless they miraculously initiated these schools some 20 years ago in order to lay the groundwork for the foreign policy orientation that Turkey pursues today, the view that these schools are "extensions" of Turkey's soft power, which the *Financial Times* report attributes to AK Party government ministers, is as well misleading, if not purposefully trying to give these apolitical civil society initiatives a political meaning. Last but not least, how can something that precedes something serve as an extension anyway?

Observing Turkey through blinkers

An attitude similar to that of the *Financial Times*' Strauss in terms of taking unsubstantiated allegations of unreferenced sources as a credible, as well as a "necessary and sufficient" premise for a conclusion about the contemporary situation in Turkey, is visible in the reporting of Anberin Zaman of *The Economist* and Berlinski, who writes for *City Journal* magazine.

In an analysis on Turkey for The German Marshall Fund of the United States, Zaman argues that there are three sources of pressure on media freedom in Turkey: first, Turkey's anti-terror laws; second, its prime minister, Erdoğan; and third, "Turkey's largest and most powerful Islamic fraternity led by Fethullah Gülen." What is her premise for such a dogma-like conclusion? She writes: "The so-called Gülenists are said to have infiltrated the bureaucracy, especially the police force. They are widely believed to be behind the arrest of Ahmet Şık and Nedim Şener." As such, she either makes the same mistake that Strauss does or pursues the same insidious method to obscure the facts and lead readers to make erroneous conclusions.

Reflections on Turkey

Who is it that says and believes so? And, why is it that an ordinary Turkish citizen with a favorable opinion of Gülen is said to have infiltrated the bureaucracy when he or she enters the civil service through legal and legitimate procedures available to any other Turkish citizen? While she does not provide any answer to this, neither does she mention that the same judiciary prosecuting Şık and Şener for their alleged involvement in alleged coup plots also opened some 400 lawsuits against journalists and reporters working for the *Zaman* newspaper for issues related to their reporting.

Finally, in her article "Prisoner of Conspiracy," Berlinski argues: "So the [Ergenekon] investigation cannot possibly lead to what its supporters say it will: the triumph of the rule of law in Turkey, a sustainable national consensus, and a verdict widely accepted as legitimate. It can only lead to more division, suspicion, and paranoia." She further argues, "Almost every Turkish citizen now deeply believes either that Ergenekon is real or that Gülen is running their country—and is truly terrified of one or the other." Does she not sound more like someone with a stake in the Ergenekon investigation than a correspondent? Or, why could she possibly be following this particular pattern in her reporting? The answer seems to be in her proposal, "The only solution I can imagine would lie in a South African-style Truth and Reconciliation Committee—an entirely public and transparent reckoning aiming not at punishment or vengeance but at reconciliation." Just like Strauss and Zaman, Berlinski, too, tries to spread the false perception that Gülen is running the show in Turkey and the Ergenekon investigation is leading to an uncertainty. Perhaps, they or those who sign their paychecks think that if they can portray Gülen as poorly and as frighteningly as possible, then the Ergenekon investigation may be brought to a halt.

WHO IS TO BLAME FOR THE TURKISH-ISRAELI DEADLOCK?[51]

T he foreign policy implications of Prime Minister Recep Tayyip Erdoğan's landslide electoral victory are yet to be seen. However, for the time being it would be safe to conclude that the
Justice and Development Party (AK Party) government is likely to interpret the steady increase in its popular support as massive approval of
its overall foreign policy orientation. In fact, during his victory speech,
Prime Minister Erdoğan alluded to how deep those implications may
be by suggesting that in this election, not only Ankara, but also Ramal-
lah, Gaza, Jenin, Nablus and Jerusalem were winners, and that Turkey
would continue to be an advocate for the righteous and the weak in
its region and beyond.

As such, it is not hard to predict that Turkish-Israeli relations are
unlikely to smoothen out in the near future, unless the Benjamin Netanyahu government compromises on two closely interrelated issues: first,
Ankara's demand for an apology and compensations for the families
of the victims of the Israeli attack on the Mavi Marmara; and second,
Washington's proposal that would enable the settlement of the so-called
Israeli-Palestinian conflict through a two-state solution on the basis of
the pre-1967 borders.

However, under normal circumstances, Tel Aviv is unlikely to do
so, not because Prime Minister Netanyahu is interested in perpetuating the Israeli-Palestinian conflict (or maybe he is), but because he has
a tendency to see everything from the perspective of Israel's survival.
Similarly, the way he understands peace is a recipe for perpetual conflict. Therefore, these may be the very reasons why Netanyahu should

---

[51] First appeared in *Today's Zaman* daily on June 17, 2011.

not be blamed for turning down President Barack Obama's proposal, as well as for creating the conditions that have caused the Turkish-Israeli deadlock.

Deciphering Benjamin

Prime Minister Netanyahu's recent visit to Washington was remarkable in that it made two points crystal clear. First, pretty much the entire world, including the Americans, the Arabs and the non-Arab nations represented within the Organization of the Islamic Conference (OIC), is willing to accept the existence of the State of Israel as a (peaceful and law-abiding) member of the international community (within its internationally agreed and recognized borders). Second, Rae Abileah, who was reportedly attacked by American Israeli Public Affairs Committee (AIPAC) members and hospitalized as a result and later arrested after she protested the Israeli occupation and war crimes during Netanyahu's address to the joint session of the US Congress, is a Jew, and hence condemnation of Israel's treatment of the Palestinians is not due to anti-Semitism.

Similar examples of many Jews so bravely opposing successive Israeli governments' illegal practices against Palestinians are a testament to that fact as well. It is obvious, based on these two recent reassertions of the widely accepted truth, that the State of Israel has, and will always have, a place among the nations.

What is not so obvious, and in fact is quite controversial, is whether the Israeli prime minister is capable of making peace at all with the Palestinians and Arabs. When Netanyahu humiliated President Obama in front of his own fellow Americans and the world by categorically rejecting what his host had proposed on the basis of the pre-1967 borders, the first question that probably entered every frustrated American taxpayer's mind was, "What else can the United States do for Israel?" After all, President Obama's proposal would not create a fully independent Palestine that has sovereign control over its landmass and air space, but an archipelago of tiny territories that are existentially dependent on Israel anyway. The issue of Palestinians' return to their homes, which have remained within the territories steadily occupied by Israel since 1967, was not even mentioned in that proposal. Nor was the militarization of the new Palestinian state.

Some explain Netanyahu's blunt defiance of President Obama as "power-intoxication." That is, Netanyahu may be thinking that there is absolutely no reason for him to be forthcoming—given the leverage he thinks he has against the president. In fact, Netanyahu has generated a kind of excitement among the current members of the US Congress which no other head of state, including President Obama, ever did. Members of Congress gave 29 standing ovations to the Israeli prime minister during his address, while they only gave 25 to President Obama during his State of the Union address. It is also clear that as he prepares to run for re-election in 2012, President Obama will have to secure the support of certain American voters that happen to heed the recommendations of Israeli leaders. So, under these circumstances, Netanyahu may be excused for not being able to recognize the historic opportunity offered to him by President Obama's proposal.

Netanyahu's 'durable peace': a recipe for conflict

However, there seems to be something more to it. According to Netanyahu, as he writes in his book *A Durable Peace: Israel and Its Place Among Nations*, the peace between Israelis and Arabs is not possible on the basis of territorial swaps because the Arabs, he believes, would use those territories for future assaults to destroy Israel. "The ceding of strategic territory to the Arabs might trigger [a] destructive process by convincing the Arab world that Israel has become vulnerable enough to attack," he argues. Moreover, he believes that the only kind of peace that would endure between the Arabs/Palestinians and the Jews is the "peace of deterrence," which is based on Israel's absolute military superiority over its immediate and distant neighbors.

Netanyahu does not believe in the international guarantees for Israel's security. He thinks that "by the time they come to save Israel, there won't be an Israel." Therefore, he argues, Israel's defense must be entrusted to its own military capabilities and forces that are willing and able to act in real time against any imminent attack or invasion. As such, Netanyahu himself explains in a way why Israel is so vigilant

248 Reflections on Turkey

against the possibility of Iran's developing military nuclear capabilities. Similarly, since he considers every threat as potentially aimed at destroying Israel, it is quite normal that he does not accept President Obama's proposal. It also explains the disproportional use of violence by Israeli forces used against the civilians on the Mavi Marmara last year. In fact, last month Netanyahu defended the Israeli forces' killing of 13 pro-Palestinian demonstrators on Nakba Day by suggesting that those demonstrators were bent on destroying Israel.

In explaining Netanyahu's overall behavior, his electorate may think that he is adamantly protecting the State of Israel, while many others may argue that he is suffering from a chronic condition in which a person has delusions, hears things that are not real and hence loses touch with reality, and as a result occasionally resorts to suicidal actions. If the latter is the case, which Mayo Clinic calls paranoid schizophrenia, Prime Minister Netanyahu certainly cannot be blamed for obstructing any peace efforts aimed at settling the Israeli-Palestinian conflict. Nor could he be blamed for the Israeli assault on the Mavi Marmara, which led to the contemporary deadlock in Turkish-Israeli relations. However, the Israeli electorate may be blamed for making the mistake of putting him in office as such, and thereby paving the way for that deadlock.

ANKARA'S SYRIAN VENTURE AND THE INSIDIOUS "KURDISH SPRING"[52]

Nowadays, Turkey, Syria and Iran seem to be undertaking measures that only adversaries would in the face of imminent threats from each another. While busy picking on each other, they are unable to recognize the looming threat, which has the potential to dwarf the so-called "Arab Spring." Whether all three genuinely like or hate each other, and if the latter is the case, whether they pose a threat to one another can only be a secondary concern when compared to the imminent threat they commonly face. It is the likely "Kurdish Spring," which started in Turkey, will rapidly spread to the other two. They will be inadvertently assisting it in becoming a reality unless they keep their direct channels of communication open at all times, and fully cooperate, in order not to suppress the Kurds' political, cultural and socioeconomic rights, but to fight terrorism perpetrated in the name of defending those rights.

What has changed in the relations all of a sudden? First, Ankara has turned increasingly critical of the Baath regime in Damascus due to the ongoing violence perpetrated against its own civilians. Prime Minister Recep Tayyip Erdoğan denounced the regime's repression of civilian protests as "savagery." Moreover, President Abdullah Gül stated that the reforms announced by President Bashar al-Assad recently during his long-awaited public address were not enough. In response, Damascus rebuked Ankara's critical stance, and warned the latter to reconsider its position for the sake of maintaining friendly relations between the two. In addition, Syria has positioned its armed forces near the country's northern border in order to control the exodus of refugees into

---

[52] First appeared in *Today's Zaman* daily on July 1, 2011.

Turkey. The Turkish military has also reinforced its troops on the Turkish side of the border. In the meantime, alarmed by the possibility of losing its only Arab ally with the possible fall of the Assad regime and hence in show of solidarity with it, Tehran has reportedly alleged that Turkey has been instigating the civilian protests, and has also reportedly armed supporters of the Baath regime.

After all, only a year ago, despite harsh criticisms from its Western allies, Turkey put itself on the frontline in order to prevent, in cooperation with Brazil, any possible military action against Iran, due to the latter's so-called civilian nuclear program. Accordingly, Tehran announced that it would continue its nuclear negotiations with the Vienna Group (US, Russia, France and the International Atomic Energy Agency [IAEA]) in Istanbul, as well as swap its low-enriched uranium for nuclear fuel rods only in Turkey. Similarly, until very recently, Syrian leadership used to proclaim that Damascus would engage in any rapprochement with Israel through the mediation of Ankara. At this point, it is questionable whether any of these pledges will materialize, yet at the same time it would be premature to conclude that relations between Turkey and Syria-Iran are irreversibly damaged.

Also, one should note that a number of obscure news reports were instrumental. According to a columnist writing for the Lebanese newspaper *Al-Akhbar*, during a recent meeting where the Syrian president voiced his concern over the critical stance Ankara has adopted, Iran's Ayatollah Ali Khamenei warned that Iran would bomb NATO and US bases in Turkey if the latter were cooperative in any NATO action against Syria. Similarly, a Kuwaiti newspaper alleged that "Turkish officials have told Western countries that Turkey might launch a military operation in Syria's north to overthrow President Bashar al-Assad's regime." Both Iranian and Turkish authorities have denied the allegations though. Even if they had not, these reports already looked like fabrications aimed at harming the trio's relations. They may well have been planted in the media as part of psychological warfare aimed at undermining the trio's relations. Nor can any of the three governments be sure that their respective authorities are not compromised by officials who would cooperate with third parties to the detriment of the governments they are supposed to represent.

Nevertheless, it is obvious that there is a tension and that the trio's relations are still brittle. The tension has resulted largely from the way Ankara positioned itself vis-à-vis the unfolding humanitarian tragedy in Syria. Primarily concerned with the security implications that a possible civil war or foreign military intervention in Syria could create for Turkey, Ankara urged President Assad to undertake reforms that would enable a peaceful democratic transition. However, those reforms are understandably difficult to implement immediately, given the intricacies of Syria's Baath regime, and apparently President Assad is far from controlling all elements of that regime, such as the intelligence service. Yet, Ankara's criticism has steadily increased. Two factors may have played a role in this: First, Prime Minister Erdoğan may have not wanted to once again remain silent about human rights violations in Syria, as was initially the case during Muammar Gaddafi's violent suppression of civilian protestors in Libya. Second, the excessive and somewhat sentimentally charged coverage of Syrian protests in Turkish media, as well as the bombastic portrayal of Prime Minister Erdoğan as the new leader of the region may have, mistakenly, led Ankara to overreact and to forget that for any democratic transition in Syria, the survival of Assad's presidency and his continuous contact with Ankara are vital.

Considering its own domestic peculiarities, however, Turkey should be extra sensitive to not ruin or even sour its relations with either Syria or Iran. These peculiarities include: first, the still alive terrorist, Abdullah Öcalan; second, the so-called Peace and Democracy Party (BDP), which is resolved to coerce the Turkish state into negotiating with terrorists over Turkey's sovereignty in its southeast region; third, the dormant but not yet dead Kurdistan Workers' Party (PKK) terror network; and finally 15-20 million ethnic Kurds, who may be more or less manipulated like any other ethnic group. Under these circumstances, its inability to counter increasing PKK terrorism in the Southeast, and possibly across the country, may force the Justice and Development Party (AK Party) government to embark on a self-destructive course with regard to the Kurdish issue.

That is, if PKK terror surges and the government appears unable to prevent it, which will be the case if Turkey cannot cooperate with both Iran and Syria, then the very same Erdoğan who recently stated that the government would have hung Öcalan if he had been in office [before the abolition of capital punishment] may be forced to seek the chief terrorist's help in appeasing the PKK's endless demands it posed as a prerequisite to ending the violence.

Could this happen really? Actually, some so-called liberal journalists/columnists in Turkey have already started to suggest that the state (practically the military) has been negotiating with Öcalan all along, therefore, so should the government in order to find a comprehensive solution to Turkey's Kurdish question. Some have even suggested a road map through which Öcalan's sentence would be turned into a five-year house arrest sentence, after which he would be a free man—if he cooperates with the government. Whether these touchy and liberal-sounding ideas can bring about an end to Turkey's more than century-old Kurdish question is questionable at best, and whether it would be prudent to release a chief terrorist is a legal and moral matter to be dealt with. However, it is for sure that no government, and probably no prime minister, can survive in a country like Turkey if Öcalan is freed during the period of rule of that government. Then, of course, how odd it would be to keep generals and other army officers, who fought Öcalan and other PKK terrorists. So, forced to follow such a course in the face of an uncontrollable PKK terror, Prime Minister Erdoğan would bring about the end not only of his government, but of himself. Given the impotency of the opposition in Turkey, which is true for Erdoğan's opponents both inside and outside the country, this may have seemed like a comprehensive solution to get rid of him and his government.

The bottom line is how Ankara positions itself in the face of tragic developments in Syria today and ones likely to occur in Iran in the future will have immediate implications for domestic Turkish politics, as Turkey's ability to cooperate with both countries has a direct effect on its ability to deal with PKK terrorism. For some capitals, it may not be risky to bash the Assad regime, but Ankara is not one of them. As it appears, there are two dimensions of Ankara's response to unraveling developments in Syria: one is practical, which is the humanitarian assistance provided to Syrian refugees escaping the violence perpetrated in their country, and the other is positional, which is characterized by increasing criticism of President Assad and the Baath regime. The best Turkey can and should do under these circumstances is to continue its constructive political engagement with President Assad and help him transform his country, while providing humanitarian assistance to Syrian refugees as they flee to the north.

BIG PICTURE – 1

Turkey's PKK Problem and the So-Called Kurdish "Mandela"[53]

The recent killing of 13 Turkish soldiers by the Kurdistan Workers' Party (PKK) ambush in Diyarbakır province has once again shaken the entire nation, adding yet another failure to the scorecard of the military and raising many questions about Turkey's more than quarter-century-old fight against terrorism. Serious allegations are openly voiced these days about some sort of cooperation between rogue elements within the Turkish Armed Forces and PKK terrorists in order to deliberately prolong Turkey's problem with terrorism and provide the self-proclaimed guardians of the regime (the generals) with leverage against the civilian governments in Ankara.

Moreover, a handful of Kurdish politicians and activists who claim to be representing all the Kurds of Turkey are becoming militant and provocative in their discourse and actions, thereby instigating the nationalist sentiments against the Kurds as well as against the Justice and Development Party (AK Party) government, which seems resolved to end PKK terrorism by introducing unprecedented political and legal reforms. In fact, today the Kurds of Turkey are enjoying the rights and freedoms which nobody could even speak about up until a decade ago. Yet, these Kurdish politicians are going as far as publicly demanding Kurdish autonomy, even though the vast majority of the Kurds do not support the idea. In addition, the so-called Kurdish movement seems to be organizing itself after the mold of South Africa's African National Congress (ANC) and tries to create a sort of "Kurdish Mandela" out of chief terrorist Abdullah Öcalan, thereby raising the suspicions about

---

[53] First appeared in *Today's Zaman* daily on July 24, 2011.

outside interference. Lastly, some naive liberal intelligentsia in the country seem to be buying the idea that the AK Party goverment's negotiation with Öcalan—as if the latter were a legitimate counterpart—is a must to solve Turkey's PKK problem.

So, what is really happening in Turkey? In order to have a grasp of it, one should have an understanding of the evolution of the Kurdish issue over the past century and should consider contemporary domestic developments in Turkey, bearing in mind Ankara's increasingly assertive and unnecessarily confrontational foreign policy orientation, especially in its relations with the traditional status quo powers within the international system.

The Kurds' misery and exploitation

Throughout the last century, the *êşandın* (pain) has manifested itself to Kurds in many ways in their daily lives. The Kurds of Turkey started to experience the repressive state policies during the last years of the Ottoman Empire under the leadership of the Ittihad ve Terakki (Union and Progress) government, the leadership of which consisted of non-Muslims—the Dönme—and the Young Turks educated in France and mired in the ethnicity-oriented nationalist ideology. The Ittihat ve Terakki's, approach to the Kurds and later, during the republican era, the Republican People Party's (CHP) approach to the Kurds was characterized ironically by both the denial of the Kurds' distinct identity and the fiercely imposed assimilation from an identity that is denied to have existed at the first place.

In addition, the outside actors deliberately made the Kurds the usual suspects in the psyche of the Turkish nationalists. The Treaty of Sèvres, which the European occupiers, namely Britain, France and Italy, forced the ailing Ottoman Empire to sign on Aug. 10, 1920, aimed to create an Armenian republic in the east and an autonomous Kurdish region in the southeast of Anatolia. As Nicole and Hugh Pope remind readers in their book, *Turkey Unveiled: A History of Modern Turkey*, although the treaty had never been ratified and implemented, such a reference to an autonomous Kurdish region has engendered the association of the ethnic Kurdish presence within the new republic, and as such any demand in relation to the Kurdish identity, with the greatest security threat posed to Turkey's territorial integrity.

In a way, the Allied powers did not succeed in partitioning the Ottoman mainland but managed to portray the Kurds, the largest ethnic group in it, as unreliable elements who would readily join the European powers at any opportune moment to carve up Turkey.

In the following decades, even though they have theoretically enjoyed equal rights and status before the law regardless of their ethnic identity, the Kurds have usually been discriminated against in the public space as well as within the state's institutions. Being a Kurd was reason enough to be ridiculed. The state's traditional disregard for the development of the Kurdish-populated regions and the Kurds' chronic lack of access to proper education had already created a natural selection process that kept the Kurds out of the political and economic opportunity spaces. So, in terms of the discrimination, bigotry and despise they suffered under the reign of Turkey's secular-fundamentalist elite up until the end of the 20th century, the misery of the Kurds resembled that of the North African Muslim immigrants living in Europe in general and in France in particular. The French discrimination has been so extreme and the French security forces' treatment of the French citizens of the North African or Muslim origin so brutal, especially under the leadership of Nicolas Sarkozy, that the brewing anger and resentment culminated in the widespread riots and violent clashes in the banlieues of Paris in October 2005.

Similarly, during Turkey's fight against PKK terrorism, the treatment of suspects and criminals of Kurdish origin looked more like it was designed to consistently provoke public opinion on both the Turkish and Kurdish sides in a manner that would reinforce the legitimacy of the fight for both sides. Just like many distinct Muslim individuals of different nationalities were abducted to secret interrogation places as well as to the infamous Guantanamo prison during the course of the so-called US war on terror, the Kurds of Turkey, too, were exposed to the extrajudicial killings, renditions and torture, fashionably called "enhanced interrogation techniques." In fact, long-time Turkey correspondents and observers Nicole and Hugh Pope suggested as early as in 1997, "[s]ummary executions and torture of Kurdish nationalists or leftist militants carried out today by unknown assailants are believed to be linked to the security forces."

However, it was not just the Kurds who were oppressed by the secular-fundamentalist elite throughout republican history. Muslims, whose rights to practice their religion in the public space and whose access to political and economic opportunity spaces were restricted, suffered a similar fate, as did the Christian minorities such as Armenians, Assyrians and Greeks, whose legal minority rights were circumscribed; the rightists and leftists, whose rights to assembly and freedom of expression were banished; and many more unknown individuals who have been left to rot in the prisons without ever receiving a fair trial.

Besides, despite all the difficulties, the Kurds in Turkey have never experienced what the African Americans in America have. For instance, the Kurds have never been enslaved; there have never been segregated transportation and other public services; and the Kurds have never been humiliated with the public displays like "Dogs and Blacks not allowed!" Nor have they ever suffered from the hate crimes similar to those Muslims in general and Turks in particular are suffering in Germany. In July 2009, a German nationalist who was openly hostile to his victim's religious identity murdered a pregnant Muslim woman in a German courtroom before the eyes of the security forces. Similarly, in the last decade only, neo-Nazi groups set the immigrant Turks' houses on fire several times, causing many deaths and injuries. Who knows how many times it happened before but has gone unreported.

BIG PICTURE – 2

Turkey's PKK Problem and the
So-Called Kurdish "Mandela"[54]

T hanks to the rapid expansion of Turkish civil society in the last decade and political, socioeconomic and legal reforms introduced during the rule of the current Justice and Development Party (AK Party) government, today the Kurds of Turkey are enjoying rights and freedoms that had remained simply unimaginable up until a decade ago.

The Kurdish language is freely used in the public space and TV and radio stations now broadcast in Kurdish. In Parliament, in addition to ethnic Kurdish deputies in various parties, some of whom have served in senior government positions, there are 36 others who have banded together under the banner of the so-called Peace and Democracy Party (BDP) and are rallying on nothing but the ethnicity ticket.

At the same time, since 2007 a massive legal investigation has been under way into the alleged Ergenekon terrorist network, which is believed to have included rogue elements from the Turkish security forces as well as Kurdistan Workers' Party (PKK) terrorists, who carried out terrorist acts in order to exacerbate and sustain Turkish-Kurdish tensions. Last but not least, Turkey is on the verge of overhauling its current Constitution, which was drafted under the tutelage of the military after the 1980 coup d'état, for a more inclusive, democratic and pluralistic one.

Yet, apparently no improvement in terms of the restoration of Kurds' individual as well as communal rights and freedoms is good

---

[54] First appeared in *Today's Zaman* daily on July 24, 2011.

enough for those 36 deputies and their political allies both inside and outside Turkey. Lately, they have begun to voice their desire for Kurdish "autonomy" in the Southeast. They argue that the AK Party government must negotiate a solution with chief terrorist Abdullah Öcalan, whom they do not refrain from, but enjoy the freedom of, calling the "national leader of Kurds," while living on salaries provided by Turkish taxpayers.

In the meantime, Öcalan, who settled for imprisonment on İmralı Island outside Istanbul in 1999 under European guarantees against his execution, after years of enjoying a posh lifestyle in his Damascus residence under the protection of the late Hafez al-Assad while countless Kurdish youth perished in the mountains, has been trying to present himself as a legitimate counterpart of the Turkish government. He has proposed a so-called "three-phase roadmap" that stipulates the establishment of a truth and reconciliation commission and the involvement of international actors such as the US, the UN, the EU and, oddly, a "Kurdish Federal Government of Iraq," which does not exist. In media organs sympathetic to, or outright supportive of, the PKK, there seems to be a systematic effort to draw parallels between the situation in Turkey and South Africa's apartheid regime and also to portray the baby killer as a sort of Kurdish "Mandela" who allegedly fought for the freedom of the Kurdish minority, served years in prison and eventually turned dovish in search for peace.

In general, these efforts are organized through the so-called Democratic Society Congress (DTK), which was established in 2010 in the mold of South Africa's African National Congress (ANC) and aims to bring together all Kurdish civil society initiatives. During its formation, the DTK announced that it would work to achieve a "Democratic Turkey, Autonomous Kurdistan."

The situation considered as a whole

So, what is really happening in Turkey with regards to the Kurdish issue and the PKK problem? Could they be analyzed independently of other domestic and foreign policy issues in Turkey? How do they all connect to each other in the big picture? It is hard to know for sure before it actually happens. However, one viable explanation may be that they are complementary parts of a concerted effort to both impede the legal investigation of the alleged Ergenekon terrorist network nested in the state and to derail Turkey's march to regional and international prominence by undermining and eventually getting rid of both Prime Minister Recep Tayyip Erdoğan and the AK Party government.

At a regional level, Turkey's two immediate neighbors and critical allies in the fight against PKK terrorism are facing existential threats that are likely to diminish their ability to cooperate with Turkey. Given precedents in Iraq, Tunisia, Egypt, Yemen and Libya, Syria will also be paralyzed by an internal conflict and instability in a way that would prevent Damascus from functioning as an effective regional partner for Ankara in the foreseeable future.

Similarly, Iran will be unable to fully cooperate with Turkey for two reasons: First, there is a naturally or deliberately growing discord between President Mahmoud Ahmadinejad and Ayatollah Ali Khamenei, which started with the former's sacking of the intelligence chief who was backed by the latter. Second, Iran is highly likely to experience popular unrest in the coming years with the demise of the aging Khamenei, who is pretty much the only bulwark before the imminent popular upheaval against Iran's revolutionary regime.

Besides, encouraged by questionable praise coming from Washington and Brussels, and increasingly critical of the regime in Syria, Ankara is diminishing its prospect of cooperation with a post-revolution establishment in this country, which would more or less remain intact with or without Bashar al-Assad. In the absence of Damascus and Tehran to cooperate with, Ankara will naturally be obliged to seek cooperation with Israel and the US in the fight against the PKK, which would of course not come for free.

On the other hand, at a national level, the Republican People's Party (CHP) and the BDP have been hindering Parliament's ability to function by creating crises over petty issues such as the taking of the parliamentary oath. DTK members are continuing to make provocative public declarations, announcing the establishment of so-called Kurdish autonomy in its alleged capital, Diyarbakır.

In the meantime, the PKK and its urban incarnation, the Kurdish Communities Union (KCK), are increasing their terrorist activities by ostensibly defying Öcalan's call for a cease-fire. In so doing, the two are not only trying to perpetuate a sense of insecurity and chaos in the country but also beefing up Öcalan's deliberately constructed false image in the eyes of the general public as a potential peacemaker.

The latest in that regard was the recent killing of 13 Turkish soldiers in Diyarbakir in a PKK ambush. CHP leader Kemal Kılıçdaroğlu was quick to blame the military's failure to prevent the incident on the AK Party government by arguing that the morale of the Turkish army had been damaged by the ongoing Ergenekon investigation. Nationalist Movement Party (MHP) leaders are publicly endorsing Erdoğan's increasingly inflammatory rhetoric against the PKK and its extensions in Parliament, as he puts it.

So, does all this mean that some dark powers are working hard to weaken or, worse, divide Turkey and create an independent Kurdish state, which would possibly be followed later by certain concessions to the Armenians, the Assyrians and the Greeks? Maybe yes, maybe no; that is not the issue of primary concern. For some, that is not even a legitimate question, but a conspiracy theory.

What is important is to recognize that there are many groups inside and outside Turkey who view the AK Party government's ouster as the only solution to secure their interests in Turkey as well as in the region. They are, and will be, working intensively to exploit the Kurdish issue in order to undermine the AK Party government's ability to work, and to diminish its popularity outside Turkey.

Similarly, one should realize that Turkey has not only foes but also friends within the international community who would not necessarily favor a more powerful and more independent Turkey on the world stage. As such, they may well be cooperating with Turkey in a fight against PKK terrorism, while also working towards developing Turkey's national issue into a much more complicated international matter that would require the involvement of many other actors as well as the United Nations, thereby making it much more difficult and costly to deal with.

At the end of the day, throughout the history of the republic and under the reign of the secular-fundamentalist elite, the Kurds of Turkey have suffered at least as much as many other vulnerable groups in Turkey, including a majority population that did not relinquish its piously Muslim identity. They seem to have also been exploited by outside actors, including the PKK, as well as rogue elements within the Turkish state as a means to interfere in Turkey's domestic affairs, to strangle civilian governments in Ankara and to create calculated tension as needed. It is no more the old Turkey but a new one, a Turkey with a growing civil society, a strengthening economy and a liberalizing political environment. It is up to the Kurds to choose either to stand up against the over-a-century-old manipulation, or continue with business as usual.

TURKISH FOREIGN POLICY
TESTS ITSELF[55]

For critics of Turkey's Justice and Development Party (AK Party) government, both inside and outside the country, the recent tension in Turkish-Syrian relations that has sprung up over the Assad regime's brutal repression of popular demands for democracy is apparently a welcome opportunity.

They seem determined to make use of it in every possible way in order to ridicule Foreign Minister Ahmet Davutoğlu's vision of Turkey as having "zero problems with [its] neighbors" and at the same time to incite, or rather draw, the AK Party government into pursuing an ever more confrontational course of action in a way that would not only cause further deterioration of Turkey's amicable image in the Middle East but also irreparably damage its relations with Iran and Syria, both of which are Turkey's natural allies in its fight against Kurdistan Workers' Party's (PKK) terrorism.

In the beginning, it looked like Prime Minister Recep Tayyip Erdoğan had come to believe that the situation in Syria was a domestic issue for Turkey. The rationale behind such a politically loaded definition of the situation was curious at best, as it was most likely to have negative implications, if continued, because most of Turkey's neighbors and allies can identify with (and potentially decide to intervene in) Turkey's domestic issues on similar grounds of ethnic-religious affinity and purely humanitarian concerns. Yet Ankara appeared resolved to go so far as to cut off its relations with Damascus, seeking an immediate end to the violence in Syria.

---

[55] First appeared in *Today's Zaman* daily on August 22, 2011.

In the meantime, a chorus of the US and European media, including *The New York Times* and *The Washington Post*, has been running news reports encouraging Ankara to be even more critical of the Assad regime, with op-ed pieces bombastically arguing that as the most powerful man in the region, only Erdoğan can stop Bashar al-Assad's crackdown. Similarly, Washington has continued to announce that the United States and Turkey share the same goals on Syria, which are an immediate end to violence and a democratic transition. Worse, the State Department spokesperson Victoria Nuland, as if speaking on behalf of her Turkish counterpart, has remarked that Turkey's patience with the Assad regime is coming to an end. Maybe not as a direct result of these remarks, but concurrently, Davutoğlu warned that there would be nothing to discuss anymore unless the Assad regime stopped the violence.

The international community paying lip service

Only recently, the Turkish intelligentsia and authorities began to realize that the international community is so far only paying lip service to stopping the violence in Syria, and has not even moved for a UN Security Council resolution: The best they have been able to produce is a weak presidential statement, condemning the Assad regime. While this is the case, what Turkey can do is extremely limited, when it comes to ending the crackdown in Syria.

Nevertheless, the ongoing humanitarian crisis in Syria, and more broadly the so-called "Arab Spring" sweeping the region, has presented probably the most daunting foreign policy challenge the AK Party government must handle as it embarks on its third term in office. How should Ankara respond to regional and international developments, given that Turkey has a number of peculiarities and contradictions, most notable among which are its need to reckon with its undemocratic past and deal with PKK terrorism, while at the same time having already achieved great economic success and vast global engagement, thanks to its expanding middle class and vibrantly active civil society.

Perhaps the best way to start would be to develop a clear understanding at all levels of the AK Party government that the status-quo, which was established in the region and has been consolidated as such over the last three or four centuries, cannot be overturned or undone in just a decade or two, or by Turkey alone. Nor can any change imposed from the outside be positively sustained, no matter how good the intentions behind it may be. That is, real change with respect to democracy and pluralism in Syria or across the Middle East cannot come about only through the revolutions organized in the streets or through public demonstrations.

A revolution is simply the replacement of those oppressing at the top with the ones oppressed at the bottom. As one Western thinker observed, the moment they come to power, the so-called revolutionaries turn into conservatives who are adamantly determined to preserve the new order. In fact, the Assad regime, which is trying to preserve its grip on the country, is the remnant of a past revolution that was waged against the perceived "defunct and corrupt" regime, which preceded it. The same fate could befall the regimes which come out of the so-called "Arab Spring," which in fact never was, and is unlikely to be, a real revolution, unless the oppressed Arabs, using legitimate and democratic means, reign in the political and economic opportunity gaps, replace the old guard, and gradually transform their respective countries.

Would it be any different in Turkey than it has been in Syria, Libya, Egypt, Yemen, or Tunisia if the Turks had revolted against the secular-fundamentalist elite, including the rogue army generals, who had so long dominated all of the country's economic and political opportunities with the help of their allies in Washington and the European capitals? That it would not be any different has been proven by each of the three bloody military interventions in the past, and still with the proven plots of rogue elements in the military to "cage" the AK Party government and smash the people's will with a "sledgehammer," so that for another hundred years no one would dare to challenge their absolute reign over the state.

It is understandably difficult, of course, for many novices within the AK Party government to recognize this fact, since they have simply parachuted into previously inaccessible political and economic positions, after the state apparatus and the political arena had been substantially transformed and democratized as a result of gradual but consistent social change across the country. Also, since they hardly understand that the AK Party is not the cause, but only one of the effects of such transformation, it is only normal for them to so readily take uncalculated risks by presuming to use powers and capabilities, which indeed they do not have.

Not all change can be administered by Turkey

Contemporary Ankara and all the Turks mesmerized by its activism should recognize that there are certain things that Turkey can succeed in changing in its region and in the international arena, but for all the rest it can only work toward preparing the conditions conducive to a change in the future. It is not a law cast in stone that all the change must be administered by today's Ankara or with today's leaders. The Turks should know this best, after suffering for the last several decades from a number of "saviors," who emerged to create a powerful Turkey, but whose personal priorities and ambitions eventually led to the hindrance of democracy in the country, which is the only source of legitimate power.

Similarly, within an international system where the status quo is enforced by states with which Turkey does not have a balance of power yet, Ankara's confrontational approach would only alert the status quo protectionists to take necessary precautions by containing Turkey's existing channels of influence, and also by blocking all the other possible ones that Ankara can utilize. Worse, Turkey's worldwide engagement with other nations would also be endangered, because the global status quo protectionists, once disturbed by Ankara's policies, would target that civil engagement by wrongfully attributing a political meaning to it.

After all, history is not at an end, and it is not up to Turkey's AK Party government to right all the wrongs in its region and across the globe. Nor would it be held responsible for not being able to do so. However, the AK Party leaders will be held responsible for their role in Turkey's democratization or for their failure to address it, if that should turn out to be the case. They will also be judged by their ability or inability to handle the political, economic and security problems of Turkey, but not those of its neighbors. The only reason why the Turks voted the AK government in for the third term with an over-whelming majority was their conviction, or hope, at least, that this government will prioritize the adoption of a new constitution, the successful completion of the so-called Ergenekon investigation into the anti-democratic formations within the state, and the maintenance of the country's high economic performance.

In the final analysis, there are many events occurring in Turkey's region, and it is up to the AK Party government to choose to get distracted by them at the expense of the priorities it was elected to address. Ankara's unsolicited involvement in these regional events could be quite costly for Turkey, given that the so-called Arab Spring now physically borders Turkey, that its inspirational effect is not confined only to Arabs, and that the anti-Turkey Kurdish separatist movement has already gained great momentum both inside and outside Turkey.

The rogue elements in the Turkish army, which are currently under investigation, may not have managed to "cage" the AK Party government as stipulated in their alleged "Cage" coup plot. However, by so readily crossing its once close neighbors, and by damaging its relationships with allies in the fight against terrorism, the AK Party government seems to be willingly stepping inside that cage. Turkey and every other nation in its region would be better off if Ankara simply got along with its friends, reached out to potential friends, and avoided any confrontation with its foes and natural rivals, while prioritizing the country's democratization and maintaining high economic performance. Ankara should immediately return to its "zero problems with neighbors" policy, which Foreign Minister Davutoğlu so masterfully devised and implemented.

DIPLOMACY BETWEEN
TURKEY AND ISRAEL[56]

"Constructive ambiguity" is probably the most useful diplomatic tool that enables the states to move forward in their relationships with their counterparts, no matter what kind of crisis they may have experienced. But it looks like it has long been kicked out of the Turkish diplomatic lexicon. Technically, the constructive ambiguity is defined as a deliberate vagueness in one's statements or position in negotiations with a view to expand the realm of maneuvering in order to advance particular political objectives.

Optimistically, the constructive ambiguity can be interpreted, as an assurance given by the parties prior or during the crisis that they are willing to revise their respective positions in order to overcome the crisis situation without losing face before their own constituencies or the international community. Both Turkish and Israeli governments have spoken with vivid clarity, however, with respect to their respective positions on the Mavi Marmara incident, where Israeli soldiers killed eight Turkish citizens and one American.

Ankara has insisted that Turkish-Israeli relations would never go back to normal unless Israel apologizes from Turkey, pays compensations to the families of the victims, and lifts the unlawful Israeli blockade on Gaza. In response, Tel Aviv has stressed that Israel would never apologize from Turkey for what Israeli soldiers did aboard the Mavi Marmara. In a way, Turkey and Israel have locked themselves up into a non-solution. After all, once announcing not only to Israel, but also to the whole world its conditions for normalization so clearly, how can the AK Party government possibly seem to be settling for anything

---

[56] First appeared in *Today's Zaman* daily on October 2, 2011.

less, or compromising to advance Turkey's long-term interests? As for the Netanyahu government; it should apologize, but hardly would do so, because doing so would be tantamount to the admission of guilt, and create a precedent, which would oblige Israel not only to apologize for its countless crimes past, present and future, but also to meet its concomitant legal obligations. Moreover, given the addition, as a third condition, of the lifting of the Gaza blockade, which is not immediately related to the Turkish-Israeli relations, the skeptics may suggest that the AK Party government is not interested in a rapid normalization anyway.

At the end of the day, the present stalemate in the Turkish-Israeli relations is a result of the political decisions made by both the AK Party government and the Netanyahu government throughout a tumultuous process, which was caused by an irresponsible act of an NGO based in Istanbul, as well as by even more irresponsible act of the Israeli armed forces. Nor this type of downgrading of the two states' relations is something abnormal. It has happened before, it may happen in the future, and as such, it is something normal.

However, the ramifications of the ensuing crisis are not confined to the diplomatic, political and economic relations between the two states only. The continued hostility between the Turkish and Israeli governments, coupled with the provocations by the zealots on both sides, are likely to instigate the emotions even further, thereby leading to irreparable damages. Therefore, the stakeholders other than the two governments such as the Turkish and Israeli peoples as well as their respective diasporas, especially in the United States, should work together to contain the potential damages of the crisis. In so doing, the onus is more on the shoulders of the American Jewish community who prioritizes the well being of the State of Israel, because relatively speaking it has far greater capability, compared to the other three, to make things much more complicated.

Spillover effect

The heat in Turkish-Israeli relations continues to increase due to the two governments' exchange of warnings and threats of sanctions. PM

Erdoğan announced that the Turkish warships would more frequently appear in the Eastern Mediterranean in order to ensure the safety of navigation, which Israel interpreted as a measure against the Israeli naval blockade on Gaza. Israeli Foreign Minister Avigdor Lieberman uttered that Israel would implement four faceted sanctions against Turkey, which includes a comprehensive travel boycott, cooperation with the Armenian diaspora, support to the terrorist Kurdish Workers Party (PKK), and portrayal of Turkey in the international fora as an oppressor of its minorities. Not surprisingly, what two prominent American political scientists, John Mearsheimer and Stephen Walt described as the Israel Lobby has rushed to mobilize each and every resource available to it within the American polity as well with the hope of punishing Turkey for going harsh on Israel. Recently, seven US senators penned a joined letter to President Barack Obama, asking the latter to "mount a diplomatic offensive" against Turkey. Similarly, Daniel Pipes and the right-wing extremist pundits alike have begun to propagate the false image of Turkey being the most dangerous country in the Middle East along with Iran. In line with this reflex, the black propaganda of the Israel Lobby against Turkey is likely to intensify in the months to come, especially during that time of the year when the US Congress is traditionally hijacked with allegations of the so-called Armenian genocide.

However, it seems like the anti-AK Party network in the US has recently diversified its targets, and now attacking Fethullah Gülen and the educational-cultural initiatives he has inspired as well. As Michael Shank of George Mason University reminds in his *Huffington Post* article, titled "Islamophobia Network Targets Top Performing American Schools," the Center for American Progress (CAP)'s recently published report on Islamophobia reveals the extend of such a defamation campaign. The CAP report, which is titled "Fear Inc: The Roots of the Islamophobia Network in America," demonstrates that the Eagle Forum, a so-called pro-family movement, and other members of the Islamophobia network have deliberately propagated an alleged Turkish threat to America: the so-called Muslim Gülen schools, which would allegedly "educate American children through the lens of Islam and teach them to hate Americans." Moreover, beside many blogosphere commentaries suffering from intellectual deficit but equally adamant in trying to defame Gülen, a recent *Newsweek* piece, titled "Erdoğan 1, Ataturk 0," referred to Gülen as "Erdoğan's friend and mentor" and to the civil society movement he has inspired as the "AKP's own 'deep state' ally, a wealthy and powerful Islamist movement directed from luxurious self-exile in the US."

Given such allegations, one is compelled to infer that the anti-AK Party network in the US is targeting Gülen and the people involved with the civil society initiatives he has inspired, probably because the members of this network assume that Gülen is the real force behind the AK Party government, and hence can be utilized to tone down its stance towards Israel. While such an assumption lacks credible evidence and remains as a mere speculation, it fails to recognize the fact that it was Gülen himself who criticized the so-called Freedom Flotilla project, which lies at the heart of the unfolding crisis between Turkey and Israel. In his interview to the *Wall Street Journal* during the days following the infamous Mavi Marmara incident, and when the entire Turkey was overwhelmed with heightened nationalistic sentiments after the Israeli murder of eight Turks and one Turkish American citizen, Gülen expressed his doubts about the true intentions behind the flotilla project and remarked that the organizers should have consulted with the authorities if the purpose was to bring humanitarian aid to Gaza. One can hardly argue that Gülen is a source of inspiration for the AK Party government, especially when it comes to foreign policy.

Track II diplomacy

Nevertheless, it is obvious that the current political crisis between Turkey and Israel bears negative implications on the non-political and totally unrelated civil society and educational initiatives. Therefore, it may be prudent to explore ways in order to prevent its further exacerbation, and contain its ramifications in form of creating anti-Turkish sentiments, or at least making the atmosphere conducive for the proliferation of such negative sentiments. In this context, the Track II diplomacy figures as a viable tool to compensate for the absence of optimistically utilized-constructive ambiguity in the Turkish-Israeli relations. Defined as a kind of informal diplomacy undertaken through exchanges between non-officials such as scholars, public intellectuals, journalists, retired officials, public figures or social activists, the Track II diplomacy is a foreign policy tool used in order to prevent further escalation of tensions, and better yet to help the parties resolve their conflict. In this regard, the non-official interactions between the Turks and the Israelis as well as between their respective diasporas in the joint initiatives such as conferences, workshops, mutual delegation visits, public declarations, and sportive or art events can be useful to increase popular demand for solution, overcome the impasse and move forward in a more constructive way.

Turks should not perceive such a civic engagement with Israelis as an acceptance of defeat in the face of the Netanyahu government's resistance to apologize from Turkey, or as a sell-out of the victims of the Israeli assault on the Mavi Marmara. Similarly, Israelis or their fellow Jews in the diaspora should not consider Turks' willingness to engage with them despite the continuing political crisis as a concession out of despair, but as an indication of their inherent constructivism. The opposite is to continue the business as usual. In that case, Turkey and Turkish-Americans would continue to be demonized. It may not be that bad after all to be demonized by such right-wing groups and fundamentalist figures as Daniel Pipes, David Yerushalmi, Robert Spencer, Frank Gaffney, Steven Emerson, Bridgette Gabriel, and Rachel Sharon-Krespin as the vast majority of Americans already know who they are, and why they do what they do. However, the situation may not be so positive for the Jewish-Americans, if the demonization of the Turks is to continue. In an America, where the criticism of Israel and the Israel Lobby reaches an unprecedented level, where high-ranking officials publicly describe Israel as an ungrateful ally and strategic liability for the US, and where according to the Anti-Defamation League figures the anti-Semitism is rampant, it is the Jewish-Americans who should be trying to avoid any action that would perpetuate or escalade the crisis between Turkey and Israel, let alone attacking those Turks who could be their only ally if the anti-Semitism gets out of control.

Finally, those Turks who do not look at the crisis between Turkey and Israel from an eschatological perspective, and hence are not beguiled with the dreams of righting all wrongs overnight with lofty speeches backed only by mediocre power would wish that the problem between the two was solved without prolonging and spilling over. Similarly, looking towards future, they may wonder if Ankara's intent to take the issue of Israeli blockade on Gaza to the International Court of Justice (ICJ) is strategically wise one. There is no doubt that Turkey has every moral right to do so. However, there is a risk associated with this move. Technically, the ICJ can consider and rule on the case only if both Turkey and Israel agree to refer it to the ICJ. Otherwise it can deliver a non-binding advisory opinion if the UN General Assembly's simple majority votes for such referral. It is clear that the first condition would never materialize. In the latter case, the advisory opinion would just add to many other UN resolutions and reports manifesting unlawful practices of Israel, but hardly have any enforcement effect. Even if in the ideal circumstance, the ICJ considers the case, and convicts Israel, which is in reality unlikely to happen; then the Security Council's permanent members have the right to stop the enforcement of the ICJ verdict. It is all too obvious which permanent member that would be.

Besides, given the black propaganda power of Turkey's opponents, which does not necessarily refer to the Netanyahu government and the right-wing extremist members of the Israel Lobby only, Turkey's such a legitimate endeavor can be portrayed as an attempt to steal leadership role from those Arab countries, who have traditionally appeared as the advocates of the Palestine cause. Worse, Turkey in general, and Turkish foreign minister in particular may be unfairly accused of embarking on yet another foreign policy objective, which is to bring Israel to justice, and leaving it unfulfilled. As such, Turkey may all of a sudden come to face the limits of its power both soft and hard in front of the international community. As Hans Morgenthau suggested, "the prestige of a nation is its reputation for power. That reputation, the reflection of the reality of power in the minds of the observers, can be as important as the reality of power itself." By the same token, an abrupt exposure of the limits of its power can ruin a nation's prestige. Of course, the policy makers in Ankara would know the best, but it may be better to not stretch further thinner, and instead just remember that some meals taste best when served cold. Turkey would be better off if it allocates its energy and resources to strengthen its democracy and economy inside, and continue to forge new partnerships outside, in line with its "zero problem with neighbors" policy. After all, only powerful Turkey can have zero problems with its neighbors, and can help the ones having problems solve theirs.

THE OIC'S XENOPHOBIC PUBLICISTS
IN THE UNITED STATES[57]

At the Organization of Islamic Cooperation (OIC), ever since Professor Ekmeleddin İhsanoğlu became secretary-general of the organization in 2005, engaging with the relevant US authorities and gaining publicity within American public opinion have continued to be priorities. After all, the OIC and the United States should be and are natural allies in dealing with a wide range of issues, which include countering inter-ethnic and intra-religious violence in both Iraq and Afghanistan as elsewhere, combating racial and religious discrimination, promoting moderation and modernization, improving mother-child health in OIC member states, encouraging the participation of women in politics, improving human rights conditions and female equality, as well as many other existing and emerging issues. The US has a vested interest in each and every single one of these areas, and the OIC is the legitimate, credible and able political body to partner with as it too shares the same interests.

Therefore, in addition to closely working with the two US presidential envoys to it, the OIC has sought the ways and means to engage with the US Senate and House, think tanks, civil society organizations and the media to introduce what it stands for and, more importantly, to understand how it can be of further help. It is unfortunate though that not many, if any, Americans are really aware of what the OIC stands for.

Ironically though, in recent months, the OIC's publicity has skyrocketed in the US, inside the Beltway at least, thanks to xenophobic and Islamophobic pundits, as well as extreme right blogs such as PipeLine-

---

[57] First appeared in *Today's Zaman* daily on December 28, 2011.

News, Family Security Matters and the like. Their continuous defamation of the OIC has intensified recently with the US State Department's
decision to invite the OIC to take part in an expert-level meeting to discuss practical steps for the implementation of United Nations Human
Rights Council (UNHRC) Resolution 16/18, which was formulated
on the basis of the eight points provided by the OIC secretary-general during one of his speeches in Geneva to promote a culture of tolerance and mutual understanding. The resolution, titled "Combating intolerance, negative stereotyping and stigmatization of, and discrimination,
incitement to violence, and violence against persons based on religion
or belief," was adopted by consensus at the UNHRC in March 2011
with the participation of the United States, European Union and OIC
member states as well as states from the other regional formations. This
week the United Nations General Assembly also adopted by consensus of 193 nations a similar resolution derived from Res. 16/18 with
the same title. The resolution simply means that the states should take
the necessary precautions—consistent with their obligations under international human rights law—so that Jews, Christians, Muslims, Buddhists, Hindus, atheists, agnostics and individuals subscribing to any
thought, belief and non-belief system are not exposed to violence and/
or discrimination due to their religion or belief.

"A form of holy war"

Oddly enough, however, Pamela Geller wrote, "the Islamized State
Department will be meeting with the Islamic supremacist Organization
of Islamic Cooperation (OIC) to discuss strategies and develop action
plans in which to impose the restriction of free speech ... under the
Sharia here in America." In the same piece, she compared the US engagement with the OIC to discuss religious tolerance to having Himmler
(military commander and leading member of the Nazi Party) meet with
Jews to condemn Jew-hatred. Similarly, Clare Lopez of the so-called
Clarion Fund speculated that Secretary of State Hillary Clinton was
due to host OIC Secretary-General Ekmeleddin İhsanoğlu in Washington to "discuss how the United States can implement the OIC agenda
to criminalize criticism of Islam." Another example of this kind is Frank

Gaffney of the Center for Security Policy, who criticized the Obama administration for facilitating the efforts of the Muslim-American organizations to "penetrate and influence the government of the United States." Gaffney thinks that these organizations are pursuing a "civilization jihad," which is allegedly a "stealthy form of holy war, designed to eliminate and destroy Western civilization from within." He too speculated that the expert-level meeting hosted by the State Department to discuss religious tolerance was a part of such a stealthy form of holy war, a civilization jihad.

The two-day Istanbul Process conference hosted by the US State Department Dec. 12-14, 2011, was in fact a dramatic step forward in implementation of the consensual decision of the US, EU, OIC member states and other signatories of the resolution toward protecting individuals or communities of the individuals subscribing to any religion or belief, against discrimination and violence. Discrimination and violence against individuals who "express" their opinion is included. The critiques argue that the US should not engage with the OIC, many members of which have blasphemy laws or restrict freedom of expression in one way or another. Actually, that is the very reason why the US should engage with the OIC. A prominent human rights advocacy organization, Human Rights First (HRF), has welcomed the UN General Assembly resolution and the US State Department meeting. Joëlle Fiss of the HRF noted that the resolution encourages open debate, human rights education and interfaith and intercultural initiatives. She also argued that the Istanbul Process conference was important to demonstrate that "states have tools at their disposal to combat violence, discrimination and hatred without restricting free speech."

The two-day conference was a follow-up to a high-level meeting, co-chaired by OIC Secretary-General İhsanoğlu and US Secretary of State Clinton in Istanbul on July 15 this year. Also participating in that high-level meeting was the EU High Representative for Foreign Affairs Catherine Ashton as well as foreign ministers and high-level representatives from some 19 countries, the Office of the UN High Commissioner for Human Rights, the African Union, the Arab League and the Vatican. In a statement issued after the meeting, they jointly "called upon all relevant stakeholders throughout the world to take seriously the call for action set forth in Resolution 16/18, which contributes to strengthening the foundations of tolerance and respect for religious diversity as well as enhancing the promotion and protection of human rights and fundamental freedoms around the world." Again at this meeting, the participants committed to "go beyond mere rhetoric and to reaffirm their commitment to freedom of religion or belief and freedom of expression by urging States to take effective measures, as set forth in Resolution 16/18, consistent with their obligations under international human rights law, to address and combat intolerance, discrimination and violence based on religion or belief."

So, does any of these look like a "stealthy form of holy war" or a "civilization jihad" waged to destroy the Western civilization? If it does, what doesn't? One would expect that in the United States the criticism within extreme right, xenophobic and Islamophobic circles targeting the OIC would be rather more sophisticated and intellectually challenging, if not constructive. However, it fails to be anything more than mere fearmongering and speculating on the basis of false information. As a matter of fact, with its new Charter revised in 2008, the OIC clearly stresses its commitment to the universally accepted principles of the UN Charter, and consequently affirms its priorities as the promotion of human rights and fundamental freedoms, good governance, transparency and accountability and the rule of law. More importantly, it consistently works toward realizing these priorities in its member states. In the end, the only good thing about the fierce defamation campaign waged against the OIC in the United States is its perpetrators' success in raising the OIC's visibility within American public opinion. Concomitantly, the only thing left to the OIC is to continue its constructive engagement with the relevant US authorities, think tanks, media, civil society organizations and other interested partners, while at the same time trying to correct the false information spread out about it.

THE SO-CALLED IRANIAN
NUCLEAR THREAT[58]

The rumor about Iran's alleged nuclear weapons program, which led to a reaction from the UN Security Council some six years ago, remains a rumor today.

Since then, a perpetually growing sense of panic has dramatically raised the prospects of either a massive regional conflict in the Persian Gulf, involving both Israel and the United States, or a regional cold war that pits Iran, Iraq and Syria against Turkey, Saudi Arabia and the Sunni Arab world. Given the council's overall approach in this matter, however, one is compelled to question if Iran's intention to build nuclear weapons, or the prevention of it from doing so, are really of primary concern. It seems that for those blowing the clarion against Iran, this country's probability of having a nuclear weapon and the pervasive fear emanating from this probability are more important than actually ensuring that it does not have, or get, one.

Following the resolution adopted by the International Atomic Energy Agency (IAEA) on Feb. 4, 2006, the Security Council issued a presidential statement in March of the same year expressing its concern about Iran's nuclear program and asking the latter to fully suspend its nuclear program and to allow the IAEA to verify its peaceful nature. Subsequently, the council adopted Resolution 1696 (2006), invoking chapter VII of the UN Charter and obliging Iran to suspend its program; Resolution 1737 (2006), imposing sanctions by cutting off nuclear cooperation and freezing the assets of individuals and entities linked to the nuclear program; Resolution 1747 (2007), expanding the list of sanctioned entities; Resolution 1803 (2008), further expanding the sanc-

[58] First appeared in *Today's Zaman* daily on January 16, 2012.

tions, imposing a travel ban on the sanctioned persons and banning the export of nuclear and missile-related dual-use goods to Iran; Resolution 1835 (2008), reaffirming all the sanctions already imposed on Iran; and finally Resolution 1929 (2010), imposing a complete arms embargo on Iran, banning it from any activities related to ballistic missiles, authorizing the inspection and seizure of shipments violating the council's sanctions and extending the asset freeze to the Iranian Revolutionary Guard Corps (IRGC) and the Islamic Republic of Iran Shipping Lines (IRISL). As should be remembered, both Turkey and Brazil voted against this resolution, believing that further sanctions on Iran would be counterproductive in trying to resolve the issue.

Resolutions that are designed not to resolve

The crux of these resolutions is captured in a specific clause on which they are all predicated: "The IAEA is unable to conclude that there are no undeclared nuclear materials or activities in Iran." Therefore, the council continues to call upon Iran to re-establish "full and sustained suspension of all enrichment-related and reprocessing activities, including research and development, to be verified by the IAEA." That is, Iran should suspend its nuclear program, even if it is in fact a peaceful one, until the IAEA makes sure that there are no undeclared nuclear materials or activities anywhere in the country. In response, the Iranian authorities argue that they have been cooperating with the IAEA as required. They also argue that they have the right to continue the enrichment for research and development in conformity with the Nuclear Non-proliferation Treaty, to which Iran is a signatory and which stipulates that the signatory states have a right to "develop research, production and use of nuclear energy for peaceful purposes without discrimination." In the meantime, the fear and panic about Iran's alleged intentions to acquire nuclear weapon capabilities have grown exponentially thanks to very well organized campaigns in the West, especially in the US.

If it is seeking nuclear weapons Iran is certainly violating international law, threatening to shift the regional balance of power and risking a massive arms race and escalation of tensions among its neighbors.

Hence, this potential threat must be dealt with before it is too late. However, the Security Council's approach to the issue is problematic. As such, the council itself hinders the resolution of the problem.

As the council considers Iran "guilty until proven innocent" as opposed to "innocent until proven guilty," this problematic approach has two dimensions, the first of which is more of a technical one. What is the reason for the IAEA's inability to fulfill its mission? Is it because of Iran's lack of cooperation, which actually does not seem to be the case, or because of the IAEA's lack of sufficient technical capabilities? Or worse, could the reason be the political pressure on the IAEA that precludes it from coming to a conclusion that would undermine the deliberately constructed fear and panic about Iran's alleged nuclear program? In the context of this connection, how should one interpret former IAEA General Director Muhammad El-Baradei's statement during his interview with the Austrian Press Agency (APA) in January 2011, in which he said, "The threat posed by Iran's nuclear program was exaggerated by the West"?

In the same interview, El-Baradei accuses the West of thwarting an agreement with Iran by making "unrealistic demands" and speaks of the second dimension of the council's approach, which is problematic, both conceptually and practically. How is it possible to ensure that Iran does not have an intention to pursue nuclear weapons? And how is it possible to ensure that there are no undeclared nuclear materials or activities in Iran? Trying to do either or both is tantamount to trying to prove that something does not exist. However, whereas discovering just one single example suffices to prove that that thing exists, proving that it does not requires one to look for it in every bit of space in order to ensure its nonexistence. Only then can one conclude that it does not exist. By this token, if the council's resolutions are to be fulfilled, the IAEA would have to search everywhere in Iran in order to ensure the nonexistence of undeclared nuclear material or activity, which is practically impossible. Even if the IAEA manages to fulfill such an unrealistic mission it is always possible that the protagonists of the alleged Iranian nuclear threat can dismiss the IAEA's conclusion by simply ridiculing it for its inability to find evidence of Iran's nuclear weapons program, which they so strongly believe exists somewhere. It is especially likely, given that the same actors had paved the way to the 2003 invasion of Iraq with similar tactics, only to admit in shame years later that they were wrong about Saddam Hussein's alleged weapons of mass destruction. In addition, the fact that Security Council members do not take similar action against another regional state, which does not deny its possession of nuclear weapons, further undermines the council's credibility vis-à-vis the alleged Iranian nuclear threat.

So, it is all quite clear that the Security Council's approach to Iran's nuclear program is designed not to eliminate but to perpetuate the suspicions about it, with a growing sense of urgency, fear and panic. It goes without saying that the protagonists of the alleged Iranian nuclear threat are the same as those who are effectively dominant in shaping and mobilizing the council's resolutions in this matter, namely the US, the EU3 (United Kingdom, France and Germany) and Israel.

Wars: destructive for some, profitable for others

As the council keeps passing one resolution after another about Iran, Israel too keeps threatening to strike Iran's nuclear facilities if diplomacy fails. The US and the EU3 have described Iran's alleged nuclear weapons program as a major threat to international security and sought to increase pressure on Iran through national sanctions along with the UN sanctions. In the meantime, although it does not single out Iran as a specific threat or target (thanks to Turkey's efforts), NATO's new strategic concept and missile defense system have been developed on the assumption that Iran is pursuing a clandestine nuclear weapons program. In reaction, Iranian officials have repeatedly warned that Iran would deliver a crushing response to any kind of military attack on its nuclear facilities, in a war that would have devastating implications far beyond the region. Moreover, Iran criticized the presence of US warships and aircraft carriers in the Persian Gulf. It warned against possible EU sanctions on Iranian oil exports by suggesting that it may shut down the Strait of Hormuz, through which about 20 percent of the world's oil is transported. In response, the US has noted that any attempt by Iran that would disrupt the flow of oil to the world markets would not be tolerated.

In the meantime, as the only winner in the invasions of Afghanistan and Iraq, Iran has been expanding its sphere of influence in the region, whereas its Sunni Arab neighbors are losing theirs as a shattering effect of the so-called Arab Spring. Iraq is now pretty much considered a Shiite state within the orbit of Iran. Syria's Alawite-dominated regime relies heavily on Tehran's support. Shiite communities all over the Arab world, including in Yemen, Bahrain and Saudi Arabia not only increase Tehran's leverage but also create a misleading sense of "Shiite emancipation from the Sunni oppressors," which can be easily manipulated. In fact, before his recent visit to Tehran, Turkish Foreign Minister Ahmet Davutoğlu warned about the existence of certain parties intending to deliberately instigate a Sunni-Shiite war in the region.

At this point, it would be a mistake to think that the US, the EU3 or Israel are seeking to prepare the ground for an invasion of Iran, or trying to instigate a Sunni-Shiite war across the region. Yet, it would be equally, if not more, mistaken to think that there are not certain special interest groups within each country, who would want to do either or both. One may be inclined to ask why they would be interested in pursuing such an agenda. But the real question one should ask is, why would they not? After all, pragmatically speaking and as seen during the course of the Iran-Iraq war as well as in the run up to the first Gulf War, sustained regional wars and the escalation of tension among the regional powers can be manipulated to become quite profitable, both politically and economically, for the United States, the European Union and, most notably, for Israel.

Nevertheless, there are strong reasons to believe that the US, the EU3 and Israel would not directly engage in a military conflict with Iran. First, neither the US nor the EU3 are financially stable enough to sustain a war with Iran, especially after a decade of military engagements both in Afghanistan and Iraq. Second, throughout its history Israel has never had any conflict with Iran beyond mere exchange of threats and condemnations. Nor is there any reason for them to do so, given that they share a similar fate in the ocean of Arabs surrounding them.

Actually, in his *Treacherous Alliance: the Secret Dealings of Israel, Iran and the United States*, Trita Parsi notes that the relationship between Tehran and Tel Aviv continued even after the so-called Islamic revolution in 1979 under the auspices of the dreaded Khomeini. Third, since the end of the Cold War the fundamental tenets of US policy towards the Middle East are to ensure safe and smooth access to energy resources and to protect Israel. Since it would be existentially detrimental to Israel, Saudi Arabia, and other Gulf countries supplying the world energy markets, any military confrontation with Iran is antithetical to the vital interests of the US. Fourth, Iran is a major energy supplier to both the EU and China. Although the EU is entertaining the idea of sanctions on Iranian crude exports, it is hardly capable of sustaining these sanctions, given that doing so would strengthen Moscow's leverage towards the EU as the only major energy supplier. Similarly, with an ever-increasing need for energy resources, China would oppose any scheme that would disrupt its energy supply from Iran.

Fifth, Iran is not like Afghanistan or Iraq. It has survived for more than three decades despite the isolation and sanctions imposed on it. In a way, these hardships enabled Iran to develop self-sufficiency and technological capabilities not only to the extent of pursuing a nuclear program but also of being able to intercept and seize possession of an American drone. Most importantly, Iran has an ideology which glorifies martyrdom from the age of seven to 77 and this could be quite costly for all of its perceived enemies. There is no need to mention that with its heavy influence over the Shiites in Iraq, Syria, Saudi Arabia and Lebanon, Iran is quite capable of burning the whole region.

From the perspective of certain elements within the US, the EU3 and Israel, the deliberate escalation of tensions and consequentially the occasional low-intensity military conflicts between Iran, Syria, Iraq and Shiite communities on one side and Turkey, Saudi Arabia, the Gulf countries and Sunni communities on the other may be considered to be a lucrative opportunity to manipulate and profit from. With the realization of this second scenario, all of the states in the region and the ethno-religious groups within each state would turn into potential customers for all kinds of military technology, from conventional weapons to long-range missiles and fighter jets and cyber-security systems. The energy suppliers on both sides would be even more willing to get their oil and gas to the world market, because only then would they be able to sustain their economic strength while engaging in an arms race or military conflict with the other side. Moreover, these countries would be much more fragile politically, economically and socially and hence easier to manipulate diplomatically. Finally, these countries would be consuming one another for a period with no foreseeable end. Of course, for this scenario to fully materialize Iran must continue to be perceived as a growing nuclear threat to regional and international security, as a major threat to the Sunni majority within the Muslim world and as an existential threat to certain Arab states, like Saudi Arabia and the Gulf emirates.

In its final analysis, the IAEA is not suggesting that Iran is pursuing a nuclear weapons program, but that the agency is "unable to conclude that there are no undeclared nuclear materials or activities in Iran." In any case, such an objective is impossible to achieve conceptually and practically. So long as that remains the objective of the IAEA, as well as the criterion for the Security Council, the perception of an "Iranian nuclear threat" will pervade and the panic is likely to increase. As a result, rather than a military conflict between the US, the EU3, Israel and Iran, a sustained escalation of tensions, military confrontations and proxy wars are likely to ensue between Iran, its allies and the rest of the region. In the end, it is up to Iran, Syria, Turkey, Saudi Arabia, the Emirates and other regional actors to allow this second scenario to materialize.

DIALECTIC, DEMAGOGY, AND CHP[59]

K arl Marx, Wilhelm Hegel and Friedrich Engels would have been mesmerized, if only they could see the piece recently published in *The Washington Post* under the name of Kemal Kılıçdaroğlu, an accidental head of Turkey's Republican People's Party (CHP) and the so-called main opposition leader.

Fathers of the dialectic materialism, the trio would be proud of Kılıçdaroğlu, as he looks as if he's trying to discuss the contradictions of Turkey's much-applauded democracy in the piece titled "Opposition being silenced in Turkey." Swimming against the current, Kılıçdaroğlu challenges the commonly accepted view that the Justice and Development Party (AK Party) may present a workable example of conservative democracy for Middle Eastern societies as they try to transform their authoritarian political systems into more democratic and pluralistic ones. He argues the AK Party government has been silencing the opposition through its manipulation of the judiciary. Therefore, he concludes the AK Party model does not hold. However, the solid distortions of the facts and the deliberate omission of critical information regarding the ongoing investigation into the so-called Ergenekon terror network nested within the state apparatus warrants the opinion that the piece published under the name of the CHP leader fails to be anything beyond mediocre demagogy.

To begin with, the question has never been whether or not the AK Party could be a model for other Muslim-majority countries in the Middle East, but rather if they could mimic Turkey's democratization experience. The widely held conclusion is that each country has its own socioeconomic and political character; as such, they have to figure out their own way to democracy; therefore, Turkey cannot be a model to

---

[59] First appeared in *Today's Zaman* daily on February 12, 2012.

these countries, but its quest for democracy and its progress in democratizing the country's highly militarized and corrupt political system can be an inspiration to them. Besides, for an AK Party model to hold, clearly there is a need for an opposition like the CHP headed by Kılıçdaroğlu. Luckily, this appears not to be the case in any of Turkey's neighbors seeking, as he puts it, to get rid of totalitarian regimes and become true democracies. It looks like Kılıçdaroğlu has remained "French," as Turks would say when describing someone who is uninformed, to the "Arab Spring" debate.

A disciple's attempt at dialectic

Speaking to the Western audience in general, and Americans in particular, Kılıçdaroğlu reports that "hundreds of journalists, publishers, military officers, academics and politicians are being held" on charges that an ultranationalist underground organization plotted to overthrow the government. He is right indeed. However, he falls short in, if not deliberately avoids, pointing out that they are being detained not because an ultranationalist underground organization plotted to overthrow the government, but because the independent prosecutors have enough reason to suspect that in their respective capacities as journalists, publishers, military officers, academics and politicians, these detainees partook in the illegal activities of an alleged terrorist organization named "Ergenekon," the existence of which has been admitted by many of the detainees, including recently by one involved in the murder of Hrant Dink, a Turkish journalist of Armenian origin.

For instance, Ahmet Şık and Nedim Şener are two journalists who have been fashionably portrayed as victims of the restrictions on freedom of expression in Turkey. Allegedly, Şık and Şener were detained because they had been investigating, as the two put it, the diffusion and influence of the so-called Gülen community within the country's police force in their respective books, titled *İmamın Ordusu* (The Imam's Army) and *Dink Cinayeti ve İstihbarat Yalanları* (The Dink Murder and Intelligence Lies). Their arrests in March 2011 have been deliberately portrayed as evidence of the government's stifling of freedom of expression. In and of itself, writing a book about anyone or any phenomenon is not, and should never be, a crime in Turkey. The presence and continuous proliferation of publications of a similar kind speak to the fact that it has not been, or at least is not, the case. It makes rather more sense that Şık and Şener may have been arrested not because they wrote these books, but because they attempted to obstruct justice and manipulate an ongoing investigation into the alleged Ergenekon terrorist network via such acts as disclosing classified information, attributing crime to innocent individuals and groups, and inciting hatred and violence against them on the basis of unfounded allegations. A similar example is that of *New York Times* journalist Judith Miller, who was jailed in 2005 for contempt of court when she refused to appear before the grand jury investigating the Valerie Plame case. Did she enjoy journalistic immunity before the law? Was what she did an exercise of freedom of expression? Or, was what federal judge Thomas Hogan did a restriction of freedom of expression? Not really.

One can certainly criticize the manner and procedure with which judicial investigations are carried out in Turkey. One can complain about the long durations of detainment without trial or conviction. After all, it is a common problem in many countries, including the United States, where individuals suspected of involvement in terrorism can be detained infinitely before hearing their indictment or standing trial. Yet, readily declaring the suspects, who happen to be journalists, innocent and all the rest, those who the suspects oppose, guilty neither serves justice nor is in line with journalistic impartiality. Especially in a country like contemporary Turkey, governed by a constitution that was made by the military with the CHP's contribution and which the CHP refuses to reform. As Mehmet Baransu of the *Taraf* daily argues, manufactured news reports and publications have long been used as evidence to depose democratically elected governments, shut down political parties and sentence people to death or to life in Turkey. He reminds us that in 1998, prosecutor Vural Savaş used a book as evidence in a lawsuit that led to the closure of the Welfare Party (RP), which had earlier been forced to resign from the government by the army. It was later confirmed that Ergün Poyraz had been commissioned to write the book, titled *Refah'ın Gerçek Yüzü* (The Real Face of Refah), by JİTEM, an element of the alleged Ergenekon terrorist network, which is currently under investigation.

Similarly, the detained "politicians" who Kılıçdaroğlu mentions are not the politicians who campaigned, got elected and were jailed because of their opposition to the government, but individuals who had been detained before the 2011 elections for their alleged involvement in the plots to overthrow the government. In the run-up to the elections, CHP leader Kılıçdaroğlu nominated these individuals as deputies for his party, despite the opposition of his colleagues and voters of the CHP. Thanks to the screwed up political party laws, which give the authority to elect deputies not to the voters but to the head of the party, these individuals were elected to Parliament from the traditionally CHP-supportive districts, where it was certain they would be elected. Kılıçdaroğlu hoped that once elected, these suspects could enjoy parliamentary immunity; but apparently, this is not the case, and it causes further resentment against him.

At the apex of demagogy

Kılıçdaroğlu reaches the apex of demagogy and hypocrisy when he brags about the universal norm of the rule of law. He rightly says, "A universal norm of the rule of law is that one is innocent until proven guilty. Another is that evidence leads to the arrest of a suspect. In today's Turkey, however, people are treated as guilty until proven innocent." Considering these words only, one can hardly say Kılıçdaroğlu is heading the political party that is almost synonymous with everything he seems to despise and every crime that he attributes to his opponent.

A quick look into the history of the Turkish Republic reveals how the CHP has persistently hindered Turkey's democratization, polarized society into different camps, deepened the ethno-religious fault lines and created the single most critical security problem the country has suffered from for decades. In 1925, the CHP first hastily adopted the Takrir-i Sükun Kanunu (Law on Ensuring Stability and Calm) in Parliament, when the majority of opposition party members were not present. This law initiated the establishment of the so-called İstiklal Mahkemeleri (Independence Courts), which were given the authority to hang anyone suspected of involvement in religious reactionaryism and schemes targeting the regime. So they exercised this authority with quite broad interpretation. In some cases, the court hanged the suspect and then asked the prosecutor to prepare the indictment. In others, the court had the corpse of a suspect excavated from his grave and hung him, just because he had died naturally before the court ruled for his hanging. The same CHP shut down its liberal opponent Terakkiperver Cumhuriyet Fırkası (Progressive Republican Party), in fact its only opponent, for some of its members' alleged involvement in the dubious Sheikh Said uprising.

Moreover, it is the same CHP that committed the Dersim massacre in 1937-1938. It involved the aerial bombardment of the predominantly Alevi towns and villages in Tunceli province, poison-gassing of the innocent people hiding out in caves, and the mass murder of people either by shooting or throwing them into the Euphrates. According to official records, which are highly likely to reflect a lower number than what it actually is, the CHP government's Dersim venture resulted in the deaths of 13,160 civilians and the relocation of 11,818. One of the Dersim Alevis who had to relocate to western Turkey, Kılıçdaroğlu did not even have the courage to condemn his party's treatment of his own kinsmen. He in fact recently silenced a member of his party who actually dared to speak up.

Similarly, the CHP just stood by and cheered for the rogue members of the army as they disrupted Turkey's democratization three-and-a-half times, respectively in 1960, 1971, 1980 and 1997. It remained silent all along as the perpetrators of the 1980 military coup turned the Diyarbakır Cezaevi (Diyarbakır Prison) into a breeding and training ground for Kurdistan Workers' Party (PKK) militants by exposing activist and non-activist Kurds to a level and kind of torture beyond human imagination. Finally, it is Kılıçdaroğlu's very same CHP that enacted and implemented laws that for so many decades equally deprived Turkey's Muslim majority and Christian minority of their rights to exercise their religion. For this reason, it is no surprise at all to see Kılıçdaroğlu and his CHP trying to have the Ergenekon suspects released, even though there is mounting evidence, both in voice recordings and signed documents, suggesting the suspects have plotted such diabolic schemes. Some of them included blowing up a museum during a children's visit and mosques during crowded prayer times, shooting down a Turkish jet and blaming it on the Greeks, assassinating prominent minority figures, and planting weapons in the apartments of college students who happen to be sympathizers of Fethullah Gülen so they can portray the ruling AK Party government as impotent to deal with the alleged rise of radicalization and terrorism.

Today, when he speaks of Turkey being "a country where people live in fear and are divided politically, economically and socially" and about Turkish democracy "regressing in terms of the separation of powers, basic human rights and freedoms and social development and justice," he sounds like he is making a mockery of his own party's legacy and himself. He also demonstrates that the real problem in Turkey is not that the governing party is silencing the opposition, but the opposition is so impotent or unsophisticated that it is incapable of meaningfully and effectively discharging its role as an opposition. Another emerging problem is that the ruling AK Party government is increasingly becoming a status quo party, giving up its reformist character.

Kılıçdaroğlu deserved credit though for recognizing that "tactics such as oppression, preying on fear and restricting freedoms can help sustain a government's rule for only so long. Never in history has a government succeeded in ruling permanently through authoritarian measures. Oppression does not endure; righteousness does. Turkey will be no exception."

Certainly, Turkey is not an exception. After all, the CHP's rule in Turkey lasted only for a quarter century from 1923 to 1948, and its probability of winning a parliamentary election in Turkey is next to none. Similarly, the so-called "dynamic forces," which disrupted Turkish democracy three-and-a-half times, strangled the democratically elected governments and kept each in a straightjacket up until very recently, seem unable to utilize tactics such as oppression, preying on fear and restricting freedoms. As Kılıçdaroğlu rightly states, oppression does not endure; so too the obstructions of Turkish democracy. Righteousness does; so will Turkey's march toward democracy.

THE SYRIAN CONUNDRUM[60]

W hat is really happening in Syria? Why is the UN Security Council unable to move forward in a way that would bring an end to the humanitarian tragedy in Homs, Hama, Daraa, Idlib and other places where the Syrian armed forces and the opposition are fighting each other?

Is the conflict in Syria a natural outcome of a popular quest for democracy and freedom in the mold of the so-called Arab Spring? Or is it a result of the power struggle between those who have been implementing a deliberate project to restructure the political sphere across the Middle East, and those who resist it, at least resist the part of that project concerning Syria? Why are some states so enthusiastic to intervene in Syria and make President Bashar al-Assad leave power? There is no doubt that the killing of even one innocent civilian is a huge tragedy and, as such, unacceptable. But is the death toll, reaching some 8,000, the primary concern of the supporters of intervention? By the way, why is the death toll rising? Is it because the Syrian armed forces are pursuing an ethnic cleansing? Or is it because the supporters of the intervention are pursuing a political strategy to prolong the conflict, further increasing the civilian death toll and, hence, gradually building legitimacy for a military intervention in Syria? In the case of a military intervention, would such an intervention be made in order to bring stability and democracy to Syria, or would it serve as a step towards laying the ground in preparation for a military assault on another country farther east such as Iran?

More specifically, when the US Secretary of State said to the Security Council, and hence to the international community that once President Assad, who has lost his legitimacy, leaves power, Syria's Alevites,

60 First appeared in *Today's Zaman* daily on March 8, 2012.

Sunnis, Druzees, Christians, Kurds and Arabs would "hand in hand" create a democratic and peaceful country, did she really believe what she said, especially after the failing examples of Afghanistan, Iraq and Libya? How could Saudi Arabia possibly vow to "take place at the forefront of any initiative" to liberate "the Syrian people, who have been oppressed for so long under the Assad family"? When Saudi Arabia and other Arab League members like Egypt and Libya pronounce such ideas as financing and arming the Syrian opposition against government forces, what could they possibly be thinking? Are these ideas aimed at ousting the Assad government? Or does it have something to do with the opportunity to deprive Iran of its only possible ally in the region?

Speaking of Syria and Iran, who happen to be Turkey's immediate neighbors and used to be its natural allies in the fight against PKK terrorism, will Turkey's national interests be best served when there is a political vacuum in Syria after President Assad's forced departure, when the ethnically and religiously divided Syrian society succumbs to a civil war, or when Turkey's Syrian border simply becomes irrelevant as a result of lawlessness and a lack of security? Or will Turkey's interests be better served if Iran becomes even more vulnerable, closer to being attacked and, hence, more reactionary? How would such a prolonged ethnic and religious conflict across Syria and a military assault targeting Iran affect Turkey's domestic politics and economy? Moreover, why has Ankara decided against political engagement with the Assad government when it opposed, at least initially, a NATO intervention against the Qaddafi regime in Libya on the grounds that such an assault would make Qaddafi resort to more violence?

Furthermore, Turkish officials stress that they have had extensive talks with President Assad, at times as long six continuous hours, in which they advised Assad what to do in order to reform his country and avoid the current crisis—a crisis Assad apparently did not see coming. Was Ankara expecting the head of another sovereign state to simply take in all the recommendations or instructions and start implementing them? Would Ankara be exonerated from the coming disasters emanating from a chaotic Syria by simply saying that we already warned Assad? Moreover, Ankara is becoming ever more daring as it likens the situation in Syria to the Srebrenica massacre, where Serbian troops massacred some 8,000 Bosnian Muslims in so-called UN safe havens. Similarly, the Turkish president has become assertive enough to say that Turkey wants President Assad to leave. One wonders if the AK Party government is capable enough to prevent future false flag operations like the recent Uludere incident, in which Turkish fighter jets bombarded 34 Kurdish civilians crossing the border. Similarly, one wonders from which international law the Turkish president gets the authority to call upon another head of state to give up power. In case the conditions were manipulated enough against Turkey, would he consider heeding such calls?

There are also a number of other questions that are hard to ask while trying to maintain political correctness. For instance, what would be Ankara's response if a group of Kurdistan Workers' Party (PKK) and Kurdish Communities Union (KCK) terrorists engaged in armed conflict with the Turkish security forces in such urban areas as Diyarbakır, Batman and Hakkari and claimed a so-called Kurdish autonomy in the name of allegedly liberating their Kurdish brethren from the century-long oppression of the Turkish state? How would Ankara react if its neighbors like Syria, Iraq and Iran were to organize and assist the militant Kurdish opposition inside Turkey in the name of taming the ultra-nationalist Turkish regime? It is not that the situation of the Kurds in Turkey resembles the situation of the opposition in Syria by any means. But that is not the point either. What matters is that certain states, which seem to be Turkey's allies at the moment, can easily exploit Turkey's fight against PKK terrorism and bring it to the attention of the international community as if it is the Turkish state's systematic oppression of the Kurdish minority.

Moreover, let us imagine that eventually the humanitarian tragedy reaches a point that a military intervention into Syria is not only legitimate, but also necessary. Given that it has the second largest army in NATO, and is an immediate neighbor to Syria, Turkey will mostly likely be expected to lead that NATO intervention, just like France led it in Libya. How would Arabs across the Middle East interpret a Turkish-led military intervention in the Syrian Arab Republic? After all, as Foreign Minister Ahmet Davutoğlu recently reminded, Turkish people must be ready to go along with the decisions made by international bodies, of which Turkey is part, must they not?

These are just some of the questions one must tackle first, before aspiring to solve the Syrian conundrum with the current approach, which Ankara also seems to have adopted. One may argue that these are hypothetical questions, or mere speculations. Similarly, one can argue that the efforts of the supporters of the intervention are aimed at stopping the violence and preventing further deaths. That is certainly something that everyone hopes for. However, the course of developments at multilateral forums does not seem to be fully convincing in that regard.

Ending vs. prolonging the conflict in Syria

First of all, one of the biggest mistakes, or perhaps one of the deliberate distortions of reality, is to view Russia and China's vetoes in the Security Council as these countries' attempt to protect the Assad government. In fact, Turkish officials, most recently President Abdullah Gül, implied that the two were acting with Cold War instincts to protect their ally, Syria. On the contrary, what these two countries oppose is not an end to the violence, but a forced regime change, in yet another sovereign state, on the pretext of aiding a humanitarian tragedy. The so-called Arab League plan and the UN General Assembly's recently adopted resolution, as well as the failed Security Council resolutions, have all aimed to start a political process through which the Syrian government is simply to dissolve itself. Understandably, both Russia and China have an interest in preserving stability in the region and avoiding any structural collapse in Syria that would precipitate region-wide chaos. Of course, when the other states supporting this approach are Iran and North Korea, others who oppose the plan aiming to change the current Syrian regime is readily declared guilty by association and labeled a pro-Assad marginal who seeks to establish a Baathist regime in Turkey.

Second, the latest news reports suggesting that the Syrian government is not allowing the UN Under-Secretary General for Humanitarian and Emergency Relief into Syria may not completely reflect the truth. Recently, the United Kingdom in its capacity as president of the Security Council for the month of March announced that the Council members were deeply disappointed that Under-Secretary General for Humanitarian Affairs Valerie Amos was not able to enter Syria in a timely manner. So the Council's disappointment is not about the Syrian authorities blocking the Under-Secretary's visit to Syria for a humanitarian assessment, but about not allowing it in a "timely manner." There is no doubt that one can quite broadly interpret what "timely manner" means. The details are not known. In fact, the Syrian Ambassador to the UN has rejected this allegation, stating that it was he who personally facilitated authorizing the Under-Secretary's entry into his country. Nevertheless, it has already been established, as if it is a fact, that Syrian authorities are not allowing humanitarian assistance while the carnage continues.

Third, all, including the Syrians, have welcomed the appointment of the former UN Secretary-General Kofi Annan as part of a joint Arab League-UN envoy for Syria. However, it is not quite clear whether that appointment is intended to end or prolong the conflict. Annan deserves credit for skillfully mediating between the Kikuyu and the Luo of Kenya in 2008, and bringing to an end the violence that broke out after rigged elections. However, he failed to act in 2003 before some 1 million Rwandans were killed in a genocide. Additionally, he is mandated not by the Security Council, but by the General Assembly. So, although the Security Council president argues that Mr. Annan's mandate is not to mediate between the Syrian government and the opposition, but to start a political process that will lead the former to abandon power, Mr. Annan lacks the full support of the Security Council to do so, as long as Russia and China are not on board. Under these circumstances, one wonders if his appointment could break the current stalemate, or simply prolong it while continuing to build the legitimacy of a military intervention as the last, inevitable option.

Then, what?

What should be then the response of the international community in general, and of Turkey in particular, in the face of mounting violence and killings in Syria? First of all, it has to be clarified whether the objective is to oust the Assad government or to stop civilian killings, or both. If it is not the first one, then the international community must clearly state that in its discourse and UN resolutions. Accordingly, it should engage with the Syrian opposition, convince it to give up arms and encourage it to fully participate in the political process, which Assad has announced, and which seems to have started with the adoption of the constitutional changes allowing a multiparty system. Once the opposition ceases its armed struggle, which can be verified by the placement of international monitors, not only would the opposition have the moral high ground, but also the government forces would have no pretext to use violence. Any further violence from the government in that case would be qualified as violence against innocent and unarmed civilians, beyond any reasonable doubt. Any violence could and would be immediately reported by the monitors to the UN, and by the Syrians themselves, to the whole world through social media. The Syrian government forces would simply be deprived of any reason to use violence. Once the violence has ceased, neither the UN nor the Arab League, but the Organization of Islamic Cooperation (OIC) should take the lead in coordinating humanitarian assistance to the victims of clashes across Syria. After all, whereas the first two have already positioned themselves as the adversaries of the Syrian government, the latter still commands relative respect and trust. There is no need to mention that the OIC has managed to continue distributing its aid, as well as aid from the UN and other international humanitarian organizations, to the Somali people all along, while Al-Shabaab expelled all but the OIC humanitarian workers from Somalia.

Despite all its inflammatory rhetoric and active involvement in organizing the opposition even during the armed conflict, Ankara still holds the highest comparative advantage to engage with the Assad government and walk it through a political process that would move Syria towards democracy. Assad may not have readily participated when Ankara first engaged with him, somewhat didactically. However, the dynamics on the ground have changed. The humanitarian situation has deteriorated tremendously. The ruling Alewite elite as well as the Sunni elite of Homs, of which President's wife Asma Assad is a member, must have already recognized that bringing the current crisis rapidly to an end is more in the interest of them and their families than anyone else. Some in Ankara would be quick to say, "We already told him this!" But the essence of diplomacy is to never cut off the channels of communication, even with a genocidal leader. It is not to favor him, but to favor his potential victims. In fact, it is the Syrian officials who often stress that they are looking up to Turkey and the international community to help them bring change to Syria. The onus is on Foreign Minister Davutoğlu because he is the foremost mediator and because there is hardly any other such prominent statesman who knows both President Assad and his government insiders. The engagement and mediation track to be led by Ankara should garner support from the international community. After all, a prolonged and bloody conflict in Syria and beyond does not serve the interests of anyone. And the choice is not between ousting the Assad government and doing nothing but watching the carnage. The choice is between stopping the carnage through engagement with the Assad government and laying the ground for a region-wide bloodbath, from which Turkey would be affected most.

GÜLEN BECOMES LITMUS TEST
FOR AMERICAN MEDIA, TOO[61]

A shade as tiny as a fly's wing that covers one's pupil enables the trickster to move, or steal for that matter, items as gigantic as mountains before the very eyes of that person without him or her even noticing. Such a trick, so long as it goes unnoticed, can serve as a source of great power and influence for anyone or any entity, be it an ordinary individual, cunning politician or formidable newspaper.

Yet, when it is exposed, the trick puts the trickster in a humiliating situation. Then, the humiliation steadily grows, or it should for any trickster with a bit of decency, as the stakeholders become increasingly suspicious about the trickster's previous seemingly genuine acts as well. So, the exposed trick threatens to ruin the trickster's entire credibility, as he or she may well have been deceptive all along. The situation becomes extremely critical if the trickster is a major newspaper, which has for so long presented itself as "the" source of public information, and as such not only shaped public opinion, but also influenced major political decisions.

Of late, American media giants *The New York Times* and the *International Herald Tribune* (IHT) have been manifestly running the risk of humiliating themselves. The tiny shade they appear to have been using is their self-claimed journalistic impartiality, and the mountain they seem to have been stealing is American public opinion. Their spin-oriented reporting, this time on world-renowned scholar Fethullah Gülen and the civic movement he has inspired, has been not only catering to a narrow political agenda but also risking their credibility.

---

[61] First appeared in *Today's Zaman* daily on April 17, 2012.

New York Times and *International Herald Tribune* play mind games

On April 18, 2012, the *International Herald Tribune* ran an almost full-page story on its front page on Mr. Gülen and the Hizmet (Service) movement, which the paper preferred to describe as the "Gülen movement." The IHT headline was "Shadow force grows in Turkey," the page featured four photos: first, of Mr. Gülen, depicting him like Don Corleone, the Godfather; second, a photo of an elementary-school kid raising a Turkish flag up a pole, with a caption that read, "So-called Gülen schools, like this one in Istanbul, are in 140 countries"; third, a photo of a secondary-school boy and girl from apparently a theater play where the boy holds a rifle in his hands; and fourth, an innocent-looking picture of a young journalist, with a caption that reads, "The journalist Ahmet Şık was jailed after writing about Gülenists." The selection and composition of these four pictures in fact speak volumes about what to expect in the news report itself.

Almost a week later, on April 24, 2012, *The New York Times* ran the exact same report with the headline "Turkey Feels Sway of Reclusive Cleric in the US," along with a photo picturing elementary school children singing what one would imagine to be the Turkish national anthem, with the caption noting, "The movement has millions of followers and schools in 140 countries." Unfamiliar with both Mr. Gülen and the civic movement he has inspired, one would most probably process this presentation of visual and textual data as follows: "Well, this Islamic leader living a posh life on a farm in the United States, avoiding other people, reigns over a worldwide network of schools. The children of 140 different countries, attending these schools, are growing up to become pro-Turkey individuals, if not Turkish nationalists. If he has millions of followers, it means that he must be ruling over a network of businesses, NGOs, media networks. He must also have followers among powerful legislators, judges, prosecutors and bureaucrats. Which then one would think explains why anyone criticizing him would be jailed. Finally, if the US government is letting this Islamic leader reside in the US, then they must have some sort of a deal." Once the reader has been more or less led through such a thinking process, then it means that the spin-oriented reporting has been successful. That is, the presentation of individually accurate data and half-truths in such a composition has manipulated the readers' thinking to make a pre-judged conclusion about the subject matter.

A brief analysis of the news report reveals the spin methods that both *The New York Times* and its global edition, the *International Herald Tribune*, have employed. As a reminder, spinning means lying without using false information, or deceiving by leading one to believe something is true, although it is not. In any case, the spinner neither uses false information nor makes false statement, and yet deceives.

Spinning for dummies

First of all, the headline "Shadow force grows in Turkey" suggests that a somewhat unlawful entity, escaping official scrutiny, is insidiously spreading its influence. Since it does not make a reference to any actual entity, the newspapers can get away with it by simply arguing that it is the inference that the reporters have made through observation. Yet, such an alarmist headline suffices to trigger fear in the readers' minds. The report starts with the half-truth that a journalist named Ahmet Şık was jailed on charges of plotting to overthrow the government, and that he believed "a secretive movement linked to a reclusive imam living in the United States was behind his arrest." It is probably true that Mr. Şık may be thinking that Mr. Gülen was behind his arrest. Similarly, it is true that when Mr. Şık was arrested last year, he had already produced a manuscript, which he claimed would be a book on Gülen's alleged influence over the Turkish police force.

Understandably, Mr. Şık has the freedom to have his own views and beliefs, no matter what they are. The news report is simply quoting him as he voices these views, saying, "If you touch them, you get burned." Yet, what the news report is missing, or deliberately hiding, is that Mr. Şık had been arrested on charges of abetting coup plots against Turkey's democratically elected government, and not on the charge of criticizing Mr. Gülen. Similarly, it ignores the fact that he is just one of many, including from army and police officers to bureaucrats, politicians and journalists, who have been arrested during the course of a comprehensive judicial investigation into the multiple alleged coup plots.

Not that it has to, but the news report also fails to provide readers with critical information: When Mr. Şık was arrested, which he claims was because he wrote a critical book on Mr. Gülen, there were already many books on the shelves attacking and defaming Mr. Gülen. The authors of these books have not only remained unburned, but also thrived economically just like Mr. Şık did, and they were largely unknown figures, just like Mr. Şık. Some of these books are "Those who perform their ablutions with blood" by Ergün Poyraz (2007), "The Pro-Fethullah Gladio" by Hikmet Çetinkaya (2008), "American Bandsman" by Hikmet Çetinkaya (2009), "Global Troublemakers and Fethullahism" by Ahmet Akgül (2010) and "The Plan to Rescue the AK Party and Gülen (Made in CIA)" by Serdar Öztürk (2011). Mr. Şık would probably remain unemployed, and his book attacking Gülen would be nothing more than yet another book on a subject losing popularity, if his arrest was not portrayed as having been allegedly caused by his critique of Gülen.

Moreover, *The New York Times/IHT* news report writes, "The [Gülen] movement's stealthy expansion of power as well as its tactics and lack of transparency are now raising accusations that Gülen supporters are using their influence in Turkey's courts, police and intelligence service to engage in witch hunts against opponents with the aim of creating a more conservative Islamic Turkey." Certainly, there are some individuals in Turkey making such allegations or who genuinely believe this. By simply noting there are some who think this way, the news report is presenting a genuine fact. However, by presenting it as if it is a majority view, or in a way that leads readers to think that it is a majority view, the news report spins the truth yet again. In fact, the reporters themselves seem to have been affected by their own spin as they use such judgmental descriptions as "stealthy expansion of power" and "lack of transparency."

Similarly, the spin-oriented reporting utilizes the tactic of "guilt by association." For instance, in saying, "With its strong influence in the media and a small army of grass roots supporters, the Gülen movement has provided indispensable support to the conservative, Islam-inspired government of Prime Minister Recep Tayyip Erdoğan," the news report directly appeals to those readers disgruntled with the current Justice and Development Party (AK Party) government for one reason or another. The implicit message that the report aims to get across is that the AK Party government is guilty for whatever reason, and so are Gülen and the people inspired by him, because the latter provide indispensable support to the former. In fact, it is true that Gülen himself and the millions of people inspired by him have provided and will mostly likely provide indispensable support to Prime Minister Erdoğan and his government as the latter continues Turkey's process of democratization. Yet, by not accurately reflecting the nature of this support, the report seeks to incite the AK Party opponents among its readership to oppose Mr. Gülen and the civic initiatives he has inspired as well.

In the meantime, the report quotes (which was later revealed to be a misquote) a founding member of the AK Party, Ayşe Böhürler, in such a way to suggest that she is disturbed by the presence and allegedly increasing power of the so-called Gülen movement. The reporters have apparently used what they misquoted Böhürler as saying as the basis for their manipulative title that portrays the movement as a shadow power in Turkey. After the *IHT* ran the report, Böhürler wrote in her column in the *Yeni Şafak* daily that she had neither referred to the Gülen movement as a shadow power nor used the phrase "kicking in shadows" in a defamatory sense when apparently referring to the absence of a central entity governing the movement. She also wrote that she had disavowed what has been attributed to her by writing to both *International Herald Tribune* and *The New York Times* editors. Neither paper has published a correction. Yet, even if they do, it will not make much of a difference. After all, the news report has come out as the editors intended it to and has already made an impression on the readers. From this point on, even if both papers publish a correction that disputes all of the information presented in the original report, it would not eradicate completely the negative impression the report has created. So, this is an essential part of the spin-oriented reporting as well: Pretend like you've made a mistake in quoting; then, publish a correction; and then use this act as evidence of your alleged journalistic impartiality.

One can go on and on illustrating the spins, half-truths and distortions in *The New York Times* and *International Herald Tribune* reports. Their spin-oriented reporting on Gülen is worrying to a certain extent. After all, even if their reporting as such is somewhat tantamount to defamation of him and millions of people around the world who respect him, this is nothing new.

Over the past four decades, the establishment papers in Turkey have run probably thousands of false reports about Gülen and the Hizmet movement. With the strong backing of the anti-democratic status quo protectionists, these papers have not felt it necessary to even look impartial. A few like-minded prosecutors have used some of these false news reports as pseudo evidence to bring charges against Gülen. Yet, as Gülen has been acquitted of each and every one of these charges, it has become increasingly evident that these newspapers were simply using their resources to manipulate Turkish public opinion to satisfy narrow political and economic interests.

In a way, Gülen had become a litmus test to gauge Turkish newspapers' credibility. As Gülen becomes an increasingly popular topic for the American media, too, the question becomes the following: What if the spin-oriented reporting on Gülen makes fellow Americans recognize that for so many decades the establishment papers like *The New York Times* and the *International Herald Tribune* have used their alleged journalistic impartiality as a tiny shade covering pupils in order to steal mountains before people's very eyes, and to manipulate American public opinion to serve certain group interests? After all, who knows what the future holds.

DESPERATE LIVES OF POWER-
INTOXICATED LEADERS[62]

D uring the annual UN General Assembly, where all the world leaders gather in New York along with their respective entourages, it is quite easy to distinguish the European countries' delegations from the Middle Eastern ones.

The European delegations are mostly small in size, composed of four or five diplomats accompanying their head of delegation, be it a president, prime minister or foreign minister. At times, it is quite difficult to tell who is the head of the delegation. On the other hand, the Middle Eastern delegations are much more crowded with many people, apart from the diplomats, looking like they do not even know why they are there. It is instantly distinguishable who the head of the delegation is, because he always walks in front, flanked by his bodyguards and tailed by tens of hangers-on. This mafia-like image is justified by the belief that it shows how powerful both the leader and the country he heads is.

The leaders take advantage of the UN's General Debate during the week in order to boost their perceived "strong leader" image by making inflammatory speeches from the General Assembly's podium and frequently posing for the international media hand-in-hand, shoulder-to-shoulder and cheek-to-cheek with other world leaders, especially with the American president. Egypt's deposed President Hosni Mubarak was one of the darlings of the Western leaders. He was the "go-to" Arab leader for any issue related to the Arab world, Islamic world or Palestine. Even he could not have predicted the situation he is in right now

---

[62] First appeared in *Today's Zaman* daily on June 17, 2012.

in his wildest nightmares, as he might have thought that he was indispensable to Western interests in the Middle East.

Similarly, Libya's Muammar Gaddafi was among those who made the most out of the UN General Assembly. After a long period of isolation, Gaddafi made a speedy return to the international stage. He never had a shoulder-to shoulder picture with the American president, but did with all the others, including European leaders and the UN secretary-general. When he tore apart and threw away the UN Charter at the podium of the General Assembly, Gaddafi, too, could not imagine that only a year or so later Libyans would tear his body apart and throw it away. Interestingly, though, both men took office in their respective countries some decades ago as heroes who people hoped would eradicate injustices and bring about prosperity. Yet, they hung on and on, every time finding a way to justify it.

As for Turkish leaders...

The addiction to power and the failure to predict the future once intoxicated with power and influence is not unique to Arab leaders. Apparently, Turkish leaders have also been suffering from what some would call a mental and emotional disorder. For instance, after a decade of unprecedented political and economic progress from 1950 to 1960, legendary Turkish Prime Minister Adnan Menderes firmly believed that there was no longer a possibility of a military coup and that he could get a piece of wood elected to Parliament if he nominated it because the public loved him so much. He and everyone else tragically realized that he was dead wrong, when months later the military junta hastily tried him on charges of treason on a remote island, and hanged him three times to exact their full revenge. On the other hand, another former prime minister and president, Süleyman Demirel, whose last name literally means "iron hand," has always prided himself as a so-called leader who left office six times but came back seven times. Demirel has avoided a similarly tragic fate largely because he preferred to cooperate with his military detractors whenever the latter reigned in. Nevertheless, his entire political career has clearly illustrated his addiction to political power, and his inability to let go of it.

Then, one is inclined to ask: While American or European leaders move to their ranches to herd their cows, establish their foundations to do charity work, go back to university to teach or retire to their mansions to write their memoirs once they finish their terms in office or are defeated, why do Arab and Turkish leaders always try to hold on to power, stay in office as long as possible or obtain a higher post? Why do they try to bend the law, at times even laws they legislated, in order to avoid legal scrutiny or to stay in power for longer? Is it because the American and European leaders are better human beings? More specifically, given the precedents in Turkish political history and its current practices, what can be said of the fate of the Justice and Development Party (AK Party) government in Turkey, and of its leaders, from Prime Minister Recep Tayyip Erdoğan at the top, down to an ordinary minister, if they cannot let go at the right time? Finally, could it be argued that Prime Minister Erdoğan is also a leader who is not able to let go in the first place?

Many both inside and outside Turkey have increasingly voiced concern over the prime minister's alleged drift toward authoritarianism. Critics have argued that he is aiming for the presidency in 2014 only to further consolidate his "one-man" control over Turkey. Some others have speculated that the so-called Strategic Vision 2023 is just a smoke screen to make it possible to keep him and his cronies in office until then. On the other hand, his supporters have preferred to defer to Erdoğan's judgment by giving him the benefit of the doubt and saying, "If he is doing it, then it must be right!" Certainly, it is impossible to read the minds of Erdoğan and his team members. As such, it would be unfair to make any conclusive judgment about their tendencies. Yet, the AK Party government's practices in its third term have so far been quite perplexing.

AK Party leaders' track record

The AK Party leaders seem to have ventured into a series of actions that may set a precedent, and judicial changes that can make one miss the anti-democratic status quo, which they were elected in 2002 to fight in the first place. First came Prime Minister Erdoğan's intervention last year in the legal process to reduce the penalty for match-fixing and other corrupt acts by prominent figures in Turkish football. Then, he waded in when a prosecutor sought to interrogate the chief of the Turkish National Intelligence Organization (MİT) as part of an investigation into the Kurdistan Communities Union (KCK) terror network. Erdoğan simply prevented the investigation by pushing through Parliament overnight legislation that makes the prime minister's approval necessary for any investigation regarding the intelligence chief, army officers and other senior bureaucrats.

Moreover, when Turkish jets reportedly mistakenly bombed 34 Turkish citizens of Kurdish ethnicity near Uludere, the government responded in such an unprofessional way that for a moment people may have wondered whether the government was expecting an apology from the families of the victims for their children and relatives being within the jets' firing range. In the meantime, various journalists have been reprimanded, and some others fired, even from newspapers that have been traditionally loyal to the AK Party, coincidentally after they have been critical of the government's handling of the Uludere incident.

These days, the AK Party leaders, under the direct supervision of the Prime Ministry, have reportedly been working to pass legislation that will, among other things, abolish the specially authorized courts' mandate to investigate organized crime, corruption, drug dealing, coups and coup attempts. Also, any investigation involving politicians, high level bureaucrats and army officers would require the approval of the prime minister, the General Staff or governors, depending on who is to be investigated. That is, if a prosecutor wants to interrogate a senior bureaucrat, they will have to first get permission from the prime minister, or from the Chief of General Staff if it is an army officer under suspicion.

The critics of the proposed legislation worry that once it is obvious that there is a pending investigation request, the suspect will either flee or destroy the possible evidence before the request is approved. Or, that approval will never be granted because of obscure reasons, as it has been the case with the prosecutor's quest to interrogate the MİT chief. Prime Minister Erdoğan has recently defended the proposed legislation in a TV interview by accusing the specially authorized courts of acting as a state within the state. He ridiculed the specially authorized prosecutors by suggesting that investigating his senior bureaucrat was tantamount to investigating the prime minister himself, as if a court's ability to investigate the prime minister was not a fundamental of any true democracy governed by the rule of law.

Injustice to journalists

Moreover, the proposed legislation stipulates that journalists who write about the voice recordings or videos put on the Internet by whistleblowers will be sentenced to between two to five years in jail. Simply put, if a voice recording of a retired or active army officer pops up on the Internet, where he is plotting to overthrow the government, or a senior bureaucrat is caught selling the state secrets, then the officer or bureaucrat in question will not be investigated unless the General Staff or prime minister approves the investigation. Yet, any journalist or newspaper reporting about that voice recording will face a jail sentence and other commensurate measures.

What is the reason for all this proposed change? Erdoğan's answer is that his government initiated the specially authorized courts in 2005, and now it was again his government's right to abolish them. Some would argue that it is the basic description of a legislative authoritarianism. Some others suggest that he is afraid that these courts may at some point launch an investigation into the AK Party government as well, and want to interrogate its officials, including himself, on corruption charges. In reality, time will show who is right, and why Erdoğan seems to be trying to deprive these courts of their freedom to investigate anyone, including himself. Time will also tell whether or not Erdoğan will be the first successful Turkish prime minister not to seek the presidency, but to retire after his third term in the office.

WHO WILL HEAR THE
ROHINGYA PEOPLE'S CRY?[63]

When it comes to hearing the cry of the oppressed, or feeling the plight of the persecuted, we seem to be quite selective. Historically, American children were at some point advised by their mothers to remember the starving Armenian children at the hands of the "terrible Turks," when they refused to eat a meal. Yet, probably none of them were told about the Muslim children who were purged from the Balkans during the same period, or about the Catholic children who perished during the French genocide of Vendée, although as General Francois J. Westermann somewhat proudly reported back to Paris: "There is no more Vendée... According to the orders that you gave me, I crushed the children under the feet of the horses, massacred the women who, at least for these, will not give birth to any more brigands. I do no have a prisoner to reproach me. I have exterminated all."

Similarly, an average American is more likely to feel "sorry" for the Muslim women around the world, because they are taught, one way or another, that Muslim men beat their wives. Yet, they are likely to be unaware that according to the National Intimate Partner and Sexual Violence Survey 2010, "22 million women in the United States had been raped in their lifetime, and that 63.84 percent of women who reported being raped, physically assaulted, and/or stalked since age 18 were victimized by a current or former husband, cohabiting partner, boyfriend, or date." Again, an average American is more likely to hear about an Afghani women's rights activist who was killed by the Taliban, than about a 32-year-old Iraqi woman, a mother of five, who was beat-

---

[63] First appeared in *Today's Zaman* daily on July 25, 2012.

en to death in California by a right-wing extremist, who left her unconscious with a note that read, "Go back to your country, you terrorist." Furthermore, some people apparently hear the whispers of the children in Darfur, but fail to hear the screams of the Palestinian children, whose flesh has literally burned and melted due to the phosphorus bombs poured onto them time and again.

The same selectivity has long seemed to be a characteristic of the international actors as well, be it states, intergovernmental organizations or world-renowned media outlets. The situation in Myanmar (Burma) provides yet another case to test their sincerity and commitment to protecting human rights, regardless of the identity of the victims. Over the past several years, the international media have rightly campaigned to bring to the world's attention, especially to that of a Western audience, the case of Aung San Suu Kyi, a Burmese politician and chairperson of the National League for Democracy, who had been kept under house arrest since 1989 by Burma's military junta which then was in power in the country. Thankfully, this campaign has borne its fruit; she has been released, and even elected to the Burmese parliament. She has been made an international celebrity, a symbol of political resistance for democracy, and awarded all kinds of prizes, including the so-called Nobel Peace Prize.

But, how about the Rohingya Muslim women raped, beaten and literally kicked back into the fire by the Buddhist Burmese as they tried to escape? (See http://t.co/pG4zQ6ov) How about the Rohingya Muslim children who are burned alive, or thrown into the river with their hands tied? Does the world even know about the decades-old persecution of the Rohingya Muslims? Oddly enough, not even Aung San Suu Kyi has spoken out against the Myanmar government's discriminatory policies and repression towards the Rohingya Muslims—an ethnic, linguistic and Muslim minority, living in the northern Rakhine (Arakan) state along Myanmar's western border. This is the moment of truth for every individual and international actor to show that their commitment to human rights is not bound by religion, race or nationality of the victims.

The last round of communal violence against the Rohingya Muslims broke out last month, on June 8, when a mob of some 300 Buddhist Rakhine dragged 10 Rohingya pilgrims out of a bus and beat them to a death in retaliation for the alleged rape and murder of a Buddhist Rakhine woman by three Rohingya Muslims in late May. In the ensuing violence, as the Burmese reported, 78 people were killed and thousands of homes were burned. Amnesty International stresses that the violence has been primarily one-sided and against the Muslims by the Rakhine Buddhists, with the security forces turning a blind eye in most cases. Reportedly, more than 1,000 Rohingya have been killed, and more than 90,000 have been left homeless as a result of the violence. According to Amnesty International, the UN High Commission for Refugees (UNHCR), Human Rights Watch and other human rights organizations, the Rohingya Muslims have long been persecuted by consecutive governments in Myanmar, and accordingly been harassed by the Buddhist majority of Rakhine state. Only today, this systematic brutality against the Rohingya has come to international attention, albeit to a much lesser extent than it should.

A worldwide awareness campaign

On Twitter, millions from around the world have joined the awareness campaign, started on the "#StopKillingBurmeseMuslims" hashtag. Again, on various social media, millions have shared the videos and pictures showing the brutal violence that the Rohingya Muslims have been exposed to. Previously, the Organization of Islamic Cooperation (OIC) initiated contacts with the Burmese government in order to stop the violence, and to send a delegation to the Rakhine state in order to assess and respond to the humanitarian situation. OIC Secretary-General Ekmeleddin İhsanoğlu appealed to the much-celebrated Aung San Suu Kyi to speak up against the ongoing discrimination and violence against the Rohingya Muslims, who are part and parcel of the very Burmese society she belongs to as well. As a matter of fact, it was under the auspices of Secretary-General İhsanoğlu that in May 2011 the senior Rohingya leaders of the diasporas came together and founded the Arakan Rohingya Union to seek a political solution to the problems faced by the Rohingya people. Moreover, various OIC countries like Turkey, Iran, Egypt, Saudi Arabia and Bangladesh voiced their concerns about the deteriorating conditions of the Rohingya Muslims. The issue is most likely to top the agenda of the OIC Islamic Summit due to take place in Mecca in mid-August.

Ghost of British colonialism haunts Rohingya Muslims

What has been happening in Rakhine (Arakan) state is not simply a humanitarian crisis. Nor is it a clash caused by religious animosity between the Muslims and the Buddhists. It is a political problem, which has been deliberately inflamed with religious animosity against the Muslims, and which has caused an unspeakably tragic humanitarian situation. It is a political problem, which is rooted in the British colonization of Burma from 1886 to 1948. Today, the Burmese government denies the very fundamental right of citizenship to the Rohingya people, arguing that they are Bengalis brought to Burma by the British colonizers; therefore they need to go back to Bangladesh. Burma's 1982 citizenship law, adopted by the military government at the time stipulates that only those ethnic and religious groups who were present within the Burmese territory when the British arrived in 1886 are considered lawful citizens of Myanmar (Burma). Obviously, the Bangladeshi government denies this claim that the Rohingya people are originally from Bangladesh, and as a result, the Rohingya people are left stateless in between Bangladesh and Burma. Burmese President Thein Sein has recently gone even so far as to state that the problem could be solved by transferring all the Rohingya to Bangladesh, or to a third state that is willing to take them.

No less important than whether or not the Rohingya people's cry is heard is who hears it. It is certainly a turning point that Muslim countries have become aware of the Rohingya people's plight, are organizing humanitarian aid campaigns, condemning the violence and calling upon the Burmese government to take necessary measures to prevent further violence. Yet, it is first and foremost the British, American, French and Canadian people that must hear the Rohingya Muslims' cry. After all, rightly or wrongly, it is the British colonizers, namely the forefathers of the British today, who are implicated in the creation of this problem more than a hundred years ago. As much responsible are the Americans, whose tax money was used to allegedly bring democracy and freedom to Myanmar (Burma). As such, it is their moral responsibility to see that every community in this country, regardless of its ethnic and religious identity, gets its rightful share from this democracy and freedom. It is their moral responsibility to pressurize Aung San Suu Kyi and her National League of Democracy to speak up for the oppressed Rohingya Muslims, just as the American taxpayers spoke up for her. Similarly, it is the moral responsibility of the French and Canadian people, whose governments are encouraging investments in Myanmar (Burma), where the fundamental human rights of the Rohingya Muslims, like the right to citizenship, the right to education, the right to freedom of movement, the right to healthcare and the right to worship among others, are deliberately denied or restricted by the Burmese government. Unless the British, American, French and Canadian public hears the Rohingya Muslims' cry, it is sad to say that cry is likely to be drowned sooner or later, just like many Rohingya children are drowning in the Naf River between Bangladesh and Burma as they try to escape death.

ANKARA IN A PRISONER'S
DILEMMA OVER SYRIA[64]

The Syrian crisis has started to take its toll on Turkish domestic politics. Public opinion is deeply divided over how Ankara should have approached the humanitarian tragedy caused by that crisis.

The main opposition Republican People's Party (CHP) holds Foreign Minister Ahmet Davutoğlu primarily responsible for all the problems that it perceives to be a result of Turkey's Syria policy and is calling for his resignation. Additionally, the continuous influx of Syrian refugees into Turkey and increased tensions over the Kurdish issue are causing socio-economic and political problems. The most unfortunate is that it was all too clear about a year or so ago that with its approach to regional developments then, Turkey would have to suffer the troubles it is facing today. At this point, there is no use in scapegoating Foreign Minister Davutoğlu, no matter how much of this is caused by his policies. It is imperative to move forward without suffering any further damage.

In that regard, the classical example of the "prisoner's dilemma" may not only represent the deeply troubling circumstances Ankara is facing vis-à-vis the situation in Syria, but also presents Turkish policymakers—provided that they stop running the country's foreign affairs solely on the basis of compassion and charity—as having the tools needed to avoid the dire consequences of that situation.

The prisoner's dilemma refers to a thought process of two supposedly rational individuals who are resolved to maximize their benefits either by cooperating and together settling for relatively lower gain

---

[64] First appeared in *Today's Zaman* daily on September 9, 2012.

or by defecting and individually going for the highest gain, to the detriment of the other. Facing charges with insufficient evidence, two suspects are separately offered by the police to testify against the other and go free. That is, if they both remain silent (cooperate), they will both be convicted of lesser charges and sentenced to four years in prison. If prisoner A (PA) testifies against prisoner B (PB), thereby defecting, but PB remains silent (cooperates), then PA goes free and PB will be sentenced to, say, 10 years. If PA remains silent (cooperates), but PB testifies against PA (and defects), then PA will be sentenced to 10 years and PB goes free. If they both testify against each other, they will both be sentenced to seven years. So, unaware of what the other will do, each prisoner is inclined to seek freedom at the expense of the other. After all, remaining silent may mean either four or ten years in prison, whereas testifying may gain one's freedom or lead to seven years in prison. So, for one to make the best decision in this case, the ultimate determinant is what the other has decided to do: testify or remain silent.

Prisoners of their own choice

A similar situation has recently emerged at the UN Security Council with respect to the situation in Syria. For Turkey to make the best decision for itself, meaning the least destructive for itself as well as for the Syrian people, it is critical for Turkey to know what the other members of the council, especially three of the permanent members—the US, the UK and France (P3)—are considering doing. After all, Turkey and these three permanent members have all seemed to be on the same page so far with respect to the future of Syria. That is, there must be a transition to a new political structure in which there is no place for President Bashar al-Assad.

Yet, meetings of the council have demonstrated that there is a major difference of opinion between Turkey and the P3 over how to get there. Turkey has made its case for establishing safe zones for refugees within Syrian territory, which would naturally require a military presence for their protection. However, none of the P3 has supported this proposal, although each has continued to call on Assad to step down. Additionally, opinions as to the legitimacy of the Syrian opposition's actions seem to be changing as well. For instance, non-permanent members of the council South Africa, India and Pakistan seem to be joining Russia and China, at least in terms of condemning the terrorist activities in Syria, referring to the explosions carried out by opposition forces.

Why should one be particularly concerned about the decisions by the P3 and Turkey? Well, as permanent members of the council, the US, the UK and France have so far seemed to be acting in sync and are in a position to directly influence the Security Council's position on Syria. They can either continue the current state of affairs by insisting on what might seem like a regime change in Syria or facilitate an end to the violence by acquiescing to the Baath regime, either with or without President Assad. Could they really agree on options that would keep either Baathist elements or Assad—or both—after all their inflammatory rhetoric so far? Surely, when it comes to politics, anything can be justified, no matter how odd it may seem.

As for Turkey, it is Syria's neighbor, hosts more than 80,000 Syrian refugees and is a regional player in a position to directly influence the direction of the Syrian crisis, although it is not a member of the Security Council. From almost the very beginning of the crisis, Ankara has lent its support to the Syrian opposition. It has clearly condemned the Assad government and asked for Assad to step down, whereas many countries—including those on the Security Council, even the UK—have condemned some or all of the explosions caused by the Syrian opposition. The UN secretary-general has called upon not only the Syrian government but also the opposition to stop their military activities, but Ankara has yet to make such a request of the opposition. Along with Saudi Arabia and Qatar, Turkey seems to be the biggest source of support for the opposition. This also puts Ankara in a position to directly influence the current state of affairs. There is no need to mention that Turkey's involvement in the Syrian crisis was inevitable as the continuity of the crisis has direct and immediate implications for Turkey's national security and interests.

Possible exit scenarios

So, what are the possible patterns the positions of the P3 and Turkey on the Syrian crisis could follow, and what are the consequences of each? First, the P3 could continue their current course of action, which seems to have two components: demanding a political transition that allows no place for Assad and supporting the opposition against the Syrian government in its struggle either by rhetoric or with arms. Ankara may prefer to do the same. That is, the P3 and Turkey may prefer to cooperate. In that case, the conflict would continue and, as a result, the number of civilian deaths would continue to rise, the ethno-religious fault lines among the different factions in Syria would deepen and the prospects for a prolonged civil war, even without Assad in place, would increase. At one level, the region would further destabilize, with Turkey having to deal with Iran and Syria as threats to national security in addition to the terrorist Kurdistan Workers' Party (PKK), and, at another level, the artificial Sunni-Shiite divide would widen with Turkey, Saudi Arabia, Qatar, Egypt and Jordan on the one side and Iran and Syria along with the Shiite communities in Sunni-dominated states on the other. This is pretty much what has been happening over the past year and a half. If it continues as such, the interests of the P3 and Turkey will be undermined, but Turkey's much more so.

Second, the P3 may signal that it will acquiesce to keeping either or both the Baathist elements and Assad in place, whereas Ankara may prefer to continue its current course and support the Syrian opposition to the Assad government. That is, the P3 may defect while Ankara cooperates. In that case, the armed Syrian opposition would rapidly lose its legitimacy in the eyes of the international community. They, along with their supporters, if any are left by then other than Turkey, may look like the only ones precluding a solution by undermining Kofi Annan's six-point plan or a new plan the new UN special envoy for Syria, Lakhdar Brahimi, may put forth. In addition, Arab public opinion, not only in Syria but in the wider region as well, may start to turn against Turkey, since Ankara would then seem to be an outsider meddling in the internal affairs of an Arab nation by supporting armed groups. There is no need to mention that such an insidious trend may be fully utilized not only by the Assad government and Iran, but also by others either inside or outside the region. So, with the P3 defecting, and Ankara continuing to cooperate, the P3 gets away with few scars to its image and relationship with the Syrian government, which would not be unusual for them historically, but Turkey would be locked out of the Arab world for quite some time, if not permanently.

Third, the P3 could continue on its current course, supporting the armed Syrian opposition and opposing any scenario that acquiesces to Assad, and Ankara could decide to revise its position given that its hitherto approach has not only failed to bring about an end to the conflict in Syria but has also started to undermine Turkey's own national security and interests. That is, while the P3 cooperates, Ankara may defect. To be more specific, while continuing to provide all possible humanitarian assistance to Syrian refugees crossing into Turkish territories, no matter how many, Ankara may renounce its support of the Syrian opposition's military activities, considering that the continuity of the armed struggle between the opposition and government forces is doing nothing but increasing casualties and further destroying the country. There is no need to mention that the continuity of that armed struggle is taking its toll on Turkey's own fight against terrorism. In that case, the Syrian opposition may feel obliged to abide by Annan's six-point plan as well as the final communiqué adopted by the Action Group for Syria in Geneva on June 30. Moreover, Ankara may revitalize its channels of communication with the Syrian government and mediate between the opposition and the government, thereby influencing the post-conflict reconciliation in and reconstruction of Syria. Again, by working with the Alawite-dominated Syrian government, Ankara will have contributed to preventing the further deepening of the artificial Sunni-Shiite divide in the region. So, with the P3 continuing to cooperate, and Ankara defecting, the P3 would preserve its ability to manipulate the course of developments with respect to the Syrian crisis. After all, they are permanent members of the Security Council. Yet, Ankara would dramatically affect it and most likely make the armed conflict come to a halt. Similarly, Ankara could contribute to preventing the further destabilization of the region by easing the recently increased tensions among Turkey, Syria, Iran, Saudi Arabia and other Arab states. But, of course, having defected, Ankara would have to endure a possible rebuke from the P3.

Finally, independent of each other, both the P3 and Ankara could renounce their support of the armed Syrian opposition and separately seek to establish channels of communication with the Syrian government in the hopes of influencing the course of developments in line with their own perceived national interests. That is, both the P3 and Ankara could defect. In that case, not only would the relationship between the P3 and Ankara suffer a massive test of trust, but the two would become rivals in terms of influencing post-conflict developments, thereby giving an opportunity to the Syrian government, and indirectly Iran, to play one against the other. As such, both the P3 and Ankara would have gained limited ability to influence the course of developments with respect to the Syrian crisis and the post-conflict process of reconciliation and reconstruction, while to a certain degree losing their credibility in the eyes of the Syrian opposition.

No solo exit

Although these four potential strategies by the P3 and Turkey for the Syrian crisis may seem distinct from each other at any given moment, on a practical level, there can be transitions from one to another. For example, after a considerable period of time during which the P3 and Ankara cooperate, as they seem to have done since the conflict started in Syria in April of 2011, the P3 may decide to defect while Ankara continues to cooperate, or vice versa. To be more specific, after a year-and-a-half or two, the P3 and Ankara may move from their (cooperate–cooperate) positions to any of the other three. No matter what the new pattern of their positions may be, the damage caused by their current positions will continue to increase until that time. That is, (1) the number of Syrian civilian deaths will continue to rise; (2) the prospects for a prolonged civil war, even without Assad, will further increase; (3) the region will be further destabilized due to increased enmity between, on the one side, Turkey, Egypt, Saudi Arabia, Qatar and Jordan and, on the other, Syria and Iran as well as the Shiite communities living in Sunni states; (4) the region will be further polarized along the Sunni-Shiite divide; (5) Turkey will increasingly have to deal with Iran and Syria as enemy states; (6) since there is no longer cooperation among Ankara, Tehran and Damascus, Turkey's fight against PKK terrorism is likely to be further undermined; (7) consequently, both Iranian and Syrian support of the PKK, and hence the PKK's terrorist activities inside Turkey, will increase, thereby creating further doubts as to the Justice and Development Party (AK Party) government's ability to deal with the security threats facing the country; (8) with the increased sense of insecurity, democracy and human rights will be subordinated to security concerns in Turkey; (9) with the artificially hyped notion of the so-called "Kurdish spring," the Peace and Democracy Party (BDP) and other Kurdish separatist factions will further provoke Turkish public opinion; and (10) finally, Turkey will be once again reduced to a country that is unable to solve its problems, open to the manipulation of the outside actors, and incapable of influencing any development in its region, let alone beyond it.

Then, what is the best option for Ankara? By the same token, what is the best option for the P3, and most importantly for the Syrian people? None of the four patterns presented in the "prisoner's dilemma" comes with no harm to Turkish national interests. Yet, some are less harmful and provide an opportunity to stop the ongoing violence in Syria. All things considered, Turkey will be better off if Ankara announces that it will welcome all Syrian refugees to the best of its ability and joins the UN secretary-general in calling on all parties in Syria, including the opposition, to stop their military activities, renounce violence and meet at the negotiating table for a political transition in the country. So will the Syrians be.

MORONIC ABUSE VERSUS RESPONSIBLE USE OF FREEDOM OF EXPRESSION[65]

Recently, four American diplomats, including the US ambassador to Libya, were killed in Benghazi by a group of morons, protesting a so-called movie insulting the Prophet Muhammad (PBUH), produced by a moron in California and supported by another moron in Florida.

While intellectuals, human rights activists, diplomats, politicians and all the other wise men and women are debating how to protect individual freedom of expression, the morons, be they American, European, Middle Eastern, Christian, Muslim, Jewish or Israeli, are exploiting that debate. These morons are causing unnecessary political crises and, most tragically, the deaths of real persons. There is no doubt that Ambassador Chris Stevens, killed in Benghazi, would be the first to defend everyone's freedom of expression. It is unfortunate that he lost his life simply because a producer had abused that very freedom in quite a moronic way—as he himself put it, in order to provoke Muslims.

What happened, really? What is the most accurate description of what the fictitious Israeli-American Sam Bacile did? Was it yet another Israeli plot to instigate hatred among Americans against Muslims? Or was it a conspiracy set up by the so-called Israel lobby against the Obama administration in order to portray it as impotent in protecting American diplomats, let alone regular citizens, abroad, especially before the upcoming election in November? Or, enjoying every bit of his or her freedom of expression, should one, be it a public official, journalist, academic or anybody, argue that the provocation intended by the film was a part of a larger plot masterminded by Israeli Prime

---

[65] First appeared in *Today's Zaman* daily on September 23, 2012.

Minister Benjamin Netanyahu against President Barack Obama, with whom he could not even get an appointment during the upcoming UN General Assembly? So where is the line, really, between the acceptable exercise of one's freedom of expression and the illegitimate abuse of that freedom for libel and defamation of an individual, group or religion?

Ideally, no one should even pay attention, let alone take to the streets in protest, when a moron threatens to burn the Quran, or produces a wretched video that insults either Islam or the Prophet. Such provocations should be confined to private spaces, and the provocateurs should not be given publicity. Morally, those perpetrating the actual violence in protest are indeed guiltier and even more moronic than those provoking the former in the first place. And, theoretically, if everyone in the world believed in the unrestricted freedom of expression, and were equally indifferent to the denigration by the others of their beliefs and religions, such unfortunate incidents would probably not take place.

But practically, in this age of digital communication and social media, when someone abuses freedom of expression to instigate hatred and violence in one part of the world, it has the potential to cause the deaths of real persons and destruction of property in the other parts. Moreover, it is almost impossible to stop the morons abroad, once they are out to harm individuals or damage property in alleged protest. Nor is it possible to know where in the world they will do so. It is rather easier and more manageable to contain the morons at home, who are abusing their constitutionally protected right to freedom of expression in order to instigate hatred and violence. In this regard, the challenge is in reaching a balance between the responsible use of freedom of expression and the moronic abuse of it to insult and demonize others.

HRC Res. 16/18 as a guide to freedom of expression

In this regard, UN Human Rights Council (HRC) Resolution 16/18, which was adopted in March 2011 in Geneva, provides a guideline for the responsible use of freedom of expression. The resolution, titled

"Combating intolerance, negative stereotyping and stigmatization of, and discrimination, incitement to violence and violence against persons based on religion or belief," was adopted by a consensus of the United States, European Union, Organization of Islamic Cooperation (OIC) member states and member states from other regional groups.

In November of the same year, the UN General Assembly in New York also adopted, by the consensus of 193 nations, a similar resolution derived from Res. 16/18 with the same title. The HRC Res. 16/18 simply suggests that states should take necessary precautions within their national legal systems consistent with their obligations under international human rights law, so that Jews, Christians, Muslims, Buddhists, Hindus, atheists, agnostics and individuals subscribing to any sort of belief, or non-belief for that matter, are not exposed to violence and/or discrimination on that basis.

Drawing on OIC Secretary-General Ekmeleddin İhsanoğlu's call for states to take specific action to foster a domestic environment of religious tolerance, peace and respect, and on the eight points he set out at the fifteenth session of the HRC, this resolution aims to contain the potential damage caused not only by morons abusing their freedom of expression to instigate hatred and violence, but also by the morons reacting to those instigations in a violent manner. It deplores "any advocacy of discrimination or violence on the basis of religion or belief." Yet it also "strongly" deplores "all acts of violence against persons on the basis of their religion or belief, as well as any such acts directed against their homes, businesses, properties, schools, cultural centers or places of worship."

That is, it deplores not only the making of the film insulting the Prophet Muhammad (PBUH), which at the end of the day demonizes Muslims, but also the violence perpetrated in the name of protesting that film. Moreover, resolution 16/18 condemns "any advocacy of religious hatred that constitutes incitement to discrimination, hostility or violence, whether it involves the use of print, audio-visual or electronic media or any other means."

Are you aware of the danger?

This consensus resolution is the outcome of an arduous and lengthy process of negotiation between the OIC member states and other stakeholders, most prominently the United States and the European Union countries. It has been produced precisely to prevent the kind of unfortunate incidents that started in Egypt and Libya and continued in Yemen and Sudan, and are likely to spread to other countries.

Thankfully, both the instigation and the violent protests it entailed have received unanimous condemnation from religious groups, political leaders, civil society organizations and other stakeholders. US Secretary of State Hillary Clinton described Sam Bacile's video as "disgusting and reprehensible" and a cynical attempt to offend people for their religious beliefs. Similarly, President Barack Obama reiterated that the US has a profound respect for people of all faiths.

OIC Secretary-General İhsanoğlu said, "While the film was a deplorable act of incitement, resorting to violence resulting in the loss of innocent lives could not be condoned." He also reminded listeners that the two unfortunate incidents, the defamatory film itself and the violent protests against it, demonstrated "the serious repercussions of abuse of freedom of expression that the OIC had consistently been warning against."

In a press statement the World Evangelical Alliance (WEA) said that it "totally condemns the defamatory and insulting video." The Islamic Networks Group (ING) and its affiliates across the US condemned in "the strongest possible terms the extremist attacks on US diplomatic compounds in Libya and Egypt." The Interfaith Center of New York joined the ING in condemning the killing of the American diplomats and the ensuing violence, while noting its conviction that "Rev. Terry Jones and the funders of [the] heinous and venomous video disrespect the memory of those who perished [in the American compound in Benghazi] and grossly warp the true tenets of Christianity and Judaism."

Another American organization, the Council on American Islamic Relations (CAIR), made a statement at a news conference on Capitol Hill condemning the attacks on the US diplomatic missions in Egypt and Libya as well as the killing of the American diplomats. It also stated that ordinary Americans and the US government should not be blamed for the religious hatred expressed in the infamous film. Similarly, Egypt's Coptic community, as well as California's, condemned the film for insulting the Prophet Muhammad and have distanced themselves from its producer, who identified himself as Egyptian Coptic Christian.

Moreover, the prominent Turkish Muslim scholar Fethullah Gülen called on all Muslims to avoid extremes. In an interview published on his website (www.herkul.org), Gülen said that while it was one extreme to remain silent in the face of systematic defamation of Islam and the Prophet, another was to resort to violence and kill innocent people in the name of allegedly protesting such defamation. He stressed that there was nothing Islamic about attacking innocent people (like the American diplomats in Benghazi) for something in which they have no involvement. "If Muslims are carrying out these violent acts, it is clear that they are not aware at all of what Islam is about. If they are carried out by others, and there are Muslims supporting these violent acts, then these Muslims are grossly insulting Islam," he said. Instead, Muslims should express their reactions in a calm and peaceful manner, he emphasized. The only consolation at this point is to see that Muslims and Christians both in the United States and the Middle East have unanimously condemned the wretched film, and united against yet another heinous attempt to sow discord among them. Yet the danger is still live and threatening to cause political turmoil in the months ahead. Even if each and every abuse of freedom of expression does not lead to bloody protests, it is likely to increase stereotypes and mar perceptions of Muslims.

Although they may seem to be most affected these days, Muslims are not the only ones threatened by deliberately constructed stereotypes under the guise of exercising freedom of expression. The defamation of the other seems to have a boomerang-like nature, and is likely to sooner or later haunt the perpetrator of such defamation. Even if this is the case, it is still unacceptable, given that, regardless of their identities, real persons are victims of it. That is, Muslims who are stereotyped today will not be better off tomorrow if Jews, Christians or others are then stereotyped and discriminated against.

The defamation of the other is a stain on the collective conscience of humanity, no matter whom it is directed at. It requires a collective and collaborative action to defeat it. While it is extremely important to name and shame the morons in our societies who deliberately abuse their freedom of expression to defame others, it is also necessary for states and civil society organizations to support initiatives like HRC Resolution 16/18 at the political level in order to encourage worldwide respect for the sanctity of the other.

TWO OBSTACLES TO
FREEDOM OF EXPRESSION[66]

Amid the ongoing international debate as to where the proper line lies between the responsible use and irresponsible abuse of freedom of expression, one can hardly deny the fact that indeed there are obstacles to freedom of expression.

After a decade of arduous debates and negotiations among states and within their respective civil societies, the international community reached a consensus on this matter, and adopted the Human Rights Council Resolution 16/18 in April of last year. Similarly, the 193-member UN General Assembly cast its support for this historic consensus in November of the same year. However, there are still two obstacles that seem to be hindering the international community's ability to put in practice the provisions of that resolution in a way that would counter incitement of hatred, violence and discrimination against persons on the basis of their religion, belief or opinion, without restricting freedom of expression.

These are the demagogues who exploit the popular fears and frustrations for their narrow political gains, and the opportunists who hijack a genuine human rights debate to demonize Islam and Muslims. The common characteristic of these two is that they have vested interest in perpetuating the crisis over the issue of freedom of expression, as well as the hostile atmosphere it generates. As such, these demagogues and opportunists join hands in manufacturing continuous cacophony in order to prevent the general public from objectively evaluating HRC Resolution 16/18 for what it really is and in persistently defaming the

---

[66] First appeared in *Today's Zaman* daily on October 30, 2012.

Organization of Islamic Cooperation (OIC) as a radical Islamist organization waging war against Western civilization.

Demagogues

By definition, the demagogues are the ones who have been exploiting the freedom of expression debate and the popular fears in that context for their narrow political gains. The leading figure within this group seems to be the far-right Dutch politician Geert Wilders, founder and leader of the Party for Freedom. According to a 2008 *Guardian* article, which described him as "Holland's rising political star," Wilders wants the Holy Quran "outlawed in Holland, the constitution rewritten to make that possible, all immigration from Muslim countries halted, Muslim immigrants paid to leave and all Muslim 'criminals' stripped of Dutch citizenship and deported 'back where they came from'." The same Wilders accused the OIC of seeking a ban on free speech. *The Guardian* article summed it up well:

> [Only two years after he formed his Party of Freedom] he was recently voted Holland's most effective politician…His Islam-bashing seems to be paying off. And not only in Holland. All across Europe, the new breed of right-wing populists are trying to revive their political fortunes by appealing anti-Muslim prejudice.

Yet, the problem is that Wilders has inspired not only other populist European politicians, but also terrorists such as Anders Breivik, who bombed government buildings in Oslo and killed 69 Norwegian youths as part of his self-appointed mission to purify Europe.

One US politician who seems to have been influenced by the radiation of Wilders' venomous rhetoric on Islam and Muslims is Michele Bachmann, Republican congresswoman from Minnesota. This year in June, extremely disturbed by the US administration's decision to purge the derogatory references to Islam and Muslims from the training materials of government officials, she, along with four of her fellow Republican congressmen, sent letters to the inspectors general of the Department of Defense, State, Justice and Homeland Security as well as the Office of the Director of National Intelligence and urged them to investigate potential Muslim Brotherhood infiltration into the US government. Moreover, she suggested that Huma Abedin, deputy chief of staff to Secretary of State Hillary Clinton, could be a Muslim Brotherhood operative, because her late father Syed Abedin founded in the late 1970s an organization called the Institute of Muslim Minority Affairs, which was supported by the Muslim World League, which according to the Pew Forum had "a longtime history of being closely aligned and partnering with the Muslim Brotherhood."

This very same Bachmann introduced the OIC as "one of the largest and most powerful organizations in the world" to her flared-up audience during the so-called Values Voter Summit in September, where she reminded them of "the objective reality," as she put it, "that there is a very radical wing of Islam that is dedicated to the destruction of America, Israel and of Israel's allies." Consequently, she alleged that the OIC intended to "internationally criminalize all or any communication or speech that is deemed by them to be insulting to Islam, even in countries like the United States." Accordingly, she accused the Obama administration and Clinton State Department of appeasing the "radical Islamist enemy" and urged them to draw an "unmistakable redline for [America's] enemies across the world" while at the same time arguing that President Barack Obama was "the most dangerous president" America has ever had.

Certainly, the demagogues are not unique to either Europe or the US. Abdulhadi Hairan of the *Huffington Post* illustrates the demagogy exercised by the Taliban in its propaganda war:

> The latest sad news is that the Christian Crusaders (Americans) have burned a copy of the Holy Quran in Wardak province and have thus shown their enmity with Islam and the Muslims...The saddest aspect of this incident is that the American invaders have committed this heinous crime in a province (Wardak) that has been known for long as home to mujahedeen (the holy warriors). The people of this province have taken active part in past and current jihadi movements. The people of this province have always defended their country

bravely and heroically. The people of this province had played a historical role in the war against British occupiers.[67]

Opportunists

In addition to those who exploit the freedom of expression debate for their political calculations, there are also individuals and groups that keep themselves relevant and cash in on hyping the public fears about the so-called "Islamic fundamentalism." Blogger of the so-called Atlas Shrugs, where she constantly posts Islamophobic and anti-Muslim opinions, Pamela Geller is infamous among the most successful in that regard. She wrote: "Islam is the most anti-Semitic, genocidal ideology in the world. The Jews have suffered unspeakable barbarity and cruelty and humiliation at the hands of Muslim rulers" in November 2010. Of course, nobody expects anyone of Geller's intellectual caliber to appreciate the historical fact that the Jews have actually survived and thrived largely under the auspices of the Muslim rulers.

Yet, it still comes as a surprise (maybe it should not) that in a *New York Times* interview a month earlier, Geller too had claimed that she had no problem with Islam, but with "political Islam." Normally, whatever Geller thinks or says would not be worthwhile to even think about. However, she obviously has some sort of following in the upper echelons inside the Beltway, given that even John Bolton, former US ambassador to the United Nations, wrote a foreword to a book, titled *The Post-American Presidency: The Obama Administration's War on America*, which she co-authored with Robert Spencer, who according to a Center for American Progress (CAP) report is one of the most notorious Islamophobes, bankrolled to pump up the Islamophobic hysteria in the US.

According to the CAP Report, titled "Fear Inc." and dated August 2011, the rise of Islamophobia across the US is not an outcome of a vast right-wing conspiracy, but of a "small, tightly networked group of misinformation experts" who reach out to millions of Americans through media and political partners as well as grassroots organizing.

---

[67] *Shahamat* (The Bravery) Magazine, 2010.

The group includes the so-called experts such as Frank Gaffney of the Center for Security Policy, David Yerushalmi of the Society of Americans for National Existence, Robert Spencer of Jihad Watch and Stop Islamization of America, and Steven Emerson of the Investigative Project on Terrorism. They manufacture misinformation and false facts about Islam and Muslims in America, and their grass roots and media partners, such as Pamela Geller, help them spread the misinformation all across the US.

Similarly, their political partners invited these so-called experts to the state or federal legislatures, where they testified calling for "a ban on the non-existing threat of Shariah law in America and proclaiming that the vast majority of mosques in [America] harbor Islamist terrorists or sympathizers." The report reveals that over the past decade these so-called experts received more than $40 million in funding from five foundations to carry out their Islamophobia campaign. Consequently, a September 2010 poll carried out by *Washington Post*-ABC News showed that "49 percent of Americans held an unfavorable view of Islam, a significant increase from 39 percent in October of 2002," which can be considered a result of the hard work (!) of these Islamophobes and of the other radical groups like al-Qaeda and the Taliban.

'Damn! The OIC is moderating'

Yet another commonality of these opportunist Islamophobes is their collective attack on the Obama administration and Clinton State Department for the latter's cooperation with the European Union and the OIC member states in adoption of the resolution, titled "Combating intolerance, negative stereotyping, stigmatization, discrimination, incitement to violence and violence against persons, based on religion or belief" by consensus both at the UN Human Rights Council in Geneva in March and at the General Assembly in November in New York last year. The resolution is historic in the sense that it signifies a major compromise from the earlier OIC-sponsored resolution, titled "Combating Defamation of Religions," which had become increasingly divisive between the US-EU on the one side, and the OIC member states and others on the other. Whereas the old resolution guarded against defaming religions, which are abstract in nature, the new resolution guards against incitement to hatred, discrimination and violence against individuals, real persons, on the basis of religion or belief, without making any reference to protecting religions against criticism.

Apparently, this is not a good development for the Islam-bashers, because one of the most lucrative sources of material for them to exploit has been vanishing with the OIC's moderation of its position under the leadership of Secretary-General Ekmeleddin İhsanoğlu. Not surprisingly, Geller described the adoption of the consensus resolution as the State Department's alleged submission to the OIC and likened Secretary Clinton to Neville Chamberlain, who appeased Adolf Hitler. Similarly, Frank Gaffney described the Istanbul Process, which was initiated jointly by Clinton and İhsanoğlu towards implementation of the said resolution, as an exploration of ways "in which [US] First Amendment rights could accommodate Shariah blasphemy laws."

Finally, the demagogues and opportunist Islamophobes often dig into the decades-old documents of the OIC such as the 1990 Cairo Declaration of Human Rights in Islam and the 1981 Universal Islamic Declaration, as if these documents are solely guiding the contemporary OIC's approach to human rights, no moderation has taken place at all, and even further moderation is not possible. It is understandable, though; for them, only an OIC, which they can continue to picture as a dangerous Islamic caliphate bent on establishing a global Islamic state is useful. Yet, their hateful discourse about Islam and their categorical opposition to anything that comes from Muslims is even more dangerous than they can possibly imagine.

When Wilders utters, "I don't have any problem with Muslim, but with Islam," and Bachmann describes her "objective reality" as somewhat "although not all Muslims are radical, there are radical Islamist enemies dedicated to the destruction of America, Israel and of Israel's allies," apparently they just do not realize that they are legitimating the very radical arguments they say they are fighting, such as, "Oh! We do not have any problem with Jews...We are only against the Jews who are controlling the global financial system, keeping politicians on payroll, manipulating public opinion through media and think tanks they own, manipulating recruitment at higher education institutions, pitting states against each other and selling weapons to them all, among all other devilish things they are doing." Well, who knows? Maybe, they do realize the consequences of what they are doing and are just unable to stop it because it pays so well for their narrow political interests. After all, they are exercising their right to freedom of expression like everyone else, aren't they?

ISRAEL'S NARRATIVE AND
THE SAME OLD MIDDLE EAST[68]

"N arratives have a powerful effect in hiding reality," argues American cognitive scientist George Lakoff, while explaining that the facts alone do not suffice to influence public opinion, nor the voters' choices when they go to the ballot box.

When the story sold suggests that the hero has defended his right to exist in the face of the continuous attacks of the villain, the third party that has already bought the story hardly pays attention to the details. The facts—such as indiscriminate civilian massacres, the killing of women, children and the elderly, flagrant violations of human rights and international law, the extrajudicial execution of individuals, and other crimes perpetrated by who is portrayed as the hero in the narrative against who is portrayed as the villain—simply become secondary issues, if not completely ignored. After all, the hero of the story is defending his right to exist against the attacks of the villain.

According to Lakoff, it happens this way because of the very way the human brain works. He reminds us that only two percent of the brain's functioning is done consciously, and its 98 percent unconscious activity includes non-stop adoption of frames, images and metaphors presented to it by the narratives, be they heard from the media, politicians, journalists, activists, propagandists, colleagues, friends or whoever. For instance, when one is told, "Muslims are not terrorists; but all the terrorists who attacked America in the past, and who constantly threaten the American way of life and freedoms, are all Muslims," he or she may not necessarily think of his or her Muslim coworker, neighbor or classmate as a terrorist. Yet, that frame associating Islam

---

[68] First appeared in *Today's Zaman* daily on December 23, 2012.

with terrorism, and as such portraying any Muslim as a potential terrorist, is injected into the brain without him or her even noticing it.
Ironically, once the frame is established, everything said to repudiate
that frame in fact reinforces it more and more. That is, when one
responds to the frame "All terrorists attacking America are Muslims"
with the opposite, "All terrorists attacking America are not Muslims,"
what is being said is basically, "Yes, there are Muslim terrorists attacking America, but not all terrorists attacking America are Muslims,"
thereby reinforcing the very same frame that puts Muslims/Islam and
terrorism together.

In international politics, Israel is by far the most successful in taking advantage of such narratives, and lucratively utilizing them for its
material and strategic gains. No matter how many Palestinian children
get killed, and houses demolished, and no matter how many times Israel's nuclear weapons outnumber those of its neighbors, when and if
they have any, Israel has so far prevailed, and is likely to do so in the
foreseeable future as well. After all, it looks like everything its neighbors,
from Turkey to Iran, from Egypt to Sudan, and from South Lebanon
to Gaza, do reinforces the narrative that in the midst of the villains
bent on destroying it, Israel is just trying to protect its citizens and its
freedom, just like any other rational state would do. In this vein, with
each and every rocket fired from Gaza, Hamas simply reactivates and
reinforces Israel's narrative in the minds of every individual, whether
or not that individual even notices it happening. Again, whenever the
Turkish prime minister roars against Israel, it may sound like music
to many ears, but in the long run, what it does is to reinforce yet another narrative: "Not even modern and secular Turkey can be trusted when
'Islamists' come to power."

A part of this success can be explained by Israel's human capital
as well as its concomitant political, legal and socioeconomic influence
in the United States and throughout Europe. Yet the larger part of
the reason why Israel always prevails is the intellectual backwardness
of the nations surrounding Israel, which includes Turkey and Iran,
their leaders' shortsightedness and strategic shallowness in their thinking. And finally, it is their intoxication with power, which they are so

afraid to give up once they seize it. The developments over the past decade, including the so-called Arab Spring, have shown that it is the same old Middle East it has been for the past century, and what has changed is hardly more than new leaders replacing old ones, and abetting Israel as it continues to prevail.

Israel the story teller

Some have argued that the so-called Arab Spring has changed the regional dynamics and that Israel will no longer enjoy its privileged status. According to Haim Bresheeth of the University of East London, the Arab popular uprisings in the name of democracy have challenged Israel's relationship with Western societies, and in particular with the American public. He argues that the West has not only developed stereotypes about Middle Eastern societies as being anti-democratic and authoritarian human rights abusers but has supported, for more than a century, the tyrants and authoritarian regimes in these countries which, in turn, justified those stereotypical frames. So long as the Arab countries remained authoritarian and anti-democratic, Israel did not have to do much to appear as the "only democracy" in the Middle East, and hence the only ally of the West. Bresheeth illustrates how this ever more reinforced framing has benefited Israel in the United States, and enabled the pro-Israeli groups, most notably the American Israeli Public Affairs Committee (AIPAC), to manipulate the American polity in favor of Israel.

Moreover, he argues, the fact that Arab societies remain backward and undemocratic has helped Israel feel safe, as the latter has enjoyed far greater superiority in military and civil technology. Israel's relative modernity as such enabled it to present itself as a sort of "European/ Western" country that happens to be geographically located in the midst of the "backward, primitive and religiously fundamentalist" Arab nations, all the while religiously describing itself as a Jewish state. This image, he argues, has helped Israel construct a "special relationship" with the United States, which in turn gave Israel a privilege to vet each and every US foreign policy towards the Middle East. However, the Arab Spring has posed a threat to Israel since it altered all the certainties that Israel and its allies had long been lucratively exploiting, the most notable of which was that the Arabs were neither capable nor worthy of democracy. As the Arabs unanimously call for democracy, pluralism, economic development, rule of law and equality, he argues, Israel is no longer in a position to claim to be the only democracy in the Middle East. Similarly, he contends, as the Arab societies continue to modernize and democratize, Israel will be viewed as what it really is—an apartheid state.

But, that is the $6 million question: Will Israel's neighbors—both Arab and non-Arab—continue to modernize and democratize? Additionally, will the change in the Middle East change anything with respect to Israel's narrative as to it being a tiny lonely democratic country constantly facing the threat of annihilation at the hands of its authoritarian neighbors?

"Fukuyamanic" leaders and postmodern authoritarianism

It is hard to say "yes" to either question, given the new Middle Eastern leaders' attitudes, actions and policies. Over the past decade, Israel's immediate and distant neighbors have been going through political and socioeconomic transformation. Consequently, the so-called former Islamists or conservative democrats have been gradually replacing the ultra-secularist establishment in their respective countries. Or at least that's what it seems like they have been doing. Long oppressed under the yoke of authoritarian regimes or dictators, they cherished democracy, pluralism, the rule of law and respect for human rights, and eventually took office either gradually through local and general elections as in the case of Turkey, or not so gradually as in the case of Egypt and Gaza.

In explaining the impact of this structural transformation, Daniel Byman of Georgetown University argues that Israel was concerned about the Arab Spring because it changed the status quo of the region that Israel had relied on. As he puts it, it meant the demise of the "devils," which Israel knew well—namely, the Arab dictators it had long been accustomed to dealing with, and has most likely supported directly or indirectly, over the past several decades. One can add to that the rogue

Turkish generals, whose interference in politics had gone as far as to administer Turkish-Israeli relations.

Byman notes that neither under the late Hafez al-Assad nor his son Bashar al-Assad had Syria ever been a friend of Israel. The latter's occupation of Syria's Golan Heights has continuously poisoned the relations between the two states. Yet, both Assads were well in the know about the balance of power between Israel and Syria, as well as between Israel and any of its other Arab neighbors. So, no matter how inflammatory the rhetoric it employed, Damascus would always stop short of taking confrontation with Israel into action. For their part, the Egyptian and Jordanian regimes were literally surviving on the economic aid and political support provided by the US, conditioned on their peace with Israel. As for Iran, Israel continued to have an official representation in this country even after the so-called Islamic revolution of 1979, and provided military assistance to it during the Iran-Iraq war. The threat Iran perceives from Sunni countries has deterred it from confronting any other enemy anyway. The Palestinians have been too divided between Fatah and Hamas to pose any credible threat to Israel. Finally, Turkey had been nothing but a friend of Israel thanks to the overwhelming influence of the generals over any civilian government.

Many, like Bresheeth and Byman, have thought that the demise of the status quo in the Middle East, and the emergence of conservative or Islamist governments paying attention to their constituency's concerns, would undermine Israel's traditional narrative of being the only democracy in the midst of authoritarian regimes bent on destroying it. Yet, it looks like the new actors of the Middle East are proving this thesis wrong by creating what İhsan Dağı of Middle East Technical University calls "postmodern authoritarianism." He argues that unlike their dictatorial predecessors who acted against the will of the masses, these governments are utilizing their electoral support to impose their will onto the entire society, and justifying their populist rhetoric and actions by arguing that they are indeed fulfilling the nation's will. Accordingly, this leads to the proliferation of bombastic speeches, promising what in fact they cannot deliver, especially with respect to fixing the injustices in the international system.

Just like Francis Fukuyama misinterpreted the end of the Cold War and capitalism's defeat of communism as the end of history, these new Middle Eastern actors seem to think that their defeat of the old authoritarian regimes and their seizure of power have brought history to an end and that no leaders or governments will replace them. They seem to think that it is them who have long been awaited to come and fix all the problems. As such, with a manic enthusiasm, they are trying to fix the region's decades- or even centuries-old problems overnight, eventually ending up further complicating them. Yet, the more their policies fail, the more inflammatory their rhetoric becomes, in order to satisfy their constituencies' sentiments. So, with these new "fukuyaman-ic" leaders in the Middle East, Israel is quite likely to continue bene-fiting lucratively from its original narrative that it is the only democ-racy in the region fighting for its right to exist in the midst of author-itarian regimes bent on destroying it. No matter who comes to power in Israel's immediate and distant neighbors, nothing will change in the Middle East unless they really democratize their countries and realize that their hatred of Israel benefits no one but Israel. Constructing a new Mid-dle East starts with the understanding of why and how not to hate Israel.

THE RISE AND FALL OF
TURKEY'S AK PARTY SAGA[69]

R ecep Tayyip Erdoğan's rise to prominence and the Justice and
Development Party (AK Party) government's first two terms
in the office, together as a political phenomenon has come
to symbolize Turkey's long-excluded masses' revenge on the Kemalist
establishment.

Shortly after he founded the AK Party with a relatively younger
generation of politicians in August 2001, Erdoğan was elected prime
minister in a landslide parliamentary election in November 2002. His
election was significant for two reasons: First, he was a young political figure who had already proven his leadership skills as the mayor of
Istanbul from 1994 to 1998, finding solutions to many pressing problems of the most complicated and cosmopolitan city in the country. Yet,
the Kemalist and secular fundamentalist elite of the country, most notably the military, staunchly opposed him; and this opposition was not
simply rhetorical.

In April 1998, Erdoğan was hastily sentenced to a 10-month prison term and banned from politics because of a poem he recited during a rally in December 1997 on charges of incitement to commit offense
and incitement to religious and racial hatred. That he was sued under
Article 312 of the Turkish Penal Code (TCK) had further ascertained
the political motivations behind his conviction. The parliamentary election law stipulated that anyone convicted under Article 312 was to be
banned for life from election to any kind of public office. Consequently, the *Hürriyet* daily—widely known as the mouthpiece of the Kemalist
establishment—announced the court decision with the somewhat joy-

[69] First appeared in *Today's Zaman* daily on March 6, 2013.

ous-sounding headline, "He cannot even become a mukhtar" (village administrator). In the eyes of many, the court decision was aimed at politically eliminating an emerging national leader who had the potential to challenge the anti-democratic Kemalist establishment.

As such, Erdoğan in a way symbolized the struggle of the sheer majority of society, which had long been pushed to the periphery, against the minority establishment of the secular fundamentalist elite, which had not only single-handedly monopolized political and economic opportunity spaces in the country and excluded the conservatives or anyone outside that elite, but also constantly perpetuated this unfair structure by manipulating the judicial, legislative and executive branches of the state.

The second reason that made Erdoğan's rise to power significant was the fact that the AK Party government would end the vicious decade of numerous coalition governments, and its concomitant political instability and economic stagnation. Describing itself as conservative democrat, with its conservatism confined to moral and social issues, the AK Party government committed itself to pursuing political and economic liberalization, as well as democratization in line with Turkey's decades-old Westernization project, namely membership in the European Union. Accordingly, it sought to reduce the influence of the military over elected officials, thereby eliminating the most effective tool that the secular fundamentalist establishment had utilized throughout the history of the republic. In the meantime, the AK Party government undertook a series of structural economic reforms that brought the country's chronically high inflation rate down to single digits in only two years and registering record high growth rates for the Turkish economy in the ensuing years.

The AK Party government shines

The AK Party government's hard work soon after started to pay off in that it expanded its popular support base across the country and across ethnic and ideological lines. Whereas it took 34.43 percent of all the votes in the 2002 general elections, it managed to raise this percentage to 41.67 in the 2004 local elections, to 46.66 in the 2007 general elections, to 38.78 in the 2009 local elections and to 49.83 in the latest general elections, which took place in June 2011. Consolidating its position as the most formidable center-right party willing to accommodate a wide span of different political ideologies, the AK Party government has managed to attract the votes of liberals, nationalists, some center-leftists and ethnic Kurds who previously supported the different derivatives of pro-Kurdish political parties. What has been particularly effective in due course was the AK Party government's willingness to tackle Turkey's various political, social and cultural taboos, the most notable of which were lifting the headscarf ban as well as liberating Kurdish ethnic identity. In February 2008, the AK Party government passed legislation amending the constitution in order to lift the headscarf ban. However, in June of the same year, the Constitutional Court announced its decision to revoke that legislation and stop its implementation. Similarly, in 2009 the government undertook an initiative that its proponents dubbed the "Democratic Opening" and opponents called the "Kurdish Opening." No matter what it was called, the government's initiative was unprecedented, radical and aimed at rehabilitating the Turkish state's problematic relationship with its ethnic Kurdish population.

In the meantime, Turkey undertook two referenda, respectively, in October 2007 and September 2010 in order to amend its constitution. Both referenda, which were adopted, respectively, by 68.95 percent of all votes in favor in 2007 and by 57.88 percent in favor in 2010, made dramatic changes to the 1982 constitution designed by the army generals after the coup. AK Party leaders have largely perceived the overwhelming popular support for the constitutional amendments spearheaded by the AK Party government as a renewal of confidence in their work. In fact, the opponents of the constitutional amendments dubbed the government's initiative as a "civilian coup," accusing it of acting with revanchist reflexes. Yet, the issue of amending the constitution did not finish with those two initiatives. Later on, in 2011 the AK Party government heavily rallied on the promise of a complete overhaul of the constitution to replace it with a new one that upholds the rule of law, protects fundamental human rights and freedoms and ensures transparency and accountability. As such, the 2011 parliamentary elections were unofficially meant to be a referendum on rewriting the Turkish constitution.

In addition to such major developments inside, Erdoğan's AK Party government has registered many unprecedented developments with respect to Turkish foreign policy as well. Turkey under the AK Party government first sought to mend its relations with all of its neighbors, including Armenia and Greece, and second reach out in all directions, breaking the confines of the strict Western orientation in foreign policy. In 2004, acting proactively in an effort to solve the Cyprus issue once and for all, Ankara supported the so-called Annan Plan, which aimed to establish one federative state on the island, where both Greek and Turkish Cypriots would have equal status and their own federal states. In 2005, the AK Party government succeeded in finally starting negotiations with the European Union for Turkey's accession to full membership in the union, for which Ankara applied in 1987 and was officially recognized as a candidate in 1999. Moreover, after 48 years, Turkey was elected to non-permanent membership on the prestigious UN Security Council, serving a two-year term in 2009-2010.

In parallel to its sustained economic development with a growth rate surpassed only by that of China, Turkey was admitted to the prestigious G20 club and grew to become the 16th biggest economy in the world as of 2012. Turkey's enviable economic performance, in addition to the political and legal reforms it has undertaken, has made it a much more visible international actor, whose opinion and involvement is sought after, especially with respect to regional affairs. In this regard, Ankara's ability to be able to speak to archenemies in the region, such as Syria and Israel or Hamas and Israel at the same time, boosted Turkey's image as a regional peacemaker. Again, Turkey's image and capabilities as an able international actor has been improved by Ankara's expansion of Turkey's diplomatic representation across the globe, as well as increased involvement in humanitarian aid and development through the Turkish Cooperation and Development Agency (TİKA) and the Turkish Red Crescent. These are all political and economic successes that Turkey achieved during the AK Party government's first two terms under the leadership of Prime Minister Erdoğan.

As the sun sets on the AK Party

However, the AK Party government in its third term has so far starkly differed from how it used to be throughout its first two terms. Ever since it won its third consecutive parliamentary election, taking 49.83 percent of all votes, the AK Party government has started to act more like a state, as opposed to an elected government accountable to its constituency. In fact, reflecting the self-confidence he has developed after the first two terms, Prime Minister Erdoğan dubbed his government's third term as the "mastership term." One would normally expect that having literally secured the support of every other voter in the country, the AK Party government would tackle the last remaining obstacles to the long-sought truly democratic Turkey. After all, it earned not only unprecedented majority seats in Parliament, but also a popular mandate through the 2010 referendum to overhaul the military-devised constitution and to abolish all the anti-democratic policies put in place by the Kemalist establishment. Moreover, from its emergence all the way through its first two terms in office, the AK Party had to endure the very same anti-democratic state practices, be it military tutelage over politics, judicial restrictions on political mobilization or restrictions on all kinds of individual freedoms from the freedom of expression to freedom of religion.

Yet, the AK Party government has got itself bogged down in endless political bickering. The list of the debates that seasonally occupied public opinion included the ones raged over the reinstatement of capital punishment, a transition to a presidential system from the parliamentary system, the prohibition of abortion and the banning of a TV series titled "Muhteşem Yüzyıl" (Magnificent Century), which in the prime minister's opinion defamed the Ottoman sultans. Moreover, AK Party leaders have turned somewhat reluctant to pursue judicial investigations into the alleged coup plots unearthed during the government's first two terms and criticized the prosecutions in a way that would raise doubt about their veracity. Erdoğan went as far as to congratulate military officers in the aftermath of a scandal where 34 ethnic Kurdish citizens were killed by a Turkish military bombardment, which was meant to target terrorist elements. Again, he prevented an investigation, which involved the chief of the National Intelligence Organization (MİT), who happens to be his confidant. Accordingly, upon his directives, Parliament passed overnight legislation that made any investigation about high-ranking military and administrative officers subject to the prime minister's personal approval.

Most importantly, efforts to overhaul the 1982 Constitution do not seem to be yielding any concrete result amid much discussion. As a matter of fact, despite its formidable political power and popular mandate, the AK Party's apparent indifference to getting results does actually raise doubts about whether it is interested in changing the constitution in the first place. Finally, with respect to its foreign policy, the AK Party government's level and manner of involvement in the so-called Arab Spring disturbed many when both Prime Minister Erdoğan and Foreign Minister Ahmet Davutoğlu said that the popular revolutions in various Middle Eastern countries were in fact Turkey's domestic matter. At the end of the day, looking at the big picture, can one point at any correlation or causation between the AK Party government's perceived grandeur in global affairs and its loss of focus on Turkey's democratization? Was there anything that compelled Erdoğan to become more and more populist both inside and outside? Who knows? Maybe. After all, to paraphrase Al Pacino in the film "The Devil's Advocate," vanity is the devil's favorite sin.

THE TURKISH CIVIL SOCIETY
THAT NEVER WAS[70]

M ore than a decade after the November 2002 elections, whoever had invested hope in the Justice and Development Party
(AK Party) government's promise to make Turkey a full-
fledged democracy must be feeling somewhat confused.

The AK Party government's performance in its third term with
respect to constitutionalizing Turkey's democratic gains is hardly anything more than disappointing. There may be many causes for the AK
Party government's reform fatigue, which range from its sense of victory in the face of its Kemalist rivals and its control over state institutions to corruption. Yet, the underlying cause that enables all other
possible causes is the lack of public criticism from conservative voters
in general, and the AK Party's own constituency in particular. That in
turn stems from the fact that Turkey has never developed a nonpartisan civil society. Turkey's history, starting from the late Ottoman era,
and all the way through the republican era until the emergence of the
AK Party government, illustrates not only how state centrism formed
and was consolidated, but also how society has come to internalize state
centrism as a norm. After a decade in office, the AK Party government
is in a position to determine what will follow. Is it going to be yet another sultanistic (either non-secularist or secularist) regime, or will it be a
full-fledged democracy, which allows any political dissent or criticism
to be voiced?

Given the developments taking place in both Turkish domestic politics and foreign policy since the AK Party government started its third
term in June 2011, there appear to be plenty of reasons for such con-

---

[70] First appeared in *Today's Zaman* daily on January 27, 2013.

fusion. The founding leader of the AK Party and current prime minister, Recep Tayyip Erdoğan, has recently lamented the separation of powers in Turkey during an address to a large audience of like-minded businessmen in the city of Konya, which is known for its conservatism. He complained that the judiciary and what he called "bureaucratic oligarchy" were acting as a hurdle before the planned projects of the government. As such, he advocated that the judiciary and legislature should first and foremost ease the work of the government, considering the benefit of the society. No matter how naïve and genuine his intentions might have been while making such an argument, Erdoğan's statement further raised concerns about the future of Turkish democracy. Even more alarming was that his comments came amid the ongoing national debate over the so-called Turkish-style presidential system, which is allegedly in the making to ensure Prime Minister Erdoğan's accession to the Çankaya presidential palace in 2014 as the 12th president of the Turkish Republic.

The issue is not simply a question of whether Prime Minister Erdoğan should be retiring to his Çamlıca residence to write his memoirs, or to Çankaya Palace to become the president. It is rather whether or not Turkey is reverting back to authoritarianism in a different form after a decade of democratization. On the one hand, under the leadership of the AK Party government in its first two terms in office from 2002 to 2011, Turkey went through a major political and economic transformation unprecedented in its entire republican history. It has carried out once-unthinkable legal and judicial reforms, weakening military control over politics, bringing military activities under the scrutiny of elected civilians, reducing the secular fundamentalist establishment's monopoly on the country's political and economic opportunity spaces and emancipating ethnic and religious identities in the country. On the other hand, Turkey has been witnessing a completely different AK Party government since it started its third term in 2011, one which seems to be hindering the previously begun legal prosecutions of actors in past coup attempts, ignoring, if not overshadowing, major political scandals and criminal acts and developing an extremely populist discourse both with respect to its domestic and foreign policies.

This is the real issue that concerns Turkish democrats. The question is as follows: Why has the AK Party government become increasingly protectionist and populist in its third term in office, having acted like a true reformist throughout its first two terms?

Armchair revolutionaries?

If the German political theorist Hannah Arendt, who once said, "The most radical revolutionary will become a conservative the day after the revolution," was asked this question, she would argue that the radical change in the AK Party government's character is nothing but normal. Given that the AK Party believes that it defeated its archenemy, the secular fundamentalist establishment, and brought the latter's protector, the military, under control, and hence established itself as the ultimate ruler of the land, it is only normal that the AK Party government would be much less inclined to take risks with further political, economic and legal reforms. Nor is there a need to mention that an AK Party loyalist would simply dismiss this question as irrelevant since the revolution which the AK Party started and successfully carried out throughout the past decade has already come to fruition, creating a Turkey which has not only solved its domestic problems and multiplied its economic power, but also become a regional and global actor, with which even the United States consults first before doing anything (at least, in the region).

However, those who believe that democratization is not an end, but a journey full of pitfalls, may point to certain factors such as corruption, cronyism, power intoxication and regional and international dynamics in explaining the change in the AK Party government. Albeit unacceptable, it is understandable that because of any of these factors, the AK Party leaders may have lost their stamina in Turkey's democratization to the extent of failing to replace the current constitution, which was drafted by the perpetrators of the 1980 military coup, with a freedom-oriented civilian one, despite all the political, legal and popular support it has. Yet, none of these factors are sufficient to explain the change in the AK Party's character. Any explanation on the basis of these factors would not be providing a full picture unless it also refers to the absence of a nonpartisan and vibrant civil society in Turkey, which closely monitors the government's policies and publically criticizes them, regardless of the identity of that government.

Enduring legacy of sultanism

The historical relationship between the state and society in Turkey has developed in a way that consolidated the state's role as a strict father and the society as his children who are not only expected to always obey the father, but also never to question his wisdom. Modernization in the late Ottoman era and both modernization and secularization in the republican era were two particular means the state establishment lucratively utilized toward that end. The result was what sociologist Şerif Mardin described as a nation composed of a small secularist core that had dominated all political, economic and cultural opportunity spaces, and a periphery, which included everyone else. Ironically, it is possible to argue that the sultanistic way of administration did not end with the demise of the Ottoman Empire but continued throughout the most of the republican era, only with a secularist core replacing the Ottoman sultan. Previously, it was the sultan who dominated, as well as manipulated, the state-society relationship through a bureaucratic administration and military loyal to him. Starting with the establishment of the new Turkish Republic in 1923, the secularist core took over the sultanistic role and effectively utilized Kemalist ideology well into the late 1990s in order to control and manipulate the state-society relationship in Turkey. Although the ideologies of the two consecutive eras were antithetical to each other, both were characterized by the sultanism, differing only in that in the first one a person was the sultan; in the second, the sultan was an elite, who called themselves "Kemalists." Similarly, they both hindered the development of a functional civil society.

Yet, one should notice that the transition period between Ottoman sultanism and Kemalist sultanism was marked by the rise of Young Turks' libertarian activism aimed at bringing down the Ottoman sultan's authoritarian regime. Once it succeeded, that libertarianism left its place to a new form of authoritarianism called "Kemalism." As such, it has become clear that the period of transition following the demise of the Ottoman sultan was not a glimpse into a truly democratic Turkey to come, but a surreal epoch of anti-authoritarianism, which was followed by yet another form of authoritarianism. Now, seemingly having triumphed over the Kemalist establishment throughout its first two terms in office, the AK Party government in its third term is in a position to determine how its entire legacy will be remembered. There are two possibilities: First, it may be remembered as yet another surreal epoch of democracy, followed by either a conservative authoritarianism under the AK Party's tutelage, or by the resurrection of secularist authoritarianism, in the event that the AK Party fails to survive the demise of its current leadership. Second, it may be remembered as the first and foundational step towards a truly democratic Turkey. The realization of the second possibility is contingent on the emergence of a vibrant nonpartisan civil society that can effectively monitor and criticize the AK Party government. For that to happen, whoever voted for the AK Party government must be the first to scrutinize anything that government does.